Catalogue of Revolutionary Soldiers and Sailors

of the

Commonwealth of Virginia

to

Whom Land Bounty Warrants Were Granted by Virginia for Military Services in the War for Independence

Compiled by
Samuel M. Wilson

HERITAGE BOOKS
2021

HERITAGE BOOKS
AN IMPRINT OF HERITAGE BOOKS, INC.

Books, CDs, and more—Worldwide

For our listing of thousands of titles see our website
at
www.HeritageBooks.com

A Facsimile Reprint
Published 2021 by
HERITAGE BOOKS, INC.
Publishing Division
5810 Ruatan Street
Berwyn Heights, Md. 20740

Copyright © 1913 Samuel M. Wilson

— Publisher's Notice —
In reprints such as this, it is often not possible to remove blemishes from the original. We feel the contents of this book warrant its reissue despite these blemishes and hope you will agree and read it with pleasure.

International Standard Book Number
Paperbound: 978-0-7884-2287-4

Bounty Allotments.

(Amounts received by Officers of various grades and also by Privates.)
Major-Generals received _____15,000 to 17,500 acres.
Brigadier-Generals received _____10,000 acres and upwards.
Colonels received _____ 5,000 to 8,888 acres.
Lieutenant-Colonels received _____ 4,500 to 6,666 acres.
Majors received _____ 4,000 to 5,333 acres.
Captains received _____ 3,000 to 4,666 acres.
Surgeons and Surgeons' Mates received_____ 2,666 to 8,000 acres.
Subalterns, i. e., Lieutenants, Ensigns and Cornets,
  received _____ 2,000 to 2,666 acres.
Every non-commissioned officer who served throughout the war__400 acres.
Every soldier and sailor under like circumstances_____200 acres.
Every non-commissioned officer, enlisted for three years, who
  served out his period of enlistment or to the end of the war____200 acres.
And every soldier and sailor under like circumstances_____100 acres.

Every officer of the Navy received the same quantity of land as an officer of equal rank in the Army.

Where any officer, soldier or sailor was killed or died in the service, his heirs or legal representatives became entitled to receive the same quantity of land as would have been due such officer, soldier or sailor respectively, had he survived the war.

NOTE.—Where a figure in a circle (e. g., ②) precedes a Warrant Number, it indicates the number of warrants issued bearing the same serial number.

Land Bounty Warrants.

Number of Warrant.	Name of Officer or Soldier.	Number of Acres.	Character of Service as Private or Officer. If Officer, what Grade.	Department of Service; Continental or State Line or Navy.	Number of Years of Service.	Date of Warrant.
	A					
1	Askew, James	100	Private	Cont. Va. Inf.	3 yrs.	Aug. 8, 1782
35	Anderson, Richard C.	6000	Lieut.-Col	Va. Cont. Line	3 yrs.	Dec. 9, 1782
49	Archer, Joseph (John Archer, heir at law)	2666⅔	Lieutenant	Va. Cont. Line	3 yrs.	Dec. 14, '82
50	Archer, Peter Field	2666⅔	Lieutenant	Va. Line	3 yrs.	Dec. 14, '82
78	Armistead, Thomas	4000	Captain	Inf. Va. State Line	3 yrs.	Dec. 28, '82
122	Allison, John	6000	Lieut.-Col	St. Line	3 yrs.	Dec. 28, '82
178	Anderson, Isaac	100	Private	Va. St. Line	3 yrs.	Feb. 11, '83
277	Austin, John W. (Dr. James McClung, assee.)	200	Serg.-Maj	Va. St. Line	3 yrs.	Mar. 13, '83
363	Alexander, Ellis	200	Private	St. Line	3 yrs.	Apr. 3, 1783
381	Atkinson, John	100	Private	Va. Line	war	Apr. 18, '83
432	Austin, John Wilson	400	Serg.-Maj	St. Line	3 yrs.	Apr. 22, '83
461	Atkinson, Thomas	400	Corporal	St. Line	war	Apr. 26, '83
529	Angle, John	200	Private	Va. St. Line	war	Apr. 28, '83
555	Anderson, Charled	200	Sergeant	Va. Cont. Line	3 yrs.	May 2, 1783
558	Anderson, Isaac	200	Private	Va. St. Line	3 yrs.	May 7, 1783
580	Anderson, Matthew	100	Private	Va. Cont. Line	war	May 8, 1783
649	Alexander, William	100	Private	Va. Art	3 yrs.	May 14, '83
645	Angel, Robert	100	Private	Va. Cont. Line	3 yrs.	May 27, '83
646	Anderson, Robert	100	Private	Art. of Va. Cont. Line	3 yrs.	May 28, '83
678	Asselin, Thomas	200	Sergeant	Va. Cont. Line	3 yrs.	May 28, '83
689	Atkinson, Reuben	100	Private	Va. Cont. Line	3 yrs.	May 29, '83
748	Atkinson, Major	100	Private	Va. Art. on Cont. Establishment	3 yrs.	May 30, '83
801	Abbott, Robert	200	Sergeant	St. Line	3 yrs.	June 5, 1783
848	Allen, Joseph	100	Private	St. Line	3 yrs.	June 13, '83
871	Archer, Isaac	200	Private	Va. Cont. Line	3 yrs.	June 17, '83
897	Anderson, James	200	Private	Va. Cont. Line	war	June 19, '83
898	Anderson, James	100	Private	Va. Cont. Line	war	June 20, '83
901	Andrews, Clairbourn	100	Private	Va. Cont. Line	war	June 20, '83
959	Ashby, Thomas	100	Private	Va. Cont. Line	3 yrs.	June 20, '83
965	Anderson, Daniel	200	Sergeant	Cont. Line		June 20, '83
970	Anderson, John	100	Private	Cont. Line	3 yrs.	June 20, '83
1021	Anderson, Henry	100	Private	Va. Cont. Line	3 yrs.	June 20, '83
1039	Adams, James	400	Corporal	Va. Cont. Line	3 yrs.	June 23, '83
1129	Abbett, Reuben	200	Private	Va. Cont. Line	war	June 24, '83
1145	Amberson, James	200	Private	Va. Cont. Line	war	June 24, '83
1153	Adams, Jacob	200	Private	Va. Cont. Line	war	June 24, '83
1172	Atkins, Lewis	233⅓	Private	Va. Cont. Line	7 yrs.	June 25, '83
1179	Aaron, William	100	Private	Va. Cont. Line	3 yrs.	June 25, '83
1207	Arrington, William	200	Private	Va. St. Line	war	June 26, '83
1347	Allen, David	2000	Lieutenant	Cont. Line	3 yrs.	July 10, '83
1348	Allen, David	666⅔	Lieutenant	Cont. Line	3 yrs.	July 10, '83
1361	Allen, Moses	200	Private	Cont. Line	war	July 12, '83
1398	Allen, Reuben	466⅔	Sergeant	Cont. Line	7 yrs.	July 19, '83
1423	Angel, James	100	Drummer	Cont. Line	3 yrs.	July 24, '83
1464	Allen, Thomas	100	Private	Cont. Line	3 yrs.	Aug. 1, 1783
1471	Aubany, Thomas	200	Private	Cont. Line	war	Aug. 1, 1783
1509	Absolom, Edmond	200	Private	Cont. Line	war	Aug. 6, 1783
1547	Andrews, Jessee	200	Sergeant	Cont. Line	3 yrs.	Aug. 11, '83
1561	Angel, William	100	Private	St. Line	3 yrs.	Aug. 12, '83
1615	Arnold, John	200	Sergeant	Cont. Line	3 yrs.	Aug. 21, '83
1649	Armstrong, Tobias	200	Private	Va. Cont. Line	war	Aug. 23, '83
1681	Altop, Thomas	200	Private	Va. Cont. Line	war	Aug. 27, '83
1685	Andrew, Benjamin	200	Sergeant	Va. St. Line	3 yrs.	Aug. 29, '83
1697	Auber, Peter (William Vause, heir at law)	100	Private	Va. Cont. Line	3 yrs.	Aug. 30, '83
1712	Anderton, John	100	Private	Va. St. Line	3 yrs.	Sept. 2, 1783
1713	Anderton, Isaac	100	Private	Va. St. Line	3 yrs.	Sept. 2, 1783
1748	Angell, William	100	Sailor	Va. St. Navy	3 yrs.	Sept. 11, '83

LAND BOUNTY WARRANTS.

Warrant.	Name.	Acres	Rank.	Department.	Term	Date.
1766	Atkinson, William	200	Private	Va. Cont. Line	war	Sept. 16, '83
1780	Armstrong, John	100	Private	Va. St. Line	3 yrs.	Sept. 20, '83
1819	Aspenwall, John	100	Private	Va. Cont. Line	3 yrs.	Oct. 3, 1783
ⓢ 1862	Anderson, John	200	Sergeant	Va. Cont. Line	3 yrs.	Nov. 3, 1783
ⓢ 1863	Armond, John	100	Private	Va. Cont. Line	3 yrs.	Nov. 6, 1783
ⓢ 1876	Anglin, Isaac	100	Private	Va. Cont. Line	3 yrs.	Nov. 7, 1783
ⓢ 1938	Allen, Edward	2666⅔	Lieutenant	Va. Cont. Line	3 yrs.	Nov. 22, '83
ⓢ 1939	Alman, William	200	Gunner	Va. St. Navy	3 yrs.	Nov. 22, '83
1952	Armistead, William	100	Private	Va. St. Line	3 yrs.	Nov. 22, '83
1976	Arnold, Gaines	100	Private	Va. Cont. Line	3 yrs.	Nov. 26, '83
1979	Arnold, Lewis (John Arnold, heir at law to)	100	Private	Va. Cont. Line	3 yrs.	Nov. 27, '83
1993	Ashburn, Luke	100	Seaman	Va. St. Navy	3 yrs.	Nov. 28, '83
2007	Adams, Thomas	100	Private	Va. Cont. Line	3 yrs.	Dec. 2, 1783
2020	Angel, Baker	100	Sailor	Va. St. Navy	3 yrs.	Dec. 6, 1783
2168	Almand, John	100	Sailor	Va. St. Navy	3 yrs.	Dec. 20, '83
2191	Aldridge, James	100	Private	Va. Cont. Line	3 yrs.	Dec. 22, '83
2193	Alva, Robert	100	Private	Va. Cont. Line	3 yrs.	Dec. 22, '83
2197	Ashby, Benjamin	2666⅔	Lieutenant	Va. Cont. Line	3 yrs.	Dec. 22, '83
2235	Anderson, Nathaniel	2666⅔	Lieutenant	Va. Cont. Line	3 yrs.	Jan. 12, '84
2237	Andrews, William	200	Sergeant	Va. Cont. Line	3 yrs.	Jan. 12, '84
2238	Alford, Jacob	100	Private	Va. Cont. Line	3 yrs.	Jan. 12, '84
2283	Ashlock, Richard	100	Private	Va. St. Line	3 yrs.	Jan. 26, '84
2327	Anderson, Henry	200	Drum Major	Va. Cont. Line	3 yrs.	Jan. 31, '84
2335	Anderton, Ralph (John Depriest, assee.)	100	Private	Va. Cont. Line	3 yrs.	Jan. 31, '84
2336	Armstrong, Adam (William Reynolds, assee.)	100	Private	Va. St. Line	3 yrs.	Jan. 31, '84
2337	Anderson, William (William Reynolds, assee.)	100	Private	Va. Cont. Line	3 yrs.	Jan. 31, '84
2348	Aspinwall, Peter	200	Private	Va. Cont. Line	war	Jan. 31, '84
2367	Anderson, John	4666⅔	Captain	Va. Cont. Line	7 yrs.	Feb. 2, 1784
2375	Armistead, William	4000	Captain	Va. St. Line	3 yrs.	Feb. 3, 1784
2389	Allen, Francis (Martin Hawkins, assee.)	200	Corporal	Va. Cont. Line	3 yrs.	Feb. 3, 1784
2431	Allen, Thomas	200	Boatswain.	St. Navy	3 yrs.	Feb. 9, 1784
2441	Arnold, William (William Forbush, assee.)	200	Corporal	Va. Cont. Line	3 yrs.	Feb. 9, 1784
2457	Aldridge, Richard (James Jenkins, assee.)	100	Private	Va. Cont. Line	3 yrs.	Feb. 11, '84
2551	Anderson, James	200	Private	Va. Cont. Line	war	Feb. 20, '84
2557	Andrews, Adam	100	Private	Va. Cont. Line	3 yrs.	Feb. 20, '84
2583	Arnold, Samuel (Isaac Arnold, heir at law)	200	Sergeant	Va. St. Line	3 yrs.	Feb. 21, '84
2607	Archer, Richard	2666⅔	Subaltern	Va. Cont. Line	war	Feb. 24, '84
2644	Ashly, John	200	Corporal	Va. Cont. Line	3 yrs.	Feb. 26, '84
2696	Armistead, Robert (James Lewis, assee.)	100	Private	Va. Cont. Line	3 yrs.	Mch. 3, 1784
2736	Ailstock, William	100	Private	St. Art	3 yrs.	Mch. 8, 1784
2803	Allen, John	100	Private	Va. Cont. Line	3 yrs.	Mch. 22, '84
2846	Anderson, William (John Stockdell, assee.)	200	Private	Va. St. Line	war	Mch. 30, '84
2852	Anderson, William	100	Private	Va. Cont. Line	3 yrs.	Apr. 1, 1784
2953	Arnold, Lindsay (Edward Valentine, assee.)	200	Private	Va. Cont. Line	war	Apr. 17, '84
2975	Akin, Joel	100	Private	Va. St. Line	3 yrs.	Apr. 20, '84
2984	Andrews, Henry	100	Private	Va. Cont. Line	3 yrs.	Apr. 21, '84
2997	Adkins, Bartlett (William Jenkins, assee.)	100	Private	Va. Cont. Line	3 yrs.	Apr. 21, '84
3010	Armstrong, Ambrose (Francis Graves, assee.)	100	Private	Va. St. Line	3 yrs.	Apr. 23, '84
3027	Amonite, Daniel (John Amonite, rep.)	100	Private	Va. Cont. Line	3 yrs.	Apr. 27, '84
3028	Armstrong, Abel	100	Private	Va. Cont. Line	3 yrs.	Apr. 27, '84
3056	Anthony, John	200	Private	Va. Cont. Line	war	May 7, 1784
3061	Archer, Robert	100	Private	Va. Cont. Line	3 yrs.	May 8, 1784
3086	Armstrong, Jesse	200	Private	Va. Cont. Line	war	May 21, '84
3115	Allen, David	200	Corporal	Va. Cont. Line	3 yrs.	June 3, '84
3142	Alexander, Geo. Dent (Robert Alexander, heir at law)	6000	Surgeon	Va. Cont. Line	3 yrs.	June 10, '84
3245	Athey, Benjamin	100	Private	Va. Cont. Line	3 yrs.	June 29, '84
3247	Athey, Thomas	100	Private	Va. Cont. Line	3 yrs.	June 29, '84
3249	Atcheson, David	233½	Private	Va. Cont. Line	7 yrs.	June 29, '84
3310	Allen, John	100	Private	Va. Cont. Line	3 yrs.	July 2, 1784
3346	Arnold, Wm. (Martha Pate, assee.)	100	Private	Va. Cont. Line	3 yrs.	July 20, '84

LAND BOUNTY WARRANTS.

Warrant	Name	Acres	Rank	Department	Term	Date
3420	ARMISTEAD, Adam	100	Private	Va. St. Line	3 yrs.	Aug. 28, '84
3441	ALEXANDER, James (William Reynolds, assee.)	100	Private	Va. St. Line	3 yrs.	Sept. 15, '84
3447	ALFORD, John	200	Private	Va. Cont. Line	war	Sept. 21, '84
3449	ARCHER, Leroy	100	Private	Va. Cont. Line	3 yrs.	Sept. 23, '84
3483	ARMSTRONG, Adam (Francis Graves, assee. of Jeremiah Watkins, assee. of)	200	Private	Va. Cont. Line	war	Oct. 26, 1784
3560	ARNOLD, Elijah (Humphrey Arnold, heir at law)	100	Private	Va. Cont. Line	3 yrs.	Dec. 8, 1784
3589	ALLEN, Daniel (Nathaniel Gray, assee.)	200	Private	Va. Cont. Line	war	Dec. 20, '84
3591	ASHBY, Steven (Res. Gen. Assby., Dec. 3, 1784)	4000	Captain			Dec. 21, '84
3597	ALLEN, John	1500	Captain	Va. St. Line	3 yrs.	Dec. 21, '84
3598	ALLEN, John	2500	Captain	Va. St. Line	3 yrs.	Dec. 21, '84
3685	ACRE, Ambrose (William Reynolds, assee. of Edward Acre, who is heir at law)	100	Private	Va. Cont. Line	3 yrs.	Jan. 11, '85
3714	AIKEN, George (James Aiken, heir at law)	200	Sergeant	Va. Cont. Line	3 yrs.	Jan. 20, '85
3732	AMMOND, Peter	233½	Private	Va. Cont. Line	7 yrs.	Feb. 7, 1785
3789	ARMSTRONG, James (Bennett Armstrong, legal rep.)	100	Private	Va. St. Line	3 yrs.	Mch. 26, '85
3790	ARMSTRONG, James (Bennett Armstrong, legal rep.)	200	Private	Va. Cont. Line	war	Mch. 26, '85
3800	ARRELL, David (Res. of Gen. Assby., Nov. 26, 1784)	400	Captain		3 yrs.	Apr. 12, '85
3821	AUBREY (alias Avery), Samuel	100	Private	Va. Cont. Line	3 yrs.	Apr. 22, '85
3841	AVERHEART, Andrew (Michael Averheart, heir at law)	200	Private	Va. Cont. Line	war	Apr. 29, '85
3977	ALLEN, Thomas (Robt. Allen, assee. of John Allen, heir at law)	200	Sergeant	Va. Cont. Line	3 yrs.	Oct. 3, 1785
4009	ADAMS, John (James Adams, heir at law)	200	Private	Va. Cont. Line	war	Nov. 25, '85
4143	ARMSTRONG, James (Joseph Armstrong, heir)	400	Sergeant	Va. Cont. Line	war	Apr. 12, '86
4159	ALEXANDER, James	200	Corporal	Va. Cont. Line	3 yrs.	May 24, '86
4171	ANDREWS, Moses	200	Private	Va. Cont. Line	war	June 14, '86
4238	ANTILL, Jacob	100	Private	Va. Cont. Line	3 yrs.	Dec. 13, '86
4271	ARCHER, Benjamin	100	Private	Va. Cont. Line	3 yrs.	Apr. 7, 1787
4274	ALDRIDGE, John	100	Private	Va. Cont. Line	3 yrs.	Apr. 7, 1787
4279	ARCHER, Jeremiah	100	Private	Va. Cont. Line	3 yrs.	Apr. 7, 1787
⑬4362	ADAMS, Mallory	100	Corporal	Va. Cont. Line	3 yrs.	Oct. 6, 1787
4419	ABNER, Simon (William Reynolds, assee. of Richard Burnett, assee. of the Rep. of)	200	Private	Va. Cont. Line	war	July 17, '88
4424	AMANDA, Ambrose (Wm. Reynolds, assee. of Christr. Stookes, assee. of)	2666⅔	Gunner	Va. St. Navy	3 yrs.	July 17, '88
4444	ALLIGROE, William (Giles Alligroe, heir at law)	200	Sailor	Va. St. Line (Navy)	war	Dec. 15, '88
4488	ALDEN, James (John W. Johnston, assee. of James Roane, assee. of the Rep. of)	100	Private	Va. St. Line	3 yrs.	Feb. 23, '90
4489	ALDEN, Samuel (Jno. W. Johnston, assee. of James Roane, assee. of the Rep.)	100	Private	Va. St. Line	3 yrs.	Feb. 23, '90
4496	ANDERSON, Richard (William Anderson, assee.)	100	Private	Va. St. Line	3 yrs.	May 28, '90
4577	APPLEBY, Samuel (Robert Carrol Appleby, heir at law)	200	Private	Cont. Line	war	

B

11	BRUSH, James	200	Sergeant	Va. Cont. Line	3 yrs.	Oct. 16, '82
17	BAY, William	100	Private	Va. Cont. Line	3 yrs.	Nov. 21, '82
43	BLAIR, John (Architald Blair, heir at law)	4000	Capt.-Lieut	Va. Cont. Art.	3 yrs.	Dec. 12, '82
48	BENTLEY, William	4000	Captain	5th Va. Cont. Reg.	3 yrs.	Dec. 14 '82
64	BOWNE, Thomas	4000	Captain	1st Va. Cont. Reg.	3 yrs.	Dec. 20, '82
71	BOOKER, Samuel	4000	Captain	Va. Cont. Line	3 yrs.	Dec. 24, '82
93	BOSWELL, Machen	4000	Captain	St. Line	3 yrs.	Jan. 11, '83
101	BAYLOR, George	6666⅔	Colonel	Lt. Drg. Cont. Line	3 yrs.	Jan. 30, '83
106	BRODIE, Lodowick	6000	Surgeon	St. Line	3 yrs.	Feb. 1, 1783

War-rant.	Name.	Acres	Rank.	Department.	Term	Date.
110	Bunch, Winston (David Clark, assee.)	100	Private	1st Va. Cont. Reg.	3 yrs.	Feb. 2, 1783
160	Ballard, William	2666⅔	Lieutenant	Art. in St. Line	3 yrs.	Mch. 7, 1783
182	Brooks, Nathaniel	100	Private	Va. Cont. Line	3 yrs.	Mch. 17, '83
195	Brown, Windsor	4666⅔	Captain	Va. St. Line	7 yrs.	Mch. 25, '83
198	Beale, Robert	4666⅔	Captain	Va. Cont. Line	7 yrs.	Mch. 26, '83
199	Butler, Lawrence	4000	Captain	Va. Line	3 yrs.	Mch. 26, '83
208	Baughan, Aris	100	Private	Va. St. Line	3 yrs.	Mch. 28, '83
209	Bland, Theodorick	6666⅔	Colonel	Cont. Cavalry	3 yrs.	Mch. 28, '83
211	Barns, Robert	100	Private	Va. Cont. Line	3 yrs.	Mch. 31, '83
224	Biggs, Benjamin	2000	Captain	Va. Cont. Line	3 yrs.	Apr. 1, 1783
225	Biggs, Benjamin	2000	Captain	Va. Cont. Line	3 yrs.	Apr. 1, 1783
241	Barbee, Thomas	4000	Captain	Va. Cont. Line	3 yrs.	Apr. 1, 1783
258	Burns, Frederick (Rev. Robert Andrews, assee.)	100	Private	St. Line	3 yrs.	Apr. 3, 1783
270	Bingley, Lewis (Dr. James McClung, assee.)	100	Private	St. Line	3 yrs.	Apr. 3, 1783
281	Bland, James	100	Private	Va. St. Line	3 yrs.	Apr. 3, 1783
285	Bohannan, Ambrose	4666⅔	Capt.-Lieut	Art. of Va. Cont. Line	7 yrs.	Apr. 3, 1783
286	Balmain, Rev. Alexander	6666⅔	Brig. Chapl.	....	3 yrs.	Apr. 3, 1783
289	Baldwin, Cornelius	6000	Surgeon	Va. Cont. Line	3 yrs.	Apr. 4, 1783
291	Bedinger, Henry	4000	Captain	Va. Cont. Line	3 yrs.	Apr. 5, 1783
292	Bedinger, Daniel	100	Private	Va. Cont. Line	3 yrs.	Apr. 5, 1783
305	Bell, Thomas	4000	Captain	Va. Cont. Line	3 yrs.	Apr. 8, 1783
318	Boston, Adam	200	Private	St. Cav	war	Apr. 12, '83
321	Bartlett, John	200	Private	Va. St. Cav	war	Apr. 12, '83
322	Brown, John L.	200	Corporal	St. Cav	3 yrs.	Apr. 12, '83
327	Barnes, William	100	Private	Va. Cont. Line	3 yrs.	Apr. 14, '83
329	Blackwell, Joseph	4000	Captain	Va. Cont. Line	3 yrs.	Apr. 14, '83
350	Bradford, Samuel K.	4000	Capt.-Lieut	Va. Art	3 yrs.	Apr. 17, '83
359	Brimer, Isaac	100	Private	St. Line	3 yrs.	Apr. 18, '83
406	Brown, John	200	Private	Va. St. Line	war	Apr. 25, '83
457	Bolware, Obediah	100	Private	St. Line	3 yrs.	Apr. 28, '83
464	Butler, John	400	Serj.-Maj	Art. in St. Line	war	Apr. 28, '83
471	Belvin, William	400	Sergeant	St. Line	war	Apr. 29, '83
476	Baker, James	200	Drummer	St. Line	war	Apr. 30, '83
480	Breadlove, William B.	200	Private	St. Line	war	Apr. 30, '83
486	Bozwell, Robert	200	Private	St. Line	war	Apr. 30, '83
494	Bailey, Michael	200	Private	St. Line	war	Apr. 30, '83
504	Brooks, or Bowles, John	200	Private	St. Line	war	May 1, 1783
532	Butler, Joseph	200	Private	St. Line	war	May 2, 1783
536	Booth, James	200	Private	St. Line	war	May 2, 1783
544	Bennett, William (William Reynolds, assee.)	200	Private	St. Line	war	May 5, 1783
553	Broadus, Robert	100	Private	Va. St. Line	.....	May 7, 1783
563	Blakey, John	100	Private	State Cont. Line	3 yrs.	May 8, 1783
571	Blankinship, Womack	200	Corporal	Va. Cont. Line	.....	May 12, '83
576	Bacon, Burwell	200	Corporal	Va. State Art. on Cont. Estab	3 yrs.	May 14, '83
585	Blakey, John	200	Corporal	St. Line	3 yrs.	May 15, '83
587	Blackwell, John	4666⅔	Captain	Va. Cont. Line	7 yrs.	May 16, '83
606	Browser, James	200	Private	Va. Cont. Line	war	May 21, '83
611	Burns, Jeremiah	200	Private	Va. Cont Line	war	May 21, '83
617	Brackenridge, Alexander	4000	Captain	Va. St. Line	3 yrs.	May 22, '83
626	Brewer, Henry	100	Drummer	Va. Cont. Line	3 yrs.	May 23, '83
628	Baylor, Walker	In part 2000	Captain	Cav. in Va. Cont. Line	3 yrs.	May 23, '83
629	Baylor, Walker	In part 2000	Captain	Cav. of the Va. Cont. Line	3 yrs.	May 23, '83
630	Brown, Jacob	3110⅔	Lieutenant	Va. Cont. Line	7 yrs.	May 23, '83
631	Baskerville, Samuel	In part 1500	Lieutenant	Va. Cont. Line	7 yrs.	May 23, '83
632	Baskerville, Samuel	In part 1610⅔	Lieutenant	Va. Cont. Line	7 yrs.	May 23, '83
650	Brooks, George	100	Private	Va. Cont. Line	3 yrs.	May 27, '83
659	Bowyer, Thomas	4000	Private	Va. Cont. Line	3 yrs.	May 28, '83
(2) 650	Burton, James	100	Private	Va. St. Line	3 yrs.	....
671	Branham, Eben	200	Sergeant	Va. Cont. Line	3 yrs.	May 29, '83
672	Brown, Henry	200	Sergeant	Va. St. Line	3 yrs.	May 29, '83
673	Buford, Abraham	6666⅔	Colonel	Va. Cont. Line	3 yrs.	May 29, '83
681	Brownlee, William	4000	Capt.-Lieut	Va. Cont. Line	3 yrs.	May 30, '83
694	Brown, William	100	Private	Va. Cont. Line	3 yrs.	May 30, '83
698	Brent, William	6666⅔	Colonel	Va. St. Line	3 yrs.	May 31, '83
711	Barron, James	7777⅞	Commodore	Va. St. Navy	7 yrs.	June 2, 1783

LAND BOUNTY WARRANTS. 7

Warrant.	Name.	Acres	Rank.	Department.	Term	Date.
712	Brown, William	6000	Reg. Surg	Va. Line	3 yrs.	June 2, 1783
722	Barron, Richard	5333⅓	Captain	Navy	3 yrs.	June 3, 1783
740	Beaver, Samuel	200	Corporal	Va. St. Line	3 yrs.	June 4, 1783
741	Bowen, John	2666⅔	Lieutenant	Va. Cont. Line	3 yrs.	June 5, 1783
764	Brown, Benjamin	100	Sailor	Va. St. Navy	3 yrs.	June 7, 1783
773	Beasley, Richard	100	Private	Va. St. Line	3 yrs.	June 9, 1783
774	Bourn, Francis	100	Drummer	Va. St. Line	3 yrs.	June 9, 1783
784	Bentley, William	666⅔	Captain	Va. Cont. Line	7 yrs.	June 10, '83
785	Bernard, William (John Bernard, heir at law to)	2666⅔	Lieutenant	Va. Cont. Line	3 yrs.	June 10, '83
813	Blake, Charles	100	Private	Va. St. Art	3 yrs.	June 13, '83
852	Beck, John	2666⅔	Lieutenant	Va. Cont. Line	3 yrs.	June 17, '83
853	Beatte, Robert	4000	Captain	Va. Cont. Line	3 yrs.	June 17, '83
863	Becam, Robert	200	Private	Va. Cont. Line		June 18, '83
872	Barnes, John	100	Private	St. Line	3 yrs.	June 19, '83
879	Brown, Thomas	400	Drum Major	Va. Cont. Line	3 yrs.	June 20, '83
889	Brent, John	100	Private	Va. Cont. Line	3 yrs.	June 20, '83
905	Ball, Burgess	7777⅞	Lieut-Col	Va. Cont. Line	7 yrs.	June 20, '83
909	Buckley, Joshua	200	Private	Va. Cont. Line	war	June 20, '83
924	Beeks, Christopher	100	Private	Va. Cont. Line	3 yrs.	June 20, '83
927	Bell, John	100	Private	Va. Cont. Line	3 yrs.	June 20, '83
929	Buckley, Abraham	100	Private	Va. Cont. Line	3 yrs.	June 20, '83
931	Brown, Absolom	100	Private	Va. Cont. Line	3 yrs.	June 20, '83
945	Brown, Isaac	100	Private	Va. Cont. Line	3 yrs.	June 20, '83
946	Black, George	100	Private	Va. Cont. Line	3 yrs.	June 20, '83
947	Botts, Archibald	200	Sergeant	Va. Cont. Line	3 yrs.	June 20, '83
948	Burgott, Cornelius	100	Private	Va. Cont. Line	3 yrs.	June 20, '83
962	Blair, Robert	100	Private	Cont. Line	3 yrs.	June 20, '83
966	Boursh, Dennis	100	Private	Cont. Line	3 yrs.	June 20, '83
968	Berkley, William	100	Private	Cont. Line	3 yrs.	June 20, '83
976	Bushop, Solomon	100	Private	Cont. Line	3 yrs.	June 20, '83
991	Brook, Walter	6666⅔	Commodore	Va. Navy	3 yrs.	June 21, '83
1029	Bruce, John	200	Sergeant	Va. Cont. Line	3 yrs.	June 23, '83
1031	Bowen, Henry	200	Sergeant	Va. Cont. Line	3 yrs.	June 23, '83
1034	Brough, William	100	Sailor	Va. St. Navy	3 yrs.	June 24, '83
1049	Barr, William	200	Private	Va. Cont. Line	war	June 24, '83
1050	Britton, John	200	Private	Va. Cont. Line	war	June 24, '83
1072	Brooks, Charles	200	Private	Va. Cont. Line	war	June 24, '83
1089	Brooks, Benjamin	200	Private	Va. Cont. Line	war	June 24, '83
1092	Bready, John	200	Private	Va. Cont. Line	war	June 24, '83
1093	Brandon, Peter	200	Private	Va. Cont. Line	war	June 24, '83
1100	Barnett, John	200	Private	Va. Cont. Line	war	June 24, '83
1103	Brute, Thomas	200	Private	Va. Cont. Line	war	June 24, '83
1110	Berry, John	200	Private	Va. Cont. Line	war	June 24, '83
1111	Bacon, Robert	200	Private	Va. Cont. Line	war	June 24, '83
1121	Beham, James	200	Private	Va. Cont. Line	war	June 24, '83
1130	Brazen, William	200	Private	Va. Cont. Line	war	June 24, '83
1133	Brumingham, William	200	Private	Va. Cont. Line	war	June 24, '83
1137	Brean, John	200	Private	Va. Cont. Line	war	June 24, '83
1169	Booker, Richardson	200	Sergeant	Va. Cont. Line	3 yrs.	June 24, '83
1173	Barbour, James (Mordecai Barbour, heir at law)	2666⅔	Lieutenant	Va. Cont. Line	3 yrs.	June 25, '83
1190	Ballenger, John	100	Private	Va. Cont. Line	3 yrs.	June 26, '83
1194	Button, Harmon	100	Private	Va. Cont. Line	3 yrs.	June 26, '83
1208	Brumley, Robert	100	Private	Va. Cont. Cav.	3 yrs.	June 26, '83
1209	Barbee, John	200	Corporal	Va. Cont. Line	3 yrs.	June 26, '83
1210	Barbee, Francis	200	Corporal	Va. Cont. Line	3 yrs.	June 26, '83
1218	Barron, Fielding	100	Private	Va. Cont. Art	3 yrs.	June 26, '83
1220	Britt, John	100	Private	Va. St. Line	3 yrs.	June 26, '83
1236	Bridgman, Joseph	200	Drummer	Va. Cont. Line	war	June 27, '83
1255	Buckley, Michael	233½	Private	Va. Cont. Line	7 yrs.	June 27, '83
1259	Burch, Samuel	100	Private	Va. Cont. Cav.	3 yrs.	June 27, '83
1273	Burton, Hutchens (John Burton, heir at law)	2666⅔	Lieutenant	Va. Cont. Line	3 yrs.	June 28, '83
1309	Baker, Thomas	100	Private	Va. St. Art	3 yrs.	June 30, '83
1324	Bartlett, John	400	Sergeant	Va. Cav	war	July 4, 1783
1340	Blalock, Zachariah	100	Private	St. Line	3 yrs.	July 9, 1783
1355	Boyle, Charles	100	Private	St. Line	3 yrs.	July 12, '83
1379	Blair, Daniel	200	Private	Cont. Line	war	July 15, '83
1384	Burfoot, Thomas	2666⅔	Lieutenant	Cont. Line	3 yrs.	July 17, '83
1385	Bristoe, Sanders	100	Private	St. Line	3 yrs.	July 17, '83
1390	Bohannon, Henry	100	Private	Cont. Line	3 yrs.	July 18, '83
1393	Brayson, Robert	200	Private	Cont. Line	war	July 18, '83
1420	Bell, Ning	100	Private	Cont. Line	3 yrs.	July 22, '83
1429	Rallow, Charles	200	Sergeant	Cont. Line	3 yrs.	July 27, '83
1487	Brittain, John	2666⅔	Sail. Master.	St. Navy	3 yrs.	Aug. 4, 1783

LAND BOUNTY WARRANTS.

Warrant.	Name.	Acres	Rank.	Department.	Ter.	Date.
1502	Bulley, John	100	Seaman	St. Navy	3 yrs.	Aug. 5, 1783
1504	Banks, James	2666⅔	Sail. Master.	St. Navy	3 yrs.	Aug. 5, 1783
1505	Banks, William	100	Sailor	St. Navy	3 yrs	Aug. 5, 1783
1520	Bailey, William	200	Private	Cont. Line	war	Aug. 7, 1783
1533	Brown, Robert	100	Trumpeter	Cont. Cav	3 yrs.	Aug. 9, 1783
1534	Bridgeman, Franklin	100	Private	St. Line	3 yrs.	Aug. 9, 1783
1545	Bowers, Philip	100	Private	Cont. Line	3 yrs.	Aug. 11, '83
1556	Bayliss, William	100	Private	St. Line	3 yrs.	Aug. 12, '83
1563	Branan, Thomas	466⅔	Sergeant	Cont. Line	war	Aug. 12, '83
1564	Baytop, James	4000	Captain	Cont. Line	3 yrs.	Aug. 13, '83
1565	Baytop, John	2666⅔	Lieutenant	Va. St. Line	3 yrs.	Aug. 13, '83
1583	Ball, Aaron	100	Private	Cont. Line	3 yrs.	Aug. 19, '83
1584	Bridgman, Thomas	200	Private	Cont. Line	war	Aug. 19, '83
1585	Bartley, William	100	Private	Cont. Line	3 yrs.	Aug. 19, '83
1594	Bransford, William	200	Private	Cont. Line	war	Aug. 20, '83
1595	Boils, David	200	Private	Cont. Line	war	Aug. 20, '83
1599	Branam, John	200	Private	Cont. Line	war	Aug. 20, '83
1601	Bigbie, William	200	Private	Cont. Line	war	Aug. 20, '83
1607	Burk, William	200	Private	Cont. Line	war	Aug. 20, '83
1610	Burnett, Ambrose	100	Private	Cont. Line	3 yrs.	Aug. 21, '83
1612	Buck, John	100	Private	St. Line	3 yrs.	Aug. 21, '83
1618	Brown, John	200	Private	Cont. Line	war	Aug. 21, '83
1620	Brady, Luke	200	Private	Cont. Line	war	Aug. 22, '83
1629	Biggs, John	200	Private	Cont. Line	war	Aug. 22, '83
1644	Bunn, Daniel	200	Private	Va. Cont. Line	war	Aug. 23, '83
1651	Burk, John	200	Fifer	Va. Cont. Line	war	Aug. 23, '83
1652	Bowyer, Henry	2666⅔	Lieutenant	Va. Cont. Line	3 yrs.	Aug. 23, '83
1653	Brackenridge, Robert	3610⅔	Lieutenant	Va. Cont. Line	7 yrs.	Aug. 23, '83
1666	Bradley, John	400	Sergeant	Va. Cont. Line	war	Aug. 25, '83
1670	Barbour, James	2666⅔	Lieutenant	Va. St. Line	3 yrs.	Aug. 26, '83
1674	Bayling, Matthew	200	Drummer	Va. Cont. Line	war	Aug. 27, '83
1682	Bailey, Edward (William Newby Bailey, heir to)	200	Sergeant	Va. St. Line	3 yrs.	Aug. 28, '83
1694	Broom, John	200	Sergeant	Va. Cont. Line	3 yrs.	Aug. 30, '83
1698	Beaver, William (John Beaver, heir at law)	100	Drummer	Va. Cont. Line	3 yrs.	Aug. 30, '83
1700	Beavers, Benjamin	200	Sergeant	Va. St. Line	3 yrs.	Sept. 1, 1783
1705	Bonner, Richard	200	Sergeant	Va. Cont. Line	3 yrs.	Sept. 2, 1783
1727	Burk, Thomas	100	Private	Va. Cont. Line	3 yrs.	Sept. 4, 1783
1739	Bowling, Thornberry	100	Private	Va. St. Line	3 yrs.	Sept. 10, '83
1755	Butten, Luke	400	Corporal	Va. Cont. Line	war	Sept. 12, '83
1765	Brett, John	200	Private	Va. Cont. Line	war	Sept. 15, '83
1767	Brishaw, John	100	Private	Va. St. Art	3 yrs.	Sept. 16, '83
1769	Bell, James	200	Sergeant	Va. Cont. Line	3 yrs.	Sept. 16, '83
1785	Brown, Samuel	200	Private	Va. Cont. Line	war	Sept. 24, '83
1788	Bates, John	200	Private	Va. Cont. Line	war	Sept. 24, '83
1800	Bishop, Joseph	100	Private	Va. Cont. Line	3 yrs.	Sept. 30, '83
1811	Blackwell, Thomas	4000	Captain	Va. Cont. Line.	yrs	Sept. 30, '83
1823	Bridgman, Hezekiah	100	Private	St. Line	3 yrs.	Oct. 6, 1783
1824	Bayley, Noah	100	Private	St. Line	3 yrs.	Oct. 6, 1783
1831	Brady, Michael	466⅔	Corporal	Cont. Line	8 yrs.	Oct. 7, 1783
1832	Blackson, Pridaux (Samuel Blackson, son and heir to)	200	Private	Cont. Line	war	Oct. 7, 1783
1834	Blackmore, George	2666⅔	Lieutenant	Cont. Line	3 yrs.	Oct. 7, 17?3
1838	Boyd, Francis	100	Private	Va. Cont. Line	3 yrs.	Oct. 9, 1783
1871	Blackwell, Samuel (John Blackwell, heir to)	4000	Captain	Va. St. Line	3 yrs.	Oct. 15, '83
1874	Brown, Robert	100	Private	Va. St. Line	3 yrs.	Oct. 15, '83
1881	Bedworth, William	200	Private	Va. Cont. Line	war	Oct. 15, '83
1898	Ballance, Willis	200	Corporal	St. Line	3 yrs.	Oct. 21, '83
1899	Ballance, Henry	200	Sergeant	St. Line	3 yrs.	Oct. 21, '83
1904	Bentley, Jeremiah	100	Private	Va. Cont. Line	3 yrs.	Oct. 23, '83
1915	Brown, James	100	Private	Va. Cont. Line	3 yrs.	Oct. 25, '83
1918	Brown, George	100	Private	Va. Cont. Line	3 yrs.	Oct. 25, '83
1930	Belvin, George	100	Private	Va. Cont. Line	3 yrs.	Oct. 29, '83
1931	Belvin, Lewis	100	Private	Va. Cont. Line	3 yrs.	Oct. 29, '83
®1840	Berry, George	4000	Captain	Va. Cont. Line	3 yrs.	Oct. 29, '83
®1843	Burnett, John	200	Private	Va. Cont. Line	3 yrs.	Oct. 31, '83
®1846	Brown, Jonathan	100	Private	Va. Cont. Line	war	Oct. 31, '83
®1849	Belfield, John	5333⅓	Major	Va. Cont. Line	3 yrs.	Nov. 1, 1783
®1857	Belcher, Robert	100	Private	Va. Cont. Line	3 yrs.	Nov. 5, 1783
®1858	Biswell, John	400	Corporal	Va. Cont. Line	war	Nov. 6, 1783
®1861	Barham, Moody	100	Private	Va. Cont. Line	3 yrs.	Nov. 6, 1783
®1877	Beal, William	400	Sergeant	Va. Cont. Line	war	Nov. 7, 1783
®1893	Bradley, William	200	Sergeant	Va. Cont. Line	3 yrs.	Nov. 12, '83
®1914	Briscoe, John	100	Private	Va. St. Navy	3 yrs.	Nov. 20, '83

LAND BOUNTY WARRANTS. 9

War-rant.	Name.	Acres	Rank.	Department.	Term	Date.
②1926	Barlow, Thomas	100	Private	Va. St. Line	3 yrs.	Nov. 22, '83
1953	Briscoe, James	200	Boatswain	Va. St. Navy	3 yrs.	Nov. 22, '83
1955	Buck, John Smith	100	Seaman	Va. St. Navy	3 yrs.	Nov. 22, '83
1957	Bully, Thomas	100	Sailor	Va. St. Navy	3 yrs.	Nov. 22, '83
1958	Burk, James	100	Gunner	Va. St. Navy	3 yrs.	Nov. 22, '83
1960	Ballard, William	2666⅔	Pilot	Va. St. Navy	3 yrs.	Nov. 24, '83
1992	Brown, John	100	Seaman	Va. St. Navy	3 yrs.	Nov. 28, '83
2003	Brann, Andrew	200	Private	Va. Cont. Line	war	Dec. 1, 1783
2013	Bailey, Anselin	100	Private	Va. St. Line	3 yrs.	Dec. 5, 1783
2021	Baylie, Peter	100	Sailor	Va. St. Navy	3 yrs	Dec. 6, 1783
2033	Beers, James	200	Private	Va. Cont. Line	war	Dec. 6, 1783
2039	Brabston, William	200	Private	Va. Cont. Line	war	Dec. 9, 1783
2051	Bond, George	100	Private	Va. Cont. Line	3 yrs.	Dec. 9, 1783
2053	Bolton, Bolling	200	Sergeant	Va. Cont. Line	3 yrs.	Dec. 9, 1783
2054	Brooks, Thomas (Samuel Griffin, assee.)	100	Private	Va. Cont. Line	3 yrs.	Dec. 9, 1783
2060	Bozwell, Robert (Samuel Griffin, assee.)	100	Private	Va. St. Line	3 yrs.	Dec. 9, 1783
2061	Bird, Thomas (Samuel Griffin, assee.)	100	Private	Va. St. Line	3 yrs.	Dec. 9, 1783
2070	Blunder, William	100	Sailor	Va. St. Navy	3 yrs.	Dec. 10, '83
2071	Blunden, Swann	100	Sailor	Va. St. Navy	3 yrs.	Dec. 10, '83
2095	Blunden, Seth	2666⅔	Midshipman	Va. St. Navy	3 yrs.	Dec. 10, '83
2099	Burns, William	200	Private	Va. Cont. Line	war	Dec. 11, '83
2113	Bailey, Thomas	100	Private	Va. Cont. Line	3 yrs.	Dec. 13, '83
2133	Burwell, Nathaniel	4666⅔	Captain	Va. Cont. Art.	7 yrs.	Dec. 15, '83
2139	Bryent, John	100	Private	Va. Cont. Line	3 yrs.	Dec. 16, '83
2149	Baldwin, John	100	Private	Va. Cont. Line	3 yrs.	Dec. 17, '83
2153	Barnes, James	200	Private	Va. Cont. Line	war	Dec. 19, '83
2155	Bradford, Henry	200	Sergenat	Va. Cont. Line	3 yrs.	Dec. 19, '83
2156	Baley, Simon	100	Private	Va. Cont. Line	3 yrs.	Dec. 19, '83
2163	Bowen, John	200	Sergeant	Va. Cont. Line	3 yrs.	Dec. 20, '83
2167	Brock, Elias	100	Private	Va. St. Line	3 yrs.	Dec. 20, '83
2172	Been, John	100	Sailor	Va. St. Navy	3 yrs.	Dec. 20, '83
2175	Butler, Edward	200	Sailor	Va. St. Navy	war	Dec. 20, '83
2180	Bennet, William	100	Private	Va. St. Line	3 yrs.	Dec. 20, '83
2181	Bully, Edward	200	Boatswain	Va. St. Navy	3 yrs.	Dec. 20, '83
2183	Bruin, Peter Bryan	5333⅓	Major	Va. Cont. Line	3 yrs.	Dec. 20, '83
2194	Balls, Nathaniel	200	Sergeant	Va. Cont. Line	3 yrs.	Dec. 22, '83
2211	Bedinger, Daniel	2666⅔	Lieutenant	Va. Cont. Line	3 yrs.	Dec. 23, '83
2221	Buns, John	100	Private	Va. St. Line	3 yrs.	Jan. 5, 1784
2227	Bernard, Thomas	200	Corporal	Va. Cont. Line	3 yrs.	Jan. 10, '84
2229	Boyd, James	100	Private	Va. Cont. Line	3 yrs.	Jan. 12, '84
2230	Bolling, Jesse	100	Private	Va. Cont. Line	3 yrs.	Jan. 12, '84
2243	Bundy, Francis	200	Private	Va. Cont. Line	war	Jan. 12, '84
2255	Bird, Reuben	200	Private	Va. Cont. Line	war	Jan. 21, '84
2256	Barrett, William	4000	Captain	Va. Cont. Line	3 yrs.	Jan. 21, '84
2257	Barrett, Chiswell	4000	Captain	Va. Cont. Line	3 yrs.	Jan. 21, '84
2261	Bell, Henry	2666⅔	Lieutenant	Va. Cont. Line	3 yrs.	Jan. 21, '84
2265	Brooke, Francis	666⅔	Lieutenant	Va. Cont. Line	war	Jan. 21, '84
2267	Brooke, John	666⅔	Lieutenant	Va. Cont. Line	war	Jan. 21, '84
2273	Buckner, Thomas	4666⅔	Captain	Va. Cont. Line	7 yrs.	Jan. 23, '84
2289	Byrd, John	100	Private	Va. St. Line	3 yrs.	Jan. 26, '84
2294	Brown, John	200	Sergeant	Va. Cont. Line	3 yrs.	Jan. 26, '84
2296	Brown, Robert	100	Private	Va. Cont. Line	3 yrs.	Jan. 26, '84
2298	Bailey, Southy	200	Private	Va. Cont. Line	war	Jan. 26, '84
2304	Berry, Nathaniel	100	Private	Va. St. Line	3 yrs.	Jan. 28, '84
2317	Baylor, George	2222	Colonel	Va. Cont. Line	8 yrs.	Jan. 29, '84
2322	Babtiste, Jean	200	Private	Va. Cont. Line	war	Jan. 30, '84
2325	Bowman, James (John Depriest, assee. of William Bowman, heir and legal rep. of)	200		Services		Jan. 31, '84
2331	Booker, Lewis	4000	Captain	Va. Cont. Line	7 yrs.	Jan. 31, '84
2332	Booker, Lewis	666⅔	Captain	Va. Cont. Line	7 yrs.	Jan. 31, '84
2355	Burton, William (Martin Hawkins, assee.)	100	Private	Va. Cont. Line	3 yrs.	Jan. 31, '84
2357	Baughan, William	100	Private	Va. Cont. Line	3 yrs.	Jan. 31, '84
2378	Bruce, George	200	Corporal	Va. Cont. Line	3 yrs.	Feb. 3, 1784
2379	Butler, Samuel	2666⅔	Lieutenant	Va. St. Line	war	Feb. 3, 1784
2394	Bryant, William (Martin Hawkins, assee.)	200	Private	Va. Cont. Line	war	Feb. 3, 1784
2400	Blys, William (Martin Hawkins, assee.)	100	Private	Va. Cont. Line	3 yrs.	Feb. 3, 1784
2436	Brandon, Lewis (Lewis Ford, assee.)	200	Sergeant	Va. Cont. Line	3 yrs.	Feb. 9, 1784

LAND BOUNTY WARRANTS.

Warrant.	Name.	Acres	Rank.	Department.	Term	Date.
2445	Barton, James	100	Private	Va. Cont. Line	3 yrs.	Feb. 10, '84
2447	Bailey, William (William Bailey, Jr., heir at law)	100	Private	Va. Cont. Line	3 yrs.	Feb. 10, '84
2453	Barbee, Elijah	200	Private	Va. Cont. Line	war	Feb. 11, '84
2462	Bowers, Jacob (David Perryman, assee. of)	100	Private	Va. Cont. Line	3 yrs.	Feb. 11, '84
2482	Bradshaw, Robert (Matthew Thompson, assee.)	200	Corporal	Va. Cont. Line	3 yrs.	Feb. 13, '84
2514	Bowles, Zachariah (James Hawkins, assee.)	100	Private	Va. St. Line	3 yrs.	Feb. 18, '84
2518	Broadus, James	2666⅔	Ensign	Va. Cont. Line	3 yrs.	Feb. 18, '84
2532	Batchelor, Peter	200	Private	Va. Cont. Line	war	Feb. 19, '84
2535	Brooking, Samuel	200	Corporal	Va. Cont. Line	3 yrs.	Feb. 19, '84
2536	Brooks, James	100	Private	Va. Cont. Line	3 yrs.	Feb. 19, '84
2537	Broadus, William	1000	Subaltern	Va. St. Line	3 yrs.	Feb. 19, '84
2538	Broadus, William	1666⅔	Subaltern	Va. St. Line	3 yrs.	Feb. 19, '84
2541	Brooke, Edmond	2666⅔	Lieutenant	Va. Cont. Line	war	Feb. 19, '84
2542	Brown, John	200	Private	Va. Cont. Line	war	Feb. 19, '84
2546	Bowles Thomas,	200	Sergeant	Va. St. Line	3 yrs.	Feb. 20, '84
2550	Broughton, William	400	Sergeant	Va. Cont. Line	war	Feb. 20, '84
2552	Brown, John	100	Private	Va. Cont. Line	3 yrs.	Feb. 20, '84
2571	Bryant, William	100	Private	Va. Cont. Line	3 yrs.	Feb. 21, '84
2573	Brown, James (Thomas Brown, Rep. and heir to)	100	Private	Va. St. Line	3 yrs.	Feb. 21, '84
2575	Brogg, William	200	Corporal	Va. St. Line	3 yrs.	Feb. 21, '84
2599	Brown, Henry	100	Private	Va. Cont. Line	3 yrs.	Feb. 23, '84
2606	Belcher, George	100	Private	Va. Cont. Line	3 yrs.	Feb. 24, '84
2618	Burgess, Dawson (Daniel Flowerree. assee.)	200	Sergeant	Va. Cont. Line	3 yrs.	Feb. 24, '84
2619	Benson, William (Daniel Flowerree, assee.)	100	Sergeant	Va. St. Line	3 yrs.	Feb. 24, '84
2620	Bayley, James (Daniel Flowerree, assee.)	200	Sergeant	Va. Cont. Line	3 yrs.	Feb. 24, '84
2649	Bramson, Benjamin (Samuel Trower, assee.)	200	Sergeant	Va. St. Line	3 yrs.	Feb. 28, '84
2665	Bradley, James	4000	Captain	Va. St. Line	3 yrs.	Mch. 2, 1784
2669	Ball, Daniel	2666⅔	Lieutenant	Va. Cont. Line	3 yrs.	Mch. 3, 1784
2687	Brasheer, Richard	4000	Captain	Va. St. Line	3 yrs.	Mch. 3, 1784
2688	Bailey, John	4000	Captain	Va. St. Line	3 yrs.	Mch. 3, 1784
2697	Brayson, Robert	33½	Private	Va. Cont. Line	7 yrs.	Mch. 3, 1784
2702	Brogg, Joel (Francis Graves, assee.)	100	Private	Va. Cont. Line	3 yrs.	Mch. 4, 1784
2705	Bedford, James	400	Sergeant	Va. Cont. Line	war	Mch. 4, 1784
2708	Burks, John	100	Private	Va. Cont. Line	3 yrs.	Mch. 5, 1784
2712	Benningfield, Henry (Thomas Aselin, assee.)	100	Artificer	Va. St. Line	3 yrs.	Mch. 5, 1784
2730	Bowman, Mackness	100	Private	Va. Cont. Line	3 yrs.	Mch. 6, 1784
2738	Bidgood, Philip	200	Private	Va. Cont. Line	war	Mch. 8, 1784
2749	Bowman, John	100	Private	Va. Cont. Line	3 yrs.	Mch. 10, '84
2772	Berry, James (James Jenkins, assee.)	100	Private	Va. Cont. Line	3 yrs.	Mch. 18, '84
2779	Brown, Duncan	100	Private	Va. St. Line	3 yrs.	Mch. 18, '84
2784	Bailey, James	100	Private	Va. St. Line	3 yrs.	Mch. 18, '84
2790	Baynham, John (Anthony New, executor)	2666⅔	Lieutenant	Va. Cont. Line	3 yrs.	Mch. 19, '84
2794	Bushop, Thomas	100	Private	Va. Cont. Line	3 yrs.	Mch. 19, '84
2822	Burns, John	100	Private	Va. St. Line	3 yrs.	Mch. 26, '84
2832	Botkins, Charles	100	Private	Va. Cont. Line	3 yrs.	Mch. 27, '84
2853	Bodkins, John	200	Sergeant	Va. Cont. Line	3 yrs.	Apr. 1, 1784
2855	Bell, William	100	Private	Va. Cont. Line	3 yrs.	Apr. 1, 1784
2856	Bedinger, Henry	666⅔	Captain	Va. Cont. Line	7 yrs.	Apr. 1, 1784
2861	Burdoin, John	200	Private	Va. Cont. Line	war	Apr. 2, 1784
2881	Boyd, John (William Boyd, rep.)	100	Private	Va. Cont. Line	3 yrs.	Apr. 5, 1784
2883	Brownloe, Thomas	100	Private	Va. Cont. Line	3 yrs.	Apr. 5, 1784
2905	Bollington, John (William Reynolds, assee.)	100	Private	Va. Cont. Line	3 yrs.	Apr. 7, 1784
2914	Brittain, John (Isham Brittain, heir at law)	200	Sergeant	Va. Cont. Line	3 yrs.	Apr. 12, '84
2918	Barnett, Michael	100	Private	Va. Cont. Line	3 yrs.	Apr. 12, '84
2929	Burrage, Charles	100	Private	Va. Cont. Line	3 yrs.	Apr. 13, '84
2937	Bland, John	100	Private	Va. St. Line	3 yrs.	Apr. 16, '84
2952	Bower, Robert (Ephemia Mitchell and Elizabeth Barnes, legal reps.)	200	Sergeant	Va. Cont. Line	3 yrs.	Apr. 17, '84
2964	Bryant, William	100	Private	Va. Cont. Line	3 yrs.	Apr. 19, '84

LAND BOUNTY WARRANTS.   11

Warrant.	Name.	Acres	Rank.	Department.	Term	Date.
2968	BARKER, Charles	100	Private	Va. Cont. Line	3 yrs.	Apr. 20, '84
2969	BRUCE, William	200	Sergeant	Va. Cont. Line	3 yrs.	Apr. 20, '84
2982	BACON, Ludwell (Lewis Ford, assee. of Burwell Bacon, who is heir at law to)	100	Private	Va. Cont. Line	3 yrs.	Apr. 21, '84
2983	BOWEN, James	100	Private	Va. Cont. Line	3 yrs.	Apr. 21, '84
2985	BUTT, Zachariah	100	Private	Va. Cont. Line	3 yrs.	Apr. 21, '84
2989	BENNETT, Arton (William Reynolds, assee.)	100	Private	Va. Cont. Line	3 yrs.	Apr. —, '84
2991	Buffington, David	200	Private	Va. Line	war	Apr. 21, '84
2996	BROWN, Robert (William Reynolds, assee.)	2666⅔	Lieutenant	Va. St. Line	3 yrs.	Apr. 21, '84
3002	BARKER, Edward	100	Private	Va. Cont. Line	3 yrs.	Apr. 22, '84
3021	BAILEY, William	100	Private	Va. St. Line	3 yrs.	Apr. 26, '84
3023	BOUSH, Charles	2666⅔	Lieutenant	Va. St. Navy	3 yrs.	Apr. 27, '84
3034	BRIDGMAN, Boswell	200	Private	Va. Cont. Line	war	May 1, 1784
3048	BRAWNER, John	200	Private	Va. Cont. Line	war	May 6, 1784
3049	BRAMHAM, John (William Reynolds, assee.)	400	Corporal	Va. Cont. Line	war	May 6, 1784
3063	BURTON, Richard (Elizabeth Burton, rep.)	100	Private	Va. St. Line	3 yrs.	May 10, '84
3084	BROWN, Aries	200	Corporal	Va. St. Line	3 yrs.	May 20, '84
3093	BOLLING, Joseph	100	Private	Va. Cont. Line	3 yrs.	May 22, '84
3097	BURKE, William	230	Private	Va. Cont. Line	war	May 24, '84
3099	BAYTOP, Thomas (Res. of Assby.)	4000	Captain	Va. Cont. Line	3 yrs.	May 25, '84
3128	BARTLEY, Joshua	200	Corporal	Va. Cont. Line	3 yrs.	June 5, 1784
3136	BLUFORD, William	100	Private	Va. Cont. Line	3 yrs.	June 8, 1784
3149	BLAND, James	200	Private	Va. Cont. Line	war	June 11, '84
3162	BROADFIELD, Charles	100	Private	Va. Cont. Line	3 yrs.	June 16, '84
3167	BAYLESS, William	2666⅔	Lieutenant	Va. Cont. Line	3 yrs.	June 17, '84
3171	BULLOCK, Rice	2000	Subaltern	Va. St. Line	3 yrs.	June 19, '84
3172	BULLOCK, Rice	666⅔	Subaltern	Va. St. Line	3 yrs.	June 19, '84
3178	BARBEE, John	200	Sergeant	Va. Cont. Line	3 yrs.	June 21, '84
3179	BARBEE, Joshua	200	Sergeant	Va. Cont. Line	3 yrs.	June 21, '84
3180	BARBEE, William	100	Private	Va. Cont. Line	3 yrs.	June 21, '84
3181	BARBEE, Daniel	200	Sergeant	Va. Cont. Line	3 yrs.	June 21, '84
3198	BROWN, John (John Stockdell, assee.)	100	Private	Va. Cont. Line	3 yrs.	June 23, '84
3211	BARKSDALE, John (William Barksdale, heir at law)	2666⅔	Lieutenant	Va. Cont. Line	3 yrs.	June 25, '84
3212	BARKER, John	100	Private	Va. Cont. Line	3 yrs.	June 26, '84
3224	BOWYER, Michael (Res. of Gen. Assby., 23d June, 1784)	4000	Captain			June 28, '84
3225	BATTERTON, Samuel	100	Private	Va. Cont. Line	3 yrs.	June 28, '84
3227	BROWN, Thomas	100	Private	Va. Cont. Line	3 yrs.	June 28, '84
3250	BOWDIRE, Lewis	100	Private	Va. Cont. Line	3 yrs.	June 30, '84
3260	BOAN, Joseph	100	Private	Va. Cont. Line	3 yrs.	June 30, '84
3265	BURK, Samuel	200	Sergeant	Va. Cont. Line	3 yrs.	June 30, '84
3270	BEATLEY, William	100	Sailor	Va. St. Navy	3 yrs.	July 1, 1784
3271	BATSON, Thomas (Sam'l Blackwell, assee.)	100	Sailor	Va. St. Navy	3 yrs.	July 1, 1784
3277	BLUNDEL, Samuel	100	Private	Va. Cont. Line	3 yrs.	July 1, 1784
3282	BEATLEY, Ralph	100	Sailor	Va. St. Navy	3 yrs.	July 1, 1784
3284	BOOTH, William	200	Mast. & Plt.	Va. St. Navy	3 yrs.	July 1, 1784
3287	BATCHELOR, Peter	200	Sergeant	Va. Cont. Line	war	July 1, 1784
3292	BECKHAM, Wm	100	Private	Va. Cont. Line	3 yrs.	July 1, 1784
3295	BALLARD, Robert	5000	Lieut.-Col.	Va. Cont. Line	3 yrs.	July 1, 1784
3341	BURK, Nicholas	100	Private	Va. St. Line	3 yrs.	July 19, '84
3343	BRIANT, James	100	Private	Va. St. Line	3 yrs.	July 19, '84
3352	BROOKES, John	200	Private	Va. Cont. Line	war	July 22, '84
3367	BYRD, Otway (Res. of Gen. Assby., June 18, 1784)	5000	Lieut.-Col.	Services		July 30, '84
3377	BELL, Thomas	100	Private	Va. St. Line	3 yrs.	Aug. 4, 1784
3378	BURFOTT, William	100	Private	Va. Cont. Line	3 yrs.	Aug. 4, 1784
3400	BAILEY, Jesse	100	Sailor	Va. St. Navy	3 yrs.	Aug. 17, '84
3403	BLODSOE, Miller	100	Private	Va. St. Line	3 yrs.	Aug. 18, '84
3405	BARTLEY, Alexander (William Bartley, legal rep.)	100	Private	Va. St. Line	3 yrs.	Aug. 20, '84
3411	BOUSH, Robert	666⅔	Subaltern	Va. St. Line	3 yrs.	Aug. 25, '84
3412	BOUSH, Robert	700	Subaltern	Va. St. Line	3 yrs.	Aug. 25, '84
3413	BOUSH, Robert	300	Subaltern	Va. St. Line	3 yrs.	Aug. 25, '84
3418	BRANHAM, William	200	Private	Va. Cont. Line	war	Aug. 27, '84
3434	BELL, William (James Fair, assee.)	100	Private	Va. Cont. Line	3 yrs.	Sept. 7, 1784
3458	BUTLER, William	100	Private	Va. St. Line	3 yrs	Oct. 7, 1784

LAND BOUNTY WARRANTS.

Warrant	Name	Acres	Rank	Department	Term	Date
3477	BRADY, Christopher (Abraham S epherd, assee. of the rep. of)	2666⅔	Subaltern .	Va. Cont. Line....	3 yrs.	Oct. 19, '84
3485	BRAGG, Benjamin (Francis Graves, assee. of)	200	Private ...	Va. Cont. Line....	war	Oct. 26, '84
3508	BUBBY (Bybby), Edward (Samuel Demovell, assee. of)	100	Sailor	Va. St. Navy......	3 yrs.	Nov. 8, 1784
3510	BAILEY, Zaddock	200	Private ...	Va. Cont. Line....	war	Nov. 8, 1784
3516	BLANKENSHIP, Daniel (Thomas Clay, assee. of Joel Blankenship, rep.)	200	Private ...	Va. St. Line......	war	Nov. 10, '84
3518	BAILEY, James	100	Private ...	Va. Cont. Line....	3 yrs.	Nov. 11, '84
3523	BERRY, David	100	Private ...	Va. Cont. Line....	3 yrs.	Nov. 15, '84
3549	BAYLES, Henry	2666⅔	Lieutenant .	Va. Cont. Line....	3 yrs.	Nov. 30, '84
3556	BRAG, John (Joseph Vanmeter, assee.)	100	Private ...	Va. Cont. Line....	3 yrs.	Dec. 6, 1784
3578	BOTTS, Leonard	400	Corporal ...	Va. Cont. Line....	war	Dec. 15, '84
3593	BIRD, Joshua	100	Private ...	Va. Cont. Line....	3 yrs.	Dec. 21, '84
3638	BERRY, John	100	Private ...	Va. St. Art.......	3 yrs.	Dec. 30, '84
3641	BERRY, Thomas	100	Private ...	Va. St. Art.......	3 yrs.	Dec. 30, '84
3642	BYNES, Thomas	100	Private ...	Va. Cont. Line....	3 yrs.	Dec. 30, '84
3665	BROWN, Robert (Henry Banks, assee.)	100	Private ...	Va. Cont. Line....	3 yrs.	Jan. 2, 1785
3669	BOYLE, Walter	100	Sailor	Va. St. Navy......	3 yrs.	Jan. 4, 1785
3671	BOYCE, William	2666⅔	Lieutenant .	Res. Gen. Assby., June 5, 1785.....		Jan. 5, 1785
3676	BROADUS, Edward (Richard Broadus, heir at law)	100	Private ...	Va. Cont. Line....	3 yrs.	Jan. 5, 1785
3680	BALL, William (William Reynolds, assee.)	200	Private ...	Va. Cont. Line....	war	Jan. 11, '85
3683	BROADUS, Richard (William Reynolds, assee.)	100	Private ...	Va. Cont. Line....	3 yrs.	Jan. 11, '85
3715	BAILEY, James	400	Corporal ...	Va. St. Line.......	war	Jan. 20, '85
3720	BARNES, John (Margaret Barnes, heir at law)	100	Private ...	Va. Cont. Line....	3 yrs.	Jan. 25, '85
3729	BARROM, Fielding	400	Sergeant ...	Va. Cont. Line....	war	Feb. 2, 1785
3741	BIRD, Thomas	400	Sergeant ..	Va. Cont. Line....	war	Feb. 7, 1785
3766	BARNES, John	200	Private ...	Va. Cont. Line....	war	Mch. 1, 1785
3770	BRIDGWATER, Levi	100	Private .	Va. Cont. Line....	3 yrs.	Mch. 5, 1785
3771	BURNS, Thomas	200	Private ...	Va. Cont. Line....	war	Mch. 8, 1785
3799	BUMBACK, Peter	200	Private ...	Va. Cont. Line....	war	Apr. 8, 1785
3803	BIRD, Richard (Lipscomb Norvell, assee. of Wm. Reynolds, assee. of John Bird, heir at law)	100	Private .	Va. St. Line.......	3 yrs.	Apr. 12, '85
3809	BAKER, Richard	400	Private ...	Va. Cont. Line....	war	Apr. 18, '85
3835	BARNES, Andrew	200	Private ...	Va. Cont. Line....	war	Apr. 29, '85
3846	BEEKHAM, James	100	Private ...	Va. Cont. Line....	3 yrs.	May 2, 1785
3849	BRUMAGEM, Patrick	200	Private ...	Va. Cont. Line....	war	May 6, 1785
3859	BUNTING, Sacker	100	Private ...	Va. St. Line......	3 yrs.	May 7, 1785
3870	BIERLY, Jacob	100	Private ...	Va. Cont. Line....	3 yrs.	May 10, '85
3873	BLAIR, Samuel	100	Private ...	Va. Cont. Line....	3 yrs.	May 10, '85
3905	BUFORD, John (William Reynolds, assee.)	200	Private ...	Va. Cont. Line....	war	June 21, '85
3909	BURK, Matthew	100	Private ...	Va. Cont. Line....	3 yrs.	June 21, '85
3918	BRUSELY, Charles	200	Private ...	Va. Cont. Line....	war	June 21, '85
3925	BALL, James	100	Private ...	Va. Cont. Line....	3 yrs.	June 21, '85
3948	BALEY, Presley (William Reynolds, assee.)	400	Corporal ...	Va. Cont. Line....	war	Aug. 10, '85
3950	BRYANT, Thomas	100	Private ...	Va. St. Line.......	3 yrs.	Aug. 10, '85
3951	BARNWELL, James	100	Private ...	Va. Cont. Line....	3 yrs.	Aug. 12, '85
3969	BLACKMORE, Thomas (George Blackemore, heir at law)	200	Private ...	Va. Cont. Line....	3 yrs.	Sept. 6, 1785
3972	BOWRY, Giles (Samuel Couch, assee.)	100	Private ...	Va. Cont. Line....	3 yrs.	Sept. 12, '85
3973	BAILEY, Pierce (Richard Couch, assce.)	200	Private ...	Va. Cont. Line....	war	Sept. 13, '85
3998	BUNCH, Winslow (Wm. Pettyjohn, assee. Joshua Humphreys, who was assee. of)	100	Private ...	Va. Cont. Line....	3 yrs.	Nov. 19, '85
4020	BROWN, George	300	Sergeant ..	Va. St. Line.......	3 yrs.	Dec. 3, 1785
4021	BOWERS, Morris (William Reynolds, assee.)	200	Private ...	Va. Cont. Line....	war	Dec. 5, 1785
4027	BRITTLE, Thomas (George Brittle, rep.)	200	Private ...	Va. Cont. Line....	war	Dec. 9, 1785
4031	BARR, Simon	100	Private ...	Va. Cont. Line....	3 yrs.	Dec. 10, '85

LAND BOUNTY WARRANTS. 13

Warrant.	Name.	Acres	Rank.	Department.	Term	Date.
4036	BERWICK, James (Res. Gen. Assby., Dec. 9, 1785).......	2666⅔	First Lieut..	Va. Cont. Line....	.....	Dec. 15, '85
4061	BLOXAM, Arthur (Arthur Bloxam, rep.)	200	Private	Va. Cont. Line....	war	Dec. 31, '85
4064	BLACKBURN, Julius·	200	Sergeant ...	Va. Cont. Line....	3 yrs.	Jan. 3, 1786
4065	BARKSDALE, Daniel	100	Private	Va. St. Line.......	3 yrs.	Jan. 5, 1786
4079	BROMFIELD, William (Robert Bromfield, heir at law).....	100	Private ...	Va. St. Line.......	3 yrs.	Jan. 14, '86
4081	BUKNALL, James (John Bucknall, heir)	100	Private	Va. Cont. Line....	3 yrs.	Jan. 17, '86
4082	BUCKNALL, Thomas (John Bucknall, heir)	100	Private	Va. Cont. Line....	3 yrs.	Jan. 17, '86
4107	BELL, John (Res. of Gen. Assby.).................	1666⅔	....	....	.....	Feb. 7, 1785
4108	BELL, John (Res. of Gen. Assby.).................	1000	....	....	.....	Feb. 7, 1786
4116	BROOK, James	200	Private	Va. Cont. Line....	war	Feb. 7, 1786
4151	BARNES, William	100	Private	Va. St. Navy......	3 yrs.	May 3, 1786
4155	BUSLEY, James	100	Private	Va. Cont. Line....	3 yrs.	May 9, 1786
4156	BUSLEY, John (Jas. Busley, heir at law)	100	Private	Va. Cont. Line....	3 yrs.	May 9, 1786
4165	BROWDER, Isham	100	Private	Va. Cont. Line....	3 yrs.	June 3, 1786
4173	BROWDER, Harrison and Frederick and Samuel (James Browder, legal rep.)........	300	Privates ...	Va. Cont. Line....	3 yrs.	June 15, '86
4197	BATES, John (Catharine Bates, rep.)	200	Private ...	Va. Cont. Line....	war	Aug. 23, '86
4206	BOY, Henry	100	Private	Va. Cont. Line....	3 yrs.	Aug. 31, '86
4240	BROMLEY, John	1000	Surg's Mate.	Va. Cont. Line....	3 yrs.	Dec. 13, '86
4241	BROMLEY, John	500	Surg's Mate.	Va. Cont. Line....	3 yrs.	Dec. 13, '86
4242	BROMLEY, John	1166⅔	Surg's Mate.	Va. Cont. Line....	3 yrs.	Dec. 13, '86
4257	BASEY, William	400	Sergeant ...	Va. Cont. Line....	war	Feb. 16, '86
4258	BASEY, William	100	Private	Va. Cont. Line....	3 yrs.	Feb. 16, '86
4260	BRAY, James	100	Private	Va. Cont. Line....	3 yrs.	Mch. 8, 1787
4263	BOND, John (William Reynolds, assee.).................	100	Private ..	Va. St. Line.......	3 yrs.	Mch. 25, '87
4265	BRADY, Joseph	200	Corporal ...	Va. Cont. Line....	3 yrs.	Mch. 28, '87
4267	BUCHANNON, John (John Smith, assee. of James Buchannon, heir at law)................	2666⅔	Lieutenant .	Va. Cont. Line....	3 yrs.	Mch. 29, '87
4280	BOULWARE, Samuel	100	Private ...	Va. St. Line.......	3 yrs.	Apr. 9, 1787
4285	BROWN, John (Charles Lewis, assee.)..................	200	Sergeant ...	Va. Cont. Line....	3 yrs.	May 24, '87
4296	BETHEL, Valentine (William Hilling, heir at law)........	100	Private	Va. Cont. Line....	3 yrs.	June 14, '87
4305	BRANN, Joseph	200	Private	Va. Cont. Line....	war	Aug. 18, '87
4312	BOURNE, John (Henry Bourne, heir at law to Jno. Bourne, decd., who was son of the elder Jno. Bourne)....... ..	100	Private	Va. Cont. Line....	3 yrs.	Oct. 15, '87
4330	BRAIN, William	200	Private	Va. Cont. Line....	war	Nov. 6, 1787
4333	BAYLES, Jesse	100	Private	Va. Cont. Line....	3 yrs.	Nov. 12, '87
4337	BROWNING, William (John Browning, heir at law).....	100	Private	Va. St. Line.......	3 yrs.	Nov. 21, '87
4353	BOSE, "alias" Booze, John....	200	Private	Va. Cont. Line....	war	Dec. 19, '87
4358	BALLARD, Dudley	100	Private	Va. Cont. Line....	3 yrs.	Jan. 4, 1788
4377	BUTLER, William (William Reynolds, assee. of the rep.)....	100	Private	Va. Cont. Line....	3 yrs.	Jan. 23, '88
4381	BLACK, Matthew (Wm. Reynolds, assee. of the rep.)....	100	Private	Va. St. Line.......	3 yrs.	Jan. 29, '88
4394	BEASLEY, Larkin (Leroy Beasley, heir at law)..........	100	Private	Va. Cont. Line....	3 yrs.	Mch. 25, '88
4414	BURNETT, Millington (William Reynolds, assee. of the rep.)	200	Corporal ...	Va. St. Line.......	3 yrs	July 17, '88
4416	BURGE, William (William Reynolds, assee. of the rep. of).	400	Sergeant ...	Va. Cont. Line....	war	July 17, '88
4437	BENNETT, Artax's	2666⅔	Gunner ...	Va. St. Navy......	3 yrs.	Oct. 22, '88
4443	BALLENGER, William	200	Sergeant ...	Va. Cont. Line....	3 yrs	Dec. 13, '88
4460	BRITTAIN, Samuel (Mary Brittain, widow)	200	Private	Va. Cont. Line....	war	June 4, 1789
4467	BRADFORD, Charles	2666⅔	Lieutenant .	Va. Cont. Line....	3 yrs.	Oct. 5, 1789
4471	BOWERS, George (Wm. Reynolds, assee. of Sam'l McCraw, assee. of Wm. Bigger, assee. of Jno. Bowers, rep.).	100	Private	Va. St. Line.......	3 yrs.	Oct. 22, '89
4485	BRIDGES, John	200	Dragoon ...	Va. Cont. Line....	war	Dec. 19, '89

LAND BOUNTY WARRANTS.

Warrant.	Name.	Acres	Rank.	Department.	Term	Date.
4492	Belvin, Robert	200	Matross	Va. Cont. Line	3 yrs.	May 11, '90
4505	Barton, Henry	100	Private	Va. Cont. Line	3 yrs.	Nov. 25, '90
4517	Bagnall, Low (James Bagnall, heir at law)	200	Private	Va. Cont. Line	war	Feb. 3, 1791
4519	Boush, Goodrich (the rep. of)	5333⅓	Captain	Va. St. Navy	war	Mch. 1, 1791
4523	Booth, George (Francis Graves, assee.)	200	Corporal	St. Line	3 yrs.	May 5, 1791
4531	Brent, John	200	Private	Cont. Line	war	Aug. 3, 1791
4559	Brown, Timothy Demon	2666⅔	Lieutenant	St. Line	war	Dec. 13, '91
4581	Branson, John (Edward Davis, assee. of Theodwick Noel, assee. of Larkin Branson, heir at law to)	200	Fifer	Cont. Line	war	June 16, '92
4610	Baumgartner, Henry	900	Private	Cont. Line	war	Apr. 15, '93
4614	Bozzell, George (the rep. or reps. of)	200	Private	Cont. Line	war	May 27, '93
4627	Bedinger, Henry	1333⅓	Captain	Cont. Line	8th yr.	Oct. 29, '93

C

9	Cabell, Samuel I.	6000	Lieut.-Col.	Va. Inf	3 yrs.	Sept. 30, '82
10	Campbell, William	4000	Captain	1st St. Reg	3 yrs.	Oct. 15, '82
16	Campbell, Samuel (Wm. Campbell, heir at law)	2666⅔	Lieutenant	Va. Cont. Line	3 yrs.	Nov. 13, '82
24	Carrington, Mayo	4000	Captain	Va. Cont. Line	3 yrs.	Nov. 29, '82
25	Croghan, William	5333⅓	Major	Va. Cont. Line	3 yrs.	Nov. 29, '82
31	Coombes, Francis	200	Private	Va. Cont. Line	war	Dec. 20, '82
32	Consolver, John	200	Private	Va. Cont. Line	war	Dec. 20, '82
52	Clay, Matthew	2666⅔	Lieutenant	Va. Line	3 yrs.	Dec. 14, '82
53	Conner, John	200	Sergeant	1st Va. St. Reg	3 yrs.	Dec. 14, '82
103	Callender, Eliazer	5333⅓	Captain	St. Navy	3 yrs.	Jan. 30, '83
140	Cash, Warren	100	Private	Va. Line	3 yrs.	Feb. 21, '83
143	Collingsworth, Edward (John Willson, assee. of Robt. Lewis, assee. of Edw. Collingsworth)	100	Private	St. Line	3 yrs.	Feb. 22, '83
144	Collingsworth, John (John Willson, assee. of Robert. Lewis, Jr., assee. of John Collingsworth)	100	Private	St. Line	3 yrs.	Feb. 22, '83
156	Coleman, Samuel	2666⅔	Lieutenant	Art. in Va. Line	3 yrs.	Mch. 4, 1783
158	Cowne, Robert	4000	Capt.-Lieut	St. Art	3 yrs.	Mch. 7, 1783
159	Cowne, Augustine	2666⅔	Lieutenant	St. Line	3 yrs.	Mch. 7, 1783
168	Crockett, Joseph	6666⅔	Lieut.-Col. Com'dant	St. Line	3 yrs.	Mch. 9, 1783
172	Clark, Jonathan	7000	Lieut.-Col.	Va. Cont. Line	7 yrs.	Mch. 10, '83
173	Cowherd, Francis	4000	Captain	Va. Cont. Line	3 yrs.	Mch. 11, '83
187	Craddock, Robert	2666⅔	Lieutenant	Va. Cont. Line	3 yrs.	Mch. 20, '83
188	Crule, John	2666⅔	Lieutenant	Va. Cont. Line	3 yrs.	Mch. 20, '83
189	Craddock, Henry	200	Sergeant	Va. Cont. Line	3 yrs.	Mch. 20, '83
193	Chavers, John	100	Private	Va. Cont. Line	3 yrs.	Mch. 24, '83
226	Coleman, Jacob	1300	Lieutenant	Va. Cont. Line	3 yrs.	Apr. 1, 1783
227	Coleman, Jacob	1366⅔	Lieutenant	Va. Cont. Line	3 yrs.	Apr. 1, 1783
257	Carnick, Patrick (Rev. Robert Andrews, assee.)	100	Private	St. Line	3 yrs.	Apr. 3, 1783
261	Creekman, William (Rev. Robt. Andrews, assee.)	100	Private	St. Line	3 yrs.	Apr. 3, 1783
265	Colden, James (Doctor James McClung, assee.)	100	Private	St. Line	3 yrs.	Apr. 3, 1783
306	Carter, John C.	4666⅔	Captain	Art. of Va. Cont Line	7 yrs.	Apr. 8, 1783
307	Clark, John	4000	Captain	Va. Cont. Line	7 yrs.	Apr. 8, 1783
308	Crawford, John	2666⅔	Lieutenant	Va. Cont. Line	3 yrs.	Apr. 9, 1783
309	Christee, James	200	Private	Va. St. Line	war	Apr. 9, 1783
319	Cole, William	200	Private	St. Cav	war	Apr. 12, '83
325	Calmes, Marquis	4000	Captain	Va. Cont. Line	3 yrs.	Apr. 12, '83
328	Clark, Edward	100	Private	Va. Art	3 yrs.	Apr. 14, '83
348	Curry, James	4000	Captain	Va. Cont. Line	3 yrs.	Apr. 16, '83
353	Carroll, Edward	400	Sergeant	St. Line	war	Apr. 17, '83
382	Connor, Philip (Philip Daw, assee.)	200	Sergeant	Va. Cont. Line	3 yrs.	Apr. 23, '83
410	Camburn, John	200	Private	Va. St. Line	war	Apr. 25, '83
434	Carroll, John	200	Private	St. Line	war	Apr. 26, '83
450	Colder, James	200	Private	St. Line	war	Apr. 28, '83
453	Crouclur, Charles	200	Private	St. Line	war	Apr. 28, '83
478	Coggin, Herbert	200	Private	St. Line	war	Apr. 30, '83

LAND BOUNTY WARRANTS. 15

Warrant.	Name.	Acres	Rank.	Department.	Term	Date.
482	COURTNEY, Thomas	200	Private	St. Line	war	Apr. 30, '83
483	CUTTS, William	200	Private	St. Line	war	Apr. 30, '83
494	CUTTS, Shadrack	200	Private	St. Line	war	Apr. 30, '83
498	CARTER, James	200	Private	St. Line	war	May 1, 1783
505	CRUMP, Abner	4000	Captain	St. Line	3 yrs.	May 1, 1783
515	CARVER, Laurence	200	Private	St. Line	war	May 1, 1783
516	CRUMP, Benjamin	400	Sergeant	St. Line	war	May 1, 1783
527	CARDER, James	400	Corporal	St. Line	war	May 2, 1783
533	COLE, Thomas	100	Private	St. Line	3 yrs.	May 2, 1783
538	CAVENDER, James	200	Private	St. Line	war	May 2, 1783
542	CROKER, William	200	Drum Maj.	St. Line	3 yrs	May 3, 1783
549	CARNES, Daniel	200	Private	St. Line	war	May 6, 1783
557	CONNER, John	400	Sergeant	St. Line	war	May 7, 1783
562	CAWTHON, Christopher	200	Sergeant	Cont. Line	3 yrs.	May 8, 1783
564	CAREY, James	100	Private	Cont. Line	3 yrs.	May 8, 1783
568	CARRINGTON, Mayo	666⅔	Captain		7 yrs.	May 10, '83
579	CARTER, Joseph	100	Private	Va. Cont. Line	3 yrs.	May 14, '83
589	COFER, George	200	Corporal	Va. St. Line	3 yrs.	May 17, '83
641	Cox, Radford	200	Corporal	Va. Cont. Line	3 yrs.	May 26, '83
645	CRUMP, Jesse	200	Sergeant	Va. St. Line	3 yrs.	May 26, '83
653	CROSS, Samuel	200	Sergeant	Va. Cont. Line	3 yrs.	May 27, '83
663	CLOD, Robert	200	Private	Va. St. Line	3 yrs.	May 28, '83
691	CARTER, John	100	Private	Va. St. Art	3 yrs.	May 30, '83
692	CLARK, James	200	Sergeant	Va. St. Line	3 yrs.	May 30, '83
697	COLE, Hamlin	200	Sergeant	Va. Cont. Line	3 yrs.	May 31, '83
701	CANNON, Luke	2666⅔	Lieutenant	Va. Cont. Line	3 yrs.	May 31, '83
723	CALVERT, John	200	Private	Va. St. Line	war	June 3, 1783
729	CASEY, Archibald	200	Private	Va. St. Line	war	June 3, 1783
738	CLEMENTS, Mace	7000	Reg. Surg.	Va. Cont. Line	7 yrs.	June 4, 1783
745	CASEY, Benjamin (Peter Casey, heir at law to)	4000	Captain	Va. Line	3 yrs.	June 5, 1783
750	CRATTON, William	200	Private	Va. Cont. Line	war	June 5, 1783
751	CHAMBERLAIN, George	4000	Lieutenant	Va. St. Navy	3 yrs.	June 5, 1783
775	CARTER, Charles	100	Private	Va. St. Line	3 yrs.	June 9, 1783
783	CUNNINGHAM, William	5333⅓	Major	Va. Cont. Line	3 yrs.	June 10, '83
789	CHAPMAN, John (Joseph Chapman, heir at law and legal rep.)	4000	Captain	St. Line	3 yrs.	June 12, '83
794	CLAYTON, Philip	2666⅔	Lieutenant	Va. Cont. Line	3 yrs.	June 12, '83
797	CRUTCHFIELD, Stapleton	100	Private	Va. Cont. Line	3 yrs.	June 12, '83
816	COLLINS, Mason	100	Private	Va. Art	3 yrs.	June 14, '83
820	COOLEY, James	100	Private	Cont. Line	3 yrs.	June 14, '83
836	COIGUHON, James	100	Private	Va. Cont. Line	3 yrs.	June 16, '83
836	COIQUHON, James	2666⅔	Lieutenant	Va. Cont. Line	3 yrs.	June 16, '83
841	COLLINS, John	200	Sergeant	Va. Cont. Line	3 yrs.	June 16, '83
845	CROWLEY, David	100	Private	Va. Cont. Line	3 yrs.	June 16, '83
851	CRAWFORD, William (John Crawford, heir at law to)	6666⅔	Colonel	Va. Cont. Line		June 17, '83
868	CHAMBERS, Alexander	100	Private	Va. Cont. Line	3 yrs.	June 19, '83
895	CAMPBELL, Archibald	200	Private	Va. Cont. Line	war	June 20, '83
902	CUMBO, Daniel	100	Private	Va. Cont. Line	3 yrs.	June 20, '83
915	CLAVENGER, Edward	100	Private	Va. Cont. Line	3 yrs.	June 20, '83
926	CHAPMAN, Thomas	100	Private	Va. Cont. Line	3 yrs.	June 20, '83
932	CASELL, William	100	Private	Va. Cont. Line	3 yrs.	June 20, '83
951	CASSE, William	100	Private	Va. Cont. Line	3 yrs.	June 20, '83
953	CRAWFORD, John	200	Sergeant	Va. Cont. Line	3 yrs.	June 20, '83
990	CAREY, Samuel	2666⅔	Lieutenant	Va. St. Line	3 yrs.	June 21, '83
994	CAREY, Robert	100	Private	Va. Cont. Line	3 yrs.	June 21, '83
995	CROPPER, John	6666⅔	Lieut.-Col.	Va. Cont. Line	3 yrs.	June 21, '83
1007	CRITTENDON, John	2666⅔	Lieutenant	Va. Cont. Line	3 yrs.	June 23, '83
1024	CRAWFORD, John	100	Private	Va. Cont. Line	3 yrs.	June 23, '83
1027	CHINWORTH, John	100	Private			3 yrs.	June 23, '83
1042	COXOR, William	200	Fifer	Va. Cont. Line	war	June 24, '83
1044	CRAWFORD, Robert	200	Private	Va. Cont. Line	war	June 24, '83
1046	CAVENEAR, Garret	200	Private	Va. Cont. Line	war	June 24, '83
1056	CARTER, Richard	200	Private	Va. Cont. Line	war	June 24, '83
1064	CONROD, Jacob	200	Private	Va. Cont. Line	war	June 24, '83
1065	CARTER, Nicholas	200	Private	Va. Cont. Line	war	June 24, '83
1069	CRAIG, Thomas	200	Private	Va. Cont. Line	war	June 24, '83
1076	CARPENTER, Christopher	200	Private	Va. Cont. Line	war	June 24, '83
1083	CUNNINGHAM, James	200	Private	Va. Cont. Line	war	June 24, '83
1088	CRAIG, William	200	Private	Va. Cont. Line	war	June 24, '83
1119	CLOYD, William or James	200	Private	Va. Cont. Line	war	June 24, '83
1128	CARDONES, John	200	Private	Va. Cont. Line	war	June 24, '83
1132	CONALLY, William	200	Private	Va. Cont. Line	war	June 24, '83
1143	CLARK, David	200	Private	Va. Cont. Line	war	June 24, '83

Warrant.	Name.	Acres	Rank.	Department.	Term	Date.
1147	Cruswell, Samuel	200	Private	Va. Cont. Line	war	June 24, '83
1154	Crawford, Charles	200	Private	Va. Cont. Line	war	June 24, '83
1177	Cabbell, Samuel J.	1000	Lieut.-Col	Cont. Line	7 yrs	June 25, '83
1181	Carrick, Patrick	200	Private	Va. St. Line	war	June 25, '83
1186	Coleman, Whitehead	4000	Captain	Va. Cont. Line	3 yrs.	June 26, '83
1193	Carter, Henry	100	Private	Va. Cont. Line	3 yrs.	June 26, '83
1197	Coons, Frederick	100	Private	Va. Cont. Line	3 yrs.	June 26, '83
1198	Catlett, Thomas (John Catlett, heir at law)	4000	Captain	Va. Cont. Line	3 yrs.	June 26, '83
1214	Carr, William	100	Private	Va. St. Line	3 yrs.	June 26, '83
1216	Carrell, Joseph	100	Private	Va. St. Line	3 yrs.	June 26, '83
1223	Collins, George	100	Private	Va. St. Line	3 yrs.	June 26, '83
1232	Cypress, Andrew	233⅓	Private	Va. Cont. Line	7 yrs.	June 27, '83
1239	Chambers, David	100	Private	Va. Cont. Line	3 yrs.	June 27, '83
1244	Crawford, David	100	Private	Va. Cont. Line	3 yrs.	June 27, '83
1248	Chrisholm, George	233⅓	Private	Va. Cont. Line	war	June 27, '83
1249	Chilton, John (Thomas Chilton, heir at law)	4000	Captain	Va. Cont. Line	3 yrs.	June 27, '83
1252	Cliffton, Joshua	233⅓	Private	Va. Cont. Line	7 yrs.	June 27, '83
1264	Conley, Asa	200	Private	Va. Cont. Line	war	June 27, '83
1297	Courtney, Samuel	233⅓	Private	Va. Cont. Line	war	June 30, '83
1302	Chapen, John	100	Private	Va. St. Line	3 yrs.	June 30, '83
1308	Cooper, William	200	Private	Va. St. Line	war	June 30, '83
1317	Carter, William	100	Private	Va. St. Line	3 yrs.	July 1, 1783
1337	Clayton, Joseph	200	Private	St. Line	war	July 8, 1783
1341	Calfrey, Charles	100	Private	Cont. Cav	3 yrs.	July 9, 1783
1356	Cox, William (Francis Cox, heir)	200	Sergeant	Cont. Cav	3 yrs.	July 12, '83
1373	Chilton, Newman	200	Corporal	St. Line	3 yrs.	July 15, '83
1392	Cowper, Richard	233⅓	Private	Cont. Line	war	July 18, '83
1413	Coverly, Thomas	2000	Lieutenant	Cont. Line	7 yrs.	July 22, '83
1414	Coverly, Thomas	1110⅔	Lieutenant	Cont. Line	7 yrs.	July 22, '83
1428	Carpenter, John	200	Sergeant	St. Line	3 yrs.	July 26, '83
1438	Climan, James	400	Sergeant	Cont. Line	war	July 28, '83
1445	Coram, William	233⅓	Private	Cont. Line	war	July 31, '83
1447	Carnal, William	200	Private	Cont. Line	war	July 31, '83
1467	Cyrus, Bartholomew	200	Private	Cont. Line	war	Aug. 1, 1783
1469	Chappin, John (Stanley Chappin, heir)	200	Private	Cont. Line	3 yrs.	Aug. 1, 1783
1478	Church, John	200	Private	Cont. Line	war	Aug. 2, 1783
1492	Carrol, Joseph	100	Private	Cont. Line	3 yrs.	Aug. 4, 1783
1493	Crawley, James	100	Private	Cont. Line	3 yrs.	Aug. 4, 1783
1498	Cooper, Ephraim	400	Sergeant	Cont. Line	war	Aug. 5, 1783
1506	Carter, Thomas	6000	Doctor	St. Navy	3 yrs.	Aug. 6, 1783
1518	Cowherd, James	200	Sergeant	Cont. Line	3 yrs.	Aug. 7, 1783
1523	Coppinger, Higgins	200	Private	Cont. Line	war	Aug. 7, 1783
1536	Clark, William	100	Private	St. Line	3 yrs.	Aug. 9, 1783
1537	Crump, Thomas	100	Private	St. Art	3 yrs	Aug. 9, 1783
1543	Cooper, Spencer	400	Corporal	Cont. Line	war	Aug. 9, 1783
1549	Cunningham, Nathaniel	200	Sergeant	Cont. Line	3 yrs.	Aug. 11, '83
1550	Canafax, Edward	100	Private	Cont. Line	3 yrs.	Aug. 11, '83
1577	Cotteral, William	2666⅔	Midshipman	St. Navy	3 yrs.	Aug. 18, '83
1614	Clift, William	200	Private	Cont. Line	3 yrs.	Aug. 21, '83
1622	Camble, Dennis	200	Private	Cont. Line	war	Aug. 22, '83
1627	Conway, Joseph	3110⅔	Lieutenant	Cont. Line	7 yrs	Aug. 22, '83
1631	Curl, Richard	200	Private	Cont. Line	war	Aug. 22, '83
1660	Carney, Patrick	200	Private	Va. Cont. Line	war	Aug. 25, '83
1661	Cox, William	200	Private	Va. Cont. Line	war	Aug. 25, '83
1683	Carter, John	100	Sailor	Va. St. Navy	3 yrs.	Aug. 29, '83
1691	Chevelier, Anthony	100	Private	Va. Cont. Line	3 yrs.	Aug. 30, '83
1696	Copland, William	200	Corporal	Va. Cont. Line	3 yrs.	Aug. 30, '83
1711	Cayner, Matthew	100	Private	Va. Cont. Line	3 yrs.	Sept. 2, 1783
1728	Carroll, Berry	100	Private	Va. St. Line	3 yrs.	Sept. 8, 1783
1733	Cavender, Joseph	400	Sergeant	Va. Cont. Line	war	Sept. 8, 1783
1744	Childress, Mosby	100	Private	Va. Cont. Line	3 yrs.	Sept. 11, '83
1746	Corbell, Peter	200	Corporal	Va. Cont. Line	3 yrs.	Sept. 11, '83
1783	Cook, William	200	Sergeant	Va. Cont. Line	3 yrs.	Sept. 23, '83
1792	Carrington, Edward	7000	Lieutenant	Va. Cont. Line	7 yrs.	Sept. 25, '83
1796	Carroll, Thomas (Samuel Coleman, assee. of)	200	Private	Va. St. Line	war	Sept 26, '83
1805	Cason, John	200	Sergeant	St. Line	3 yrs.	Sept. 30, '83
1806	Cason, William	100	Private	St. Line	3 yrs.	Sept. 30, '83
1807	Cason, James	100	Private	St. Line	3 yrs.	Sept. 30, '83
1840	Carrell, John	200	Sergeant	Va. Cont. Line	3 yrs.	Oct. 9, 1783
1850	Charles, William	100	Private	Va. St. Line	3 yrs.	Oct. 11, '83
1857	Clark, Moses	200	Private	Va. Cont Line	war	Oct. 13, '83

LAND BOUNTY WARRANTS. 17

Warrant.	Name.	Acres	Rank.	Department.	Term	Date.
1880	Corbett, John	200	Private	Va. Cont. Line	war	Oct. 15, '83
1882	Collins, Peter	200	Private	Va. Cont. Line	war	Oct. 15, '83
1912	Christie, Dr. Thomas	7000	Surgeon	Va. Cont. Line	7 yrs.	Oct. 25, '83
1919	Case, William	100	Private	Va. Cont. Line.*.	3 yrs.	Oct. 25, '83
1924	Cogwell, Frederick (Zachariah Cogwell, heir at law to)	100	Private	Va. Cont. Line	3 yrs.	Oct. 27, '83
1935	Carrington, George	2666⅔	Lieutenant	Va. Cont. Line	3 yrs.	Oct. 31, '83
②1855	Cox, Presley	100	Private	Va. Cont. Line	3 yrs.	Nov. 4, 1783
②1860	Charles, Samuel	200	Sergeant	Va. Cont. Line	3 yrs.	Nov. 6, 1783
②1868	Culbertson, James	4000	Captain	Va. Cont. Line	3 yrs.	Nov. 6, 1783
②1881	Carter, Armstead	100	Private	Va. Cont. Line	3 yrs.	Nov. 10, '83
②1882	Carter, Robert	200	Sergeant	Va. Cont. Line	3 yrs.	Nov. 10, '83
②1896	Chilton, Thomas, "alias" Sheldon	5333½	*Five* Major	Va. Cont. Line	8 yrs.	Nov. 12, '83
②1909	Cartwright, Justinian	466⅔	Sergeant	Va. Cont. Line	7 yrs.	Nov. 19, '83
②1923	Croghan, William	6420	Major	Res. of Gen Assby. Nov. 18, 1783..	7 yrs.	Nov. 21, '83
③1922	Croghan, William	888⅔	Major	Va. Cont. Line	7 yrs.	Nov. 21, '83
1970	Compton, Augustine	100	Private	Va. Cont. Line	3 yrs.	Nov. 26, '83
1978	Colvin, Jeremiah (John Colvin, heir at law)	200	Sergeant	Va. Cont. Line	3 yrs.	Nov. 27, '83
1982	Cherry, William	1000	Captain	Va. Cont. Line	3 yrs.	Nov. 28, '83
1983	Cherry, William	3000	Captain	Va. Cont. Line	3 yrs.	Nov. 28, '83
1989	Crowder, Robert	100	Seaman	Va. St. Navy	3 yrs.	Nov. 28, '83
1998	Cockran, William	200	Sergeant	Va. Cont. Line	3 yrs.	Nov. 29, '83
2011	Conant, John	200	Private	Va. Cont. Line	war	Dec. 4, 1783
2014	Campbell, Archibald	2666⅔	Lieutenant	Va. Cont. Line	3 yrs.	Dec. 5, 1783
2024	Craig, James	4000	Captain	Va. Cont. Line	3 yrs.	Dec. 6, 1783
2031	Cave, James	100	Private	Va. Cont. Line	3 yrs.	Dec. 6, 1783
2038	Case, William	200	Private	Va. Cont. Line	war	Dec. 9, 1783
2069	Causey, James	100	Seaman	Va. St. Navy	3 yrs.	Dec. 10, '83
2084	Cocke, Michael	100	Private	Va. Cont. Line	3 yrs.	Dec. 10, '83
2089	Craine, James	4000	Captain	Va. Cont. Line	3 yrs.	Dec. 10, '83
2091	Cassidy, Michael	100	Private	Va. Cont. Line	3 yrs.	Dec. 10, '83
2093	Carnahan, John	100	Private	Va. Cont. Line	3 yrs.	Dec. 10, '83
2101	Cruze, Redman	100	Private	Va. Cont. Line	3 yrs.	Dec. 11, '83
2105	Canary, William	100	Private	Va. Cont. Line	3 yrs.	Dec. 12, '83
2124	Chapman, John	200	Sergeant	Va. St. Line	3 yrs.	Dec. 15, '83
2129	Cornelius, Josiah	100	Private	Va. Cont. Line	3 yrs.	Dec. 15, '83
2141	Coleman, John (James Coleman, heir at law)	2666⅔	Ensign	Va. St. Line	3 yrs.	Dec. 16, '83
2184	Cook, Joseph (Thomas Cook, heir at law)	200	Private	Va. Cont. Line	war	Dec. 20, '83
2196	Childress, Henry	100	Private	Va. Cont. Line	3 yrs.	Dec. 22, '83
2200	Campbell, William (Charles Campbell, son and heir to)	5000	General	Res., Gen. Assby., Dec. 19, 1783		Dec. 23, '83
2223	Carnes, Patrick	4000	Captain	Va. Cont. Line	3 yrs.	Jan. 7, 1784
2239	Carrington, Clement	2666⅔	Ensign	Va. Cont. Line	war	Jan. 12, '84
2240	Coleman, Richard (Francis Coleman, heir at law)	4000	Captain	Va. Cont. Line	3 yrs.	Jan. 12, '84
2249	Carr, William	200	Private	Va. Cont. Line	war	Jan. 16, '84
2259	Clarke, William	100	Private	Va. Cont. Line	3 yrs.	Jan. 21, '84
2260	Call, Richard	5333½	Major	Va. Cont. Line	3 yrs.	Jan. 21, '84
2278	Clay, Thomas	4000	Captain	Va. St. Line	3 yrs.	Jan. 23, '84
2284	Crittindon, William	100	Private	Va. St. Line	3 yrs.	Jan. 26, '84
2286	Clark, Thomas	200	Private	Va. St. Line	war	Jan. 26, '84
2292	Clark, George Rogers	10000	Brig. Gen	Va. St. Line	3 yrs.	Jan. 26, '84
2323	Cocke, Colin	4666⅔	Captain	Va. Cont. Line	7 yrs.	Jan. 30, '84
2347	Claiborne, Richard	2666⅔	Lieutenant	Va. Cont. Line	war	Jan. 31, '84
2359	Clarke, Edmund	2666⅔	Lieutenant	Va. Cont. Line	3 yrs.	Feb. 2, '84
2372	Cochran, Samuel	200	Sergeant	Va. Cont. Line	3 yrs.	Feb. 3, 1784
2382	Crocket, Presley	100	Private	Va. Cont. Line	3 yrs.	Feb. 3, 1784
2395	Chewning, Thomas (Martin Hawkins, assee.)	100	Private	Va. Cont. Line	3 yrs.	Feb. 3, 1784
2410	Claverius, James (Benjamin Claverius, rep.)	4000	Capt.-Lieut.	Va. St. Line	3 yrs.	Feb. 5, 1784
2419	Carter, Robert	200	Private	Va. Cont. Line	war	Feb. 6, 1784
2421	Cardwell, John	100	Private	Va. Cont. Line	3 yrs.	Feb. 6, 1784
2432	Cornelius, William	200	Gunner	St. Navy	3 yrs.	Feb. 9, 1784
2435	Coleman, Wyatt	3110⅔	Lieutenant	Va. St. Line	7 yrs.	Feb. 9, 1784
2511	Cogay, John (James Hawkins, assee.)	100	Private	Va. St. Line	3 yrs.	Feb. 18, '84
2513	Cawthorn, William (James Hawkins, assee.)	100	Private	Va. St. Line	3 yrs.	Feb. 18, '84

LAND BOUNTY WARRANTS.

Warrant.	Name.	Acres	Rank.	Department.	Term	Date.
2543	Conway, Samuel (Francis Graves, assee.)	200	Corporal	Va. Cont. Line	3 yrs.	Feb. 19, '84
2559	Cougall, John	100	Private	Va. Cont. Line	3 yrs.	Feb. 20, '84
2562	Crawford, John	444	Lieutenant	Va. Cont. Line	7th yr	Feb. 20, '84
2563	Camp, James, (Thomas Camp, heir to)	100	Private	Va. Cont. Line	3 yrs.	Feb. 20, '84
2574	Chisam, James	100	Private	Va. St. Line	war	Feb. 21, '84
2588	Callahan, Major (Francis Graves, assee.)	100	Private	Va. Cont. Line	3 yrs.	Feb. 23, '84
2592	Creamer, William (Francis Graves, assee.)	100	Private	Va. Cont. Line	3 yrs.	Feb. 23, '84
2616	Cox, Samuel (Daniel Flowerree, assee.)	100	Private	Va. Cont. Line	3 yrs.	Feb. 24, '84
2642	Cowherd, Francis	666⅔	Captain	Va. Cont. Line	7th yr	Feb. 26, '84
2652	Cuthburt, William (Samuel Trower, assee.)	200	Corporal	Va. Cont. Line	3 yrs.	Feb. 28, '84
2660	Crosslick, Edward	100	Private	Va. St. Art.	3 yrs.	Mch. 1, 1784
2679	Calvert, Joseph	2666⅔	Lieutenant	Va. St. Line	3 yrs.	Mch. 3, 1784
2681	Clarke, William	2666⅔	Lieutenant	Va. St. Line	3 yrs.	Mch. 3, 1784
2683	Chaplain, Abraham	2666⅔	Lieutenant	Va. St. Line	3 yrs.	Mch. 3, 1784
2684	Clarke, Richard	2666⅔	Lieutenant	Va. St. Line	3 yrs.	Mch. 3, 1784
2693	Coleman, Thomas (Martin Hawkins, assee.)	200	Sergeant	Va. Cont. Line	3 yrs.	Mch. 3, 1784
2719	Coleman, Joseph	200	Sergeant	Va. Cont. Line	3 yrs.	Mch. 6, 1784
2724	Cheseround, John	100	Private	Va. Cont. Line	3 yrs.	Mch. 6, 1784
2737	Coats, George	100	Private	Va. Cont. Line	3 yrs.	Mch. 8, 1784
2782	Clarke, James	100	Private	Va. Cont. Line	3 yrs.	Mch. 18, '84
2785	Carrick, James	100	Private	Va. Cont. Line	3 yrs.	Mch. 18, '84
2789	Charity, Charles	200	Private	Va. Cont. Line	war	Mch. 18, '84
2792	Cole, John	200	Sergeant	Va. Cont. Line	3 yrs.	Mch. 19, '84
2797	Coleman, Thomas	100	Private	Va. Cont. Line	3 yrs.	Mch. 19, '84
2799	Camp, Thomas (William Camp, heir at law)	400	Corporal	Va. Cont. Line	war	Mch. 20, '84
2809	Childress, Meredith	100	Private	Va. Cont. Line	3 yrs.	Mch. 23, '84
2821	Cooke, William (James Hawkins, assee.)	400	Sergeant	Va. Cont. Line	war	Mch. 26, '84
2833	Campbell, William	100	Private	Va. Cont. Line	3 yrs.	Mch. 27, '84
2836	Carter, John	200	Sergeant	Va. St. Line	3 yrs.	Mch. 27, '84
2884	Colvin, James	100	Private	Va. Cont. Line	3 yrs.	Apr. 5, 1784
2888	Coon, Anthony	100	Private	Va. Cont. Line	3 yrs.	Apr. 5, 1784
2901	Cartwright, Jesse	100	Private	Va. Cont. Line	3 yrs.	Apr. 7, 1784
2902	Carbine, Henry	100	Private	Va. Cont. Line	3 yrs.	Apr. 7, 1784
2904	Chatham, John	200	Private	Va. Cont. Line	war	Apr. 7, '84
2909	Coleman, Richard	100	Private	Va. St. Line	3 yrs.	Apr. 8, 1784
2946	Curtis, James	100	Private	Va. Cont. Line	3 yrs.	Apr. 17, '84
2966	Christian, Nicholas	200	Steward	Va. St. Navy	3 yrs.	Apr. 19, '84
2970	Cleveland, John (William Taylor, assee.)	100	Private	Va. Cont. Line	3 yrs.	Apr. 20, '84
2978	Connor, John	100	Private	Va. Cont. Line	3 yrs.	Apr. 20, '84
2999	Campbell, Dennis (John Rinns, assee.)	200	Private	Va. Cont. Line	war	Apr. 21, '84
3001	Campbell, Richard (Archibald Campbell, heir at law)	6000	Lieut.-Col.	Va. Cont. Line	3 yrs.	Apr. 22, '84
3042	Collins, John	200	Private	Va. Cont. Line	3 yrs.	May 4, 1784
3050	Clemens, John	200	Private	Va. Cont. Line	war	May 6, 1784
3051	Carlton, William (Edward Valentine, assee.)	100	Private	Va. Cont. Line	3 yrs.	May 6, 1784
3055	Carter, William	100	Private	Va. Cont. Line	3 yrs	May 7, 1784
3077	Cosby, Sydnor	400	Sergeant	Va. Cont. Line	war	May 14, '84
3079	Camron, Hugh (Duncan Camron, heir at law)	100	Private	Va. Cont. Line	3 yrs.	May 17, '84
3083	Collins, Adam (William Reynolds, assee.)	100	Private	Va. St. Line	3 yrs.	May 20, '84
3138	Clark, John	100	Private	Va. St. Line	3 yrs.	June 9, 1784
3156	Carpenter, George (John Carpenter, heir at law)	100	Private	Va. St. Line	3 yrs.	June 14, '84
3161	Clarke, Henry	200	Sergeant	Va. Cont. Line	3 yrs.	June 16, '84
3165	Clayton, Henry	100	Private	Va. St. Line	3 yrs.	June 16, '84
3185	Colbert, Elisha (Bazel Colbert, heir at law)	100	Private	Va. Cont. Line	3 yrs.	June 22, '84
3189	Chunn, Sylvester	100	Private	Va. Cont. Line	3 yrs	June 23, '84
②3200	Clough, John	400	Sergeant	Va. Cont. Line	war	June 23, '84
3201	Chambers, Robert (Jacob Dorin, assee.)	200	Sergeant	Va. Cont. Line	3 yrs.	June 24, '84
3205	Collins, Richard (Thomas Collins, heir at law)	100	Private	Va. St. Line	3 yrs.	June 24, '84

LAND BOUNTY WARRANTS. 19

Warrant.	Name.	Acres	Rank.	Department.	Term	Date.
3223	Cocke, Pleasant (Robt. Boyd, Mart'a, his wife, and Miss Theodocia Cocke, heirs and reps.)	4000	Captain	Va. Cont. Line	3 yrs.	June 28, '84
3229	Carlton, Lewis (James Lewis, assee.)	100	Private	Va. Cont. Line	3 yrs.	June 29, '84
3237	Clark, Edmond (Benjamin Smith, assee.)	200	Sergeant	Va. Cont. Line	3 yrs.	June 29, '84
3246	Conner, James	200	Sergeant	Va. Cont. Line	3 yrs.	June 29, '84
3251	Crews, Edward	100	Private	Va. Cont. Line	3 yrs.	June 30, '84
3266	Carter, Thomas (Thos. Pinkhard, assee.)	100	Captain	Va. Cont. Line	3 yrs.	July 1, 1784
3272	Cockrell, Littleton (Samuel Blackwell, assee.)	100	Sailor	Va. St. Navy	3 yrs.	July 1, 1784
3278	Curtice, Henry	100	Sailor	Va. St. Navy	3 yrs.	July 1, 1784
3305	Colbert, John	100	Private	Va. Cont. Line	3 yrs.	June 2, 1784
3322	Casey, James	200	Sergeant	Va. Cont. Line	3 yrs.	July 13, '84
3334	Conore, Andrew	200	Private	Va. St. Line	war	July 19, '84
3336	Coldwater, John	200	Private	Va. St. Line	war	July 19, '84
3351	Conley, Timothy	200	Private	Va. Cont. Line	war	July 22, '84
3376	Croxton, Richard	100	Private	Va. Cont. Line	3 yrs.	Aug. 4, 1784
3384	Carter, Obadiah (Samuel McCraw, assee.)	200	Sergeant	Va. Cont. Line	3 yrs.	Aug. 6, 1784
3391	Consolver, Charles (Mary Consolver, rep.)	100	Private	Va. Cont. Line	3 yrs.	Aug. 13, '84
3417	Croxton, John	100	Private	Va. Cont. Line	3 yrs.	Aug. 27, '84
3426	Coller, James (William Reynolds, assee.)	100	Private	Va. St. Line	3 yrs.	Aug. 28, '84
3442	Christian, James (William Reynolds, assee. of Richard Christian, legal rep.)	400	Corporal	Va. Cont. Line	war	Sept. 15, '84
3456	Carny, Anthony (Thos. Kennon, assee. of Wm. Carny, who was heir at law to)	400	Sergeant	Va. Cont. Line	war	Oct. 7, 1784
3459	Carr, Joseph	400	Sergeant	Va. Cont. Line	war	Oct. 12, '84
3472	Cooper, Leonard	4000	Captain	Va. Cont. Line	7 yrs.	Oct. 18, '84
3473	Cooper, Leonard	1000	Captain	Va. Cont. Line	7 yrs.	Oct. 18, '84
3474	Cooper, Leonard	1000	Captain	Va. Cont. Line	7 yrs.	Oct. 18, '84
3475	Cooper, Leonard	1000	Captain	Va. Cont. Line	7 yrs.	Oct. 18, '84
3476	Cooper, Leonard	666⅔	Captain	Va. Cont. Line	7 yrs.	Oct. 18, '84
3484	Casey, John (Francis Graves, assee. of Robert Broadus, who was assee. of John Casey)	200	Private	Va. Cont. Line	war	Oct. 26, '84
3493	Craig, John	100	Private	Va. Cont. Line	3 yrs.	Nov. 2, 1784
3497	Carter, John (Richard Carter, heir at law)	200	Sergeant	Va. Cont. Line	3 yrs.	Nov. 4, 1784
3503	Chavers, Robert W	100	Private	Va. Cont. Line	3 yrs.	Nov. 4, 1784
3505	Cosby, Thomas	100	Private	Va. Cont. Line	3 yrs.	Nov. 5, 1784
3513	Casey, John	200	Private	Va. Cont. Line	war	Nov. 9, 1784
3575	Carter, George	100	Private	Va. St. Line	3 yrs.	Dec. 15, '84
3582	Carter, Dale	100	Private	Va. St. Line	3 yrs.	Dec. 16, '84
3599	Capts, Obadiah	100	Private	Va. St. Line	3 yrs.	Dec. 21, '84
3602	Cross, John (John Bartlett, assee.)	200	Private	Va. Cont. Line	war	Dec. 21, '84
3609	Cook, William	100	Private	Va. St. Line	3 yrs.	Dec. 22, '84
3621	Clarke, Robert	100	Private	Va. St. Line	3 yrs.	Dec. 23, '84
3637	Crosby, William	100	Private	Va. Cont. Line	3 yrs.	Dec. 30, '84
3670	Cope, Thomas	100	Private	Va. Cont. Line	3 yrs.	Jan. 4, 1785
3691	Clerk, Hezekiah	100	Private	Va. Cont. Line	3 yrs.	Jan. 20, '85
3692	Custard, George	100	Private	Va. Cont. Line	3 yrs.	Jan. 20, '85
3701	Custard, John	100	Private	Va. Cont. Line	3 yrs.	Jan. 20, '85
3713	Childress, Alexander (William Dillen, assee.)	100	Private	Va. Cont. Line	3 yrs.	Jan. 20, '85
3717	Chavers, James	100	Private	Va. Cont. Line	3 yrs.	Jan. 22, '85
3731	Casady, James	466⅔	Sergeant	Va. Cont. Line	7 yrs.	Feb. 7, 1785
3748	Cummins, George	100	Private	St. Line	3 yrs.	Feb. 9, 1785
3754	Cooper, Charles	100	Private	Va. Cont. Line	3 yrs.	Feb. 14, '85
3758	Clarke, John	100	Private	Va. Cont. Line	3 yrs.	Feb. 19, '85
3763	Chandler, Thomas (Mitchell Chandler, legal rep.)	1466⅔	Lieutenant	St. Navy	3 yrs.	Feb. 28, '85
3764	Chandler, Thomas Mitchell (Chandler, legal rep.)	'200	Lieutenant	St. Navy	3 yrs.	Mch. 17, '85
3774	Collins, Thomas	200	Sergeant	Va. Cont. Line	3 yrs.	Feb. 28, '85
3775	Chenault, John	100	Private	Va. St. Line	3 yrs.	Mch. 11, '85
3781	Carnes, Joshua	200	Private	Va. St. Line	war	Mch. 12, '85

20 LAND BOUNTY WARRANTS.

War-rant.	Name.	Acres	Rank.	Department.	Term	Date.
3789	Conner, Edward (Mary Rodes and Elizabeth Hitchcock, legal reps.)	2666⅔	Cornet	Va. Cont. Line	3 yrs.	Mch. 25, '85
3795	Cooper, Reuben	200	Sergeant	Va. Cont. Line	3 yrs.	Apr. 5, 1785
3826	Crawson, John Hanson	100	Private	Va. Cont. Line	3 yrs.	Apr. 26, '85
3843	Coleman, James	100	Private	Va. Cont. Line	3 yrs.	Apr. 30, '85
3845	Cralle, Rodham K	100	Private	Va. Cont. Line	3 yrs.	May 2, 1785
3852	Chapin, Solomon	100	Private	Va. Cont. Line	3 yrs.	May 6, 1785
3857	Crook, Joseph	200	Sergeant	Va. Cont. Line	3 yrs	May 6, 1785
3862	Cropper, James	200	Private	Va. Cont. Line	war	May 7, 1785
3872	Conolly, Philip	100	Private	Va. Cont. Line	3 yrs.	May 10, '85
3876	Cartright, Peter	100	Private	Va. Cont. Line	3 yrs	May 10, '85
3921	Cullickan, John	200	Private	Va. Cont. Line	war	June 21, '85
3926	Chambers, James	100	Private	Va. Cont. Line	3 yrs.	June 21, '85
3927	Conard, James	100	Private	Va. Cont. Line	3 yrs.	June 21, '85
3940	Clarke, Robert	266⅔	Private	Va. Cont. Line	7 yrs.	Aug. 2, 178>
3962	Cardiff, Miles	100	Private	Va. Cont. Line	3 yrs.	Aug. 13, '85
3968	Connor, Terrence	200	Private	Va. Cont. Line	3 yrs.	Sept. 6, 1785
3971	Casey, James (Samuel Couch, assee.)	100	Private	Va. Cont. Line	3 yrs.	Sept. 12, '85
3979	Campbell, David	200	Sergeant	Va. St. Line	3 yrs.	Oct. 15, '85
3989	Crews, Joseph	200	Private	Va. Cont. Line	war	Oct. 29, '85
3999	Chavious, James (Wm. Pettyjohn, assee. of Joshua Humphrey, who was assee. of)	100	Private	Va. St. Line	3 yrs.	Nov. 19, '85
4003	Chavers, Samuel (Wm. Pettyjohn, assee. of Joshua Humphrey, who was assee. of)	100	Private	Va. Cont. Line	3 yrs.	Nov. 19, '85
4004	Chizham, James (Wm. Chizham, heir at law)	100	Private	Va. Cont. Line	3 yrs.	Nov. 23, '85
4010	Cumberford, Isaac (Henry Banks, assee.)	100	Private	Va. Cont. Line	3 yrs.	Dec. 2, 1785
4042	Cruidson, Benjamin	200	Private	Cont. Line	war	Dec. 15, '85
4104	Camp, James (Thos. Camp, heir at law)	100	Private	Va. Cont. Line	3 yrs.	Feb. 6, 1786
4°27	Camp, Marshall (Thos. Camp, heir at law)	200	Private	Va. Cont. Line	war	Mch. 18, '86
4129	Carving, Jeremiah	200	Private	Va. Cont. Line	war	Mch. 18, '86
4144	Cook, Zachariah	100	Private	Va. Cont. Line	3 yrs.	Apr. 13, '86
4145	Clement, Edward W	100	Private	Va. Cont. Line	3 yrs.	Apr. 19, '86
4176	Cock, Benjamin	100	Private	Va. Cont. Line	3 yrs.	June 20, '86
4216	Campbell, Thomas (Sam'l Lamm, assee. of Wm. Reynolds, assee. of)	100	Private	Va. Cont. Line	3 yrs.	Oct. 4, 1786
4223	Currel, Jacob	100	Sailor	Va. St. Navy	3 yrs.	Nov. 1, 1786
4224	Cornelius, William	100	Sailor	Va. St. Line (Navy)	3 yrs.	Nov. 1, 1786
4230	Coats, Samuel (John Coats, heir at law)	100	Sailor	Va. St. Navy	3 yrs.	Nov. 16, '86
4239	Cole, William	100	Private	Va. Cont. Line	3 yrs.	Dec. 13, '86
4249	Chambers, James	200	Private	Va. Cont. Line	war	Jan. 6, 1787
4255	Collins, Thomas (Bartlett Collins, heir at law)	200	Private	Va. Cont. Line	war	Jan. 31, '87
4276	Covey, Drury	100	Private	Va. Cont. Line	3 yrs.	Apr. 7, 1787
4283	Cooper, Thomas	100	Private	Va. Cont. Line	3 yrs	Apr. 16, '87
4294	Carpenter, John (James Carpenter, heir at law)	200	Private	Va. Cont. Line	war	June 14, '87
4316	Caswell, Michael	100	Private	Va. Cont. Line	3 yrs.	Oct. 23, '87
4329	Cook, William	2666⅔	Gunner	Va. St. Navy	3 yrs.	Nov. 3, 1787
4332	Colgin, William	100	Private	Va. Cont. Line	3 yrs.	Nov. 12, '87
4338	Cooper, Appoles (Robert Cooper, heir at law)	2666⅔	Lieutenant	Va. Cont. Line	3 yrs.	Nov. 23, '87
4341	Campbell, John	100	Private	Va. Cont. Line	3 yrs.	Nov. 28, '87
4342	Carr, William	100	Private	Va. St. Line	3 yrs.	Nov. 28, '87
4344	Chewing, Christopher (Charles Chewing, heir at law)	100	Private	Va. Cont. Line	3 yrs.	Nov. 23, '87
4351	Cosby, William	400	Sergeant	Va. Cont. Line	war	Dec. 6, 1787
4357	Crossen, Gustavus	100	Private	Va. St. Line	3 yrs.	Dec. 28, '87
4373	Childress, Meredith (William Reynolds, assee.)	100	Private	Va. St. Line	3 yrs.	Jan. 23, '88
4405	Cardwell, William	100	Private	Va. Cont. Line	3 yrs.	June 12, '88
4413	Cain, Matthias (John Bailey, assee. of the rep. of)	200	Private	Va. Cont. Line	war	July 17, '88
4431	Clendeny, George	100	Sailor	Va. St. Navy	3 yrs.	Aug. 4, 1788
4451	Cross, Ric'ard (Drury Cross, heir at law)	100	Private	Va. Cont. Line	3 yrs.	Feb. 26, '89
4473	Currell, James	1333⅓	Midshipman	Va. St. Navy	3 yrs.	Oct. 29, '89

LAND BOUNTY WARRANTS. 21

Warrant.	Name.	Acres	Rank.	Department.	Term	Date.
4474	Currell, James	1333⅓	Midshipman.	Va. St. Navy	3 yrs.	Oct. 29, '89
4482	Chandler, Jesse	200	Private	Va. Cont. Line	war	Dec. 4, 1789
4511	Carr, Samuel (Peter Carr, heir at law)	4666⅔	Captain	Va. St. Navy	war	Dec. 8, 1789
4520	Campbell, John	100	Private	St. Line	3 yrs.	Apr. 19, '91
4532	Creed, Thomas	466⅔	Sergeant	Cont. Line	3 yrs.	Apr. 19, '91
4533	Cottle, William (William McClung, assee.)	200	Private	Cont. Line	war	Oct. 18, '91
4535	Curtis, John	200	Private	Cont. Line	war	Oct. 18, '91
4550	Coleman, Samuel	100	Private	Cont. Line	war	Nov. 10, '91
4565	Chapen, Benjamin (Hiram Chapen, Gurdon Chapen, Richard W. Ashton and Eliza, his wife, Chas. Ashton and Margaret, his wife, and Anne Chapen, the said Hiram being heir at law to Benjamin Chapen)	6000	Surgeon	St. Navy	war	Jan. 21, '92
4569	Carter, William, Sr.	6000	Surgeon	Cont. Hospital	war	Feb. 7, 1792
4579	Coffin, John (the rep. of)	100	Private	Cont. Line	3 yrs.	June 16, '92
4580	Coffin, Lemuel	100	Private	Cont. Line	3 yrs.	June 16, '92
4611	Crawford, Nehemiah	100	Private	Cont. Line	3 yrs.	May 27, '93

D

5	Downs, John	100	Private	Va. Cont. Line	3 yrs.	Aug. 29, '82
23	Drew, Thomas Haines	4000	Captain	Va. Cont. Line	3 yrs.	Nov. 29, '82
27	Dudley, Henry	4000	Captain	Va. St. Line	3 yrs.	Nov. 30, '82
28	Dabney, Charles	6666⅔	Lieut.-Col. Com.			
47	Drew, Thomas H	4000	Captain	Va. St. Line	3 yrs.	Nov. 30, '82
77	Dandridge, John	4000	Captain	St. Gar. Reg.	3 yrs.	Dec. 14, '82
83	Davies, Doctor Joseph (Thos. Overton, assee.)	6000	Surgeon	Art. of Cont. Line	3 yrs.	Dec. 28, '82
94	Dillon, Jesse (Benjamin Dillon, heir at law)	200	Corporal	2d Va. Cont. Reg.	3 yrs.	Dec. 31, '82
121	Davis, John	200	Sergeant	Cont. Line		Jan. 14, '83
130	Diggs, Dudley	2666⅔	Lieutenant	Va. Line	3 yrs.	Feb. 10, '83
142	Driver, Francis	200	Sergeant	Cav. in St. Line	3 yrs.	Feb. 18, '83
152	Dix, Thomas	4000	Capt.-Lieut	St. Line	3 yrs.	Feb. 22, '83
157	Dugar, Robert	200	Sergeant	Art. in Va. Cont. Line	3 yrs.	Feb. 27, '83
207	Dickerson, Edmund (Robert Gibbins, heir at law)	5333⅓	Major	Va. Cont. Line	3 yrs.	Mch. 6, 1783
232	Dawson, Henry	1300	Lieutenant	Va. Line	3 yrs.	Mch. 27, '83
233	Dawson, Henry	1366⅔	Lieutenant	Va. Cont. Line	3 yrs.	Apr. 1, 1783
273	Dunn, Richard (Dr. James McClung, assee.)	100	Private	Va. Cont. Line	3 yrs.	Apr. 1, 1783
330	Davis, John	200	Private	St. Line	3 yrs.	Apr. 3, 1783
346	Duel, Henry	200	Private	St. Cav	war	Apr. 14, '83
357	Dean, John	200	Private	St. Cav	war	Apr. 16, '83
391	Duntor, Stephen	200	Private	St. Line	war	Apr. 17, '83
417	Davis, Lewis C	100	Private	Va. St. Line	war	Apr. 24, '83
426	Davis, Joseph	200	Private	Va. St. Line	3 yrs.	Apr. 26, '83
444	Davis, William	200	Private	Va. St. Line	war	Apr. 26, '83
472	Drury, Benjamin	200	Private	St. Line	war	Apr. 26, '83
507	Dunn, John	200	Private	St. Line	war	Apr. 29, '83
586	Duff, Edward	6000	Surgeon	Va. Cont. Line	3 yrs.	May 1, 1783
591	Duffey, James	100	Private	Va. Cont. Line	3 yrs.	May 16, '83
618	Dihouse, Edward	200	Private	Va. St. Line	war	May 17, '83
635	Denholm, Archibald	4000	Captain	Va. Cont. Line	3 yrs.	May 22, '83
682	Daviee, Richard	200	Sergeant	Va. St. Cav	3 yrs.	May 24, '83
713	Dagnell, Stephen	200	Private	Va. St. Cav	war	May 30, '83
727	Dandridge, Robert	2666⅔	Lieutenant	Va. Cont. Art	3 yrs.	June 2, 1783
730	Dupriest, John	200	Sergeant	Va. St. Art	3 yrs.	June 3, 1783
787	Dichic, William	100	Private	Va. Art	3 yrs.	June 11, '83
812	Darke, William	6666⅔	Lieut.-Col	Va. Cont Line	3 yrs.	June 13, '83
843	Davies, William	200	Private	Va. Cont. Line	war	June 16, '83
857	Dowell, William	100	Private	Va. Cont. Line	3 yrs.	
866	Danley, John (John Danley, heir at law to)	100	Private	Va. Cont. Line	3 yrs.	June 19, '83
880	Dougherty, Patrick	200	Private	Va. Cont. Line	3 yrs.	June 20, '83
910	Death, William	100	Serg.-Major.	Cont. Line	3 yrs.	June 20, '83
911	Dean, Michael	100	Private	Va. Cont. Line	3 yrs.	June 20, '83
912	Dean, Joseph	100	Private	Va. Cont. Line	3 yrs.	June 20, '83
955	Doller, William	100	Private	Va. Cont. Line	3 yrs.	June 20, '83

LAND BOUNTY WARRANTS.

Warrant.	Name.	Acres	Rank.	Department.	Term	Date.
960	DEMSEY, John	100	Private	Va. Cont. Line	3 yrs.	June 20, '83
967	DRAKE, Andrew	100	Private	Cont. Line	3 yrs.	June 20, '83
993	DODD, William	100	Private	Va. Cont. Line	3 yrs.	June 21, '83
1014	DUNBARR, James	200	Sergeant	Va. Cont. Line	3 yrs.	June 23, '83
1070	DUFFEY, James	200	Private	Va. Cont. Line	war	June 24, '83
1113	DOCHERTY, John	200	Private	Va. Cont. Line	war	June 24, '83
1148	DENNISON, Joseph	200	Private	Va. Cont. Line	war	June 24, '83
1156	DRAPER, George	2000	Reg. Surg.	Va. Cont. Line	3 yrs.	June 24, '83
1157	DRAPER, George	2000	Reg. Surg.	Va. Cont. Line	3 yrs.	June 24, '83
1158	DRAPER, George	2000	Reg. Surg.	Va. Cont. Line	3 yrs.	June 24, '83
1160	DEVERE, Isaac	200	Private	Va. Cont. Line	3 yrs.	June 24, '83
1168	DUDLEY, Robert (Ambrose Dudley, heir at law of)	2666⅔	Lieutenant	Va. Cont. Line	3 yrs.	June 24, '83
1212	DULANY, Thomas	100	Private	Va. St. Line	3 yrs.	June 26, '83
1213	DYER, Samuel	100	Private	Va. Cont. Line	3 yrs.	June 26, '83
1215	DRURY, Samuel	100	Private	Va. Cont. Line	3 yrs.	June 26, '83
1224	DANDRIDGE, Alexander Spottswood	in part 1000	Captain	Va. Cav	3 yrs.	June 26, '83
1225	DANRDIDGE, Alexander Spottswood	in part 1000	Captain	Va. Cont. Cav.	3 yrs.	June 26, '83
1226	DANDRIDGE, Alexander Spottswood	in part 1000	Captain	Va. Cont. Cav.	3 yrs.	June 26, '83
1227	DANDRIDGE, Alexander Spottswood	in part 1000	Captain	Va. Cont. Cav.	3 yrs.	June 26, '83
1228	DANIEL, John	200	Corporal	Va. St. Line	3 yrs.	June 26, '83
1246	DEAN, John	200	Sergeant	Va. St. Art.	3 yrs.	June 27, '83
1290	DOLLENS, William	200	Private	Va. Cont. Line	war	June 28, '83
1299	DARBY, Nathaniel	3110⅔	Lieutenant	Va. Cont. Line	7 yrs.	June 30, '83
1310	DRIVER, Edward	200	Sergeant	Va. Cont. Line	3 yrs.	June 30, '83
1313	DAVIS, John	100	Private	Va. St. Line	3 yrs.	June 30, '83
1320	DUNETH, John	200	Private	Va. St. Line	3 yrs.	June 30, '83
1332	DELAPLANE, James	2666⅔	Lieutenant	Va. Cont. Line	war	July 2, 1783
1335	DAWSON, Thomas	100	Private	St. Line	3 yrs.	July 5, 1783
1372	DAVIS, James	100	Private	Cont. Line	3 yrs.	July 5, 1783
1380	DEAN, Joshua (Frederick Smith, assee.)	100	Private	Cont. Line	3 yrs.	July 14, '83
1399	DEWNEY, John	200	Sergeant	St. Line	3 yrs.	July 16, '83
1446	DAVIS, Spillsby	400	Sergeant	Cont. Line	3 yrs.	July 21, '83
1473	DUNCAN, Charles	100	Private	Cont. Line	war	July 31, '83
1482	DAVIS, William	200	Sergeant	Cont. Line	3 yrs.	Aug. 1, 1783
1484	DRUMMOND, John	466⅔	Sergeant	Cont. Line	3 yrs.	Aug. 2, 1783
1486	DOBSON, Robert	2666⅔	Sail. Mast'r.	St. Navy	7 yrs.	Aug. 2, 1783
1521	DYLLARD, John	200	Private	Cont. Line	3 yrs.	Aug. 4, 1783
1530	DAILEY, James	200	Drummer	Cont. Line	war	Aug. 7, 1783
1532	DUNN, John	200	Private	Cont. Line	war	Aug. 8, 1783
1560	DEPRIEST, Robert	100	Private	Cont. Line	3 yrs.	Aug. 8, 1783
1568	DOBBINS, Charles	200	Drummer	St. Line	3 yrs.	Aug. 12, '83
1586	DAVIS, John (John Davis, heir at law)	100	Private	Cont. Line	war	Aug. 14, '83
1587	DOE, John	200	Private	Cont. Line	3 yrs.	Aug. 20, '83
1641	DOYLE, Robert	200	Private	Va. Cont. Line	war	Aug. 23, '83
1657	DENER, Jacob	400	Sergeant	Va. Cont. Line	war	Aug. 23, '83
1667	DEINER, Jacob	200	Drum Major	Va. Cont. Line	3 yrs.	Aug. 26, '83
1686	DICKSON, James	200	Private	Va. Cont. Line	war	Aug. 29, '83
1688	DENNIS, Henry	233⅓	Private	Va. Cont. Line	7 yrs.	Aug. 30, '83
1719	DYKES, Robert	100	Seaman	Va. St. Navy	3 yrs.	Sept. 2, 1783
1762	DAULTON, Moses	200	Sergeant	Va. Cont. Line	3 yrs.	Sept. 13, '83
1768	DUGMORE, John	100	Private	Va. St. Line	3 yrs.	Sept. 16, '83
1779	DUNN, James	200	Private	Va. Cont. Line	war	Sept. 20, '83
1809	DARNOLD, Aaron	100	Drummer	Va. Cont. Line	3 yrs.	Sept. 30, '83
1814	DAVENPORT, Clairborne	100	Private	Va. Cont. Line	3 yrs.	Oct. 2, 1783
1836	DUNN, Joshua	100	Private	Cont. Line	3 yrs.	Oct. 7, 1783
1846	DURHAM, James	100	Private	Cont. Line	3 yrs.	Oct. 10, '83
1866	DAVIS, Samuel	100	Private	Va. Cont. Line	3 yrs.	Oct. 14, '83
1888	DRAKE, Michael	200	Private	Va. Cont. Line	3 yrs.	Oct. 17, '83
1921	DOWELL, William	100	Sergeant	Va. Cont. Line	3 yrs.	Oct. 27, '83
④1904	DICKEY, Alexander	233⅓	Private	Va. Cont. Line	7 yrs.	Nov. 18, '83
④1916	DEVIER, John	100	Private	Va. St. Line	3 yrs.	Nov. 20, '83
④1931	DENTON, John	100	Private	Va. St. Line	3 yrs.	Nov. 22, '83
1965	DAWSON, Francis	400	Sergeant	Va. Cont. Line	war	Nov. 25, '83
1968	DYE, Jonathan (Nancy Dye, heir at law)	2666⅔	Lieutenant	Va. Cont. Line	3 yrs.	Nov. 26, '83
2010	DOIL, Robert	200	Private	Va. Cont. Line	war	Dec. 2, 1783
2044	DENNY (Drury), Henry	466⅔	Sergeant	Va. Cont. Line	7 yrs.	Dec. 9, 1783
2065	DIXON, James (Samuel Griffin, assee.)	100	Private	Va. St. Line	3 yrs.	Dec. 9, 1783

LAND BOUNTY WARRANTS.   23

Warrant.	Name.	Acres	Rank.	Department.	Term	Date.
2097	Day, George	100	Sailor	Va. St. Navy	3 yrs.	Dec. 10, '83
2118	Delozer, Aza	200	Private	Va. Cont. Line	war	Dec. 13, '83
2137	Dixon, Anthony F.	1000	Reg. Surg	Va. St. Line	3 yrs.	Dec. 16, '83
2138	Dixon, Anthony F.	5000	Reg. Surg	Va. St. Line	3 yrs.	Dec. 16, '83
2146	Donnakin, Daniel	100	Private	Va. Cont. Line	3 yrs.	Dec. 18, '83
2171	Davis, James	100	Private	Va. St. Line	3 yrs.	Dec. 20, '83
2187	Dogan, Henry	100	Private	Va. Cont. Line	3 yrs.	Dec. 22, '83
2201	Drew, John	1000	Lieutenant	Va. Cont. Line	war	Dec. 23, '83
2212	Drew, John	1666⅔	Lieutenant	Va. Cont. Line	war	Dec. 23, '83
2218	Dupe, William	200	Private	Va. Cont. Line	war	Jan. 5, 1784
2268	Dishman, James	200	Private	Va. Cont. Line	war	Jan. 21, '84
2285	Dungie, James	100	Private	Va. St. Line	3 yrs.	Jan. 26, '84
2302	Dick, Alexander	5333⅓	Major	Va. St. Line	3 yrs.	Jan. 27, '84
2312	Dade, Francis	4000	Captain	Va. Cont. Line	3 yrs.	Jan. 29, '84
2342	Davis, William (William Reynolds, assee.)	200	Private	Va. St. Line	war	Jan. 31, '84
2386	Dell, Joseph (Martin Hawkins, assee.)	100	Private	Va. Cont. Line	3 yrs.	Feb. 3, 1784
2391	Davenport, Joel (Martin Hawkins, assee.)	100	Private		3 yrs.	Feb. 3, 1784
2415	Davenport, Opie	2666⅔	Lieutenant	Va. St. Line	war	Feb. 5, 1784
2416	Davison, Josiah	100	Private	Va. Cont. Line	3 yrs.	Feb. 6, 1784
2452	Davies, William	7777⅞	Colonel	Va. Cont. Line	7 yrs.	Feb. 11, '84
2458	Day, John (Henry Banks, assee.)	200	Private	Va. Cont. Line	war	Feb. 11, '84
2483	Duval, Daniel	4000	Captain	Va. Cont. Line	3 yrs.	Feb. 13, '84
2495	Danby, Jonathan (Francis Graves, assee. of)	100	Private	Va. Cont. Line	3 yrs.	Feb. 14, '84
2516	Downey, Michael	100	Private	Va. St. Line	3 yrs.	Feb. 18, '84
2584	Doyle, John (Farrell O'Neal, assee.)	200	Private	Va. Cont. Line	war	Feb. 23, '84
2591	Dyles, John	100	Sailor	Va. St. Navy	3 yrs.	Feb. 23, '84
2624	Drummond, Joshua (Daniel Flowerree, assee.)	100	Private	Va. St. Line	3 yrs.	Feb. 24, '84
2654	Driskill, Dennis	100	Private	Va. St. Line	3 yrs.	Mch. 1, 1784
2661	Davidson, Joseph (James Bedford, assee.)	100	Private	Va. Cont. Line	3 yrs.	Mch. 1, 1784
2703	Dillard, Edward (Francis Graves, assee.)	100	Private	Va. Cont. Line	3 yrs.	Mch. 4, 1784
2819	Downton, William	200	Gunner	Va. St. Navy	3 yrs.	Mch. 25, '84
2826	Dewit, Henry	100	Private	Va. Cont. Line	3 yrs.	Mch. 26, '84
2848	Dunstan, Warner	100	Private	Va. St. Line	3 yrs.	Mch. 30, '84
2874	Demoss, John	200	Private	Va. Cont. Line	war	Apr. 5, 1784
2948	Doren, Terence	100	Private	Va. Cont. Line	3 yrs.	Apr. 17, '84
2955	Davis, James	100	Private	Va. Cont. Line.	3 yrs.	Apr. 17, '84
3062	Dunnevent, Abraham	100	Private	Va. St. Line	3 yrs.	May 10, '84
3065	Dunston, Alman (Edward Valentine, assee.)	100	Private	Va. St. Line	3 yrs.	May 10, '84
3088	Davison, Ambrose (James Vaughan, assee.)	100	Private	Va. Cont. Line	3 yrs.	May 22, '84
3089	Davison, Joshua (James Vaughan, assee.)	200	Private	Va. Cont. Line	war	May 22, '84
3092	Decker, Samuel	100	Private	Va. Cont. Line	3 yrs.	May 22, '84
3111	Davis, Samuel	200	Private	Va. Cont. Line	war	May 29, '84
3117	DeKlauman, C. C.	1000	Major	Va. St. Line	3 yrs.	June 4, 1784
3118	DeKlauman, C. C.	1000	Major	Va. St. Line	3 yrs.	June 4, 1784
3119	DeKlauman, Christian C.	1000	Major	Va. St. Line	3 yrs.	June 4, 1784
3120	DeKlauman, Christian C.	2333⅓	Major	Va. St. Line	3 yrs.	June 4, 1784
3122	Davis, Joseph (William Reynolds, assee.)	200	Private	Va. St. Line	war	June 5, 1784
3126	Delaney, Anthony (Daniel Delaney, heir to)	200	Corporal	Va. Cont. Line	3 yrs.	June 5, 1784
3157	Delph, Daniel (Michael Delph, heir at law)	100	Private	Va. St. Line	3 yrs.	June 23, '84
3160	Darby, Darmon	100	Pilot	Va. St. Navy	3 yrs.	June 23, '84
3190	Daniel, George	100	Sailor	Va. St. Navy	3 yrs.	June 26, '84
3191	Daniel, Thomas	100	Sailor	Va. St. Navy	3 yrs.	June 14, '84
3192	Dee, John	100	Private	Va. St. Line	3 yrs.	June 15, '84
3219	Demoville, Samuel	100	Seaman	St. Navy	3 yrs.	June 29, '84
3231	Dear, Benjamin (James Marney, assee.)	100	Private	Va. Cont. Line	3 yrs.	June 29, '84
3274	Davison, David	200	Private	Va. Cont. Line	war	July 1, 1784
3279	Dogget, Clement	100	Sailor	Va. St. Navy	3 yrs.	July 1, 1784
3293	Davis, Nicholas	100	Private	Va. Cont. Line	3 yrs.	July 1, 1784
3374	Davis, John	200	Sergeant	Va. St. Line	3 yrs.	Aug. 3, 1784

24 LAND BOUNTY WARRANTS.

War-rant.	Name.	Acres	Rank.	Department.	Term	Date.
3380	Dowdy, Clairborne (James Faris, assee.)	100	Private	Va. Cont. Line	3 yrs.	Aug. 5, 1784
3383	Dodman, Samuel	200	Sergeant	Va. Cont. Line	3 yrs.	Aug. 5, 1784
3423	Davis, John (William Reynolds, assee.)	200	Private	Va. St. Line	war	Aug. 28, '84
3444	Dawson, James	200	Private	Va. Cont. Line	war	Sept. 20, '84
3471	Dunn, James (Joshua Dunn, heir at law)	100	Private	Va. St. Line	3 yrs.	Oct. 19, '84
3544	Day, William	100	Private	Va. Cont. Line	3 yrs.	Nov. 29, '84
3550	Dunlop, John (Samuel Dunlop, heir at law)	200	Private	Va. Cont. Line	war	Dec. 2, 1784
3555	Dewitt, Peter (Joseph Vanmeter, assee.)	100	Private	Va. Cont. Line	3 yrs.	Dec. 6, 1784
3567	Deamon, Robert (John Deamon, heir at law)	200	Sergeant	Va. Cont. Line	3 yrs.	Dec. 9, 1784
3572	Downton, George	200	Private	Va. St. Line	3 yrs.	Dec. 15, '84
3603	Davis, Acquilla	200	Private	Va. St. Line	war	Dec. 21, '84
3615	Dangerfield, William	400	Sergeant	Va. Cont. Line	war	Dec. 23, '84
3640	Davis, John	100	Seaman	Va. St. Navy	war	Dec. 30, '84
3684	Dally, George (William Reynolds, assee. of Edward Valentine, who was assee. of)	200	Private	Va. Cont. Line	war	Jan. 11, '85
3709	Decker, Nicholas	100	Private	Va. Cont. Line	3 yrs.	Jan. 20, '85
3726	Draper, Robert	100	Private	Va. Cont. Line	3 yrs.	Jan. 31, '85
3739	Drummond, Alexander	200	Private	Va. Cont. Line	war	Feb. 7, 1785
3743	Doland, John	200	Private	Va. Cont. Line	war	Feb. 7, 1785
3749	Dunbar, Hamilton (Andrew Dunbar, heir at law)	200	Sergeant	Va. Cont. Line	3 yrs.	Feb. 9, 1785
3776	Dixon, Edward	100	Private	Va. St. Line	3 yrs.	Mch. 12, '85
3802	Day, Thomas (Lipscomb Norvell, assee. of Wm. Reynolds, who was assee. of)	100	Private	Va. St. Line	3 yrs.	Apr. 12, '85
3847	Dixon, Joseph (William Jackson, assee.)	200	Private	Va. Cont. Line	war	May 2, 1785
3881	Dunn, Patrick	100	Private	Va. Cont. Line	3 yrs.	May 23, '85
3891	Dallis, Robert (Robert Rankins, assee.)	100	Private	Va. Cont. Line	3 yrs.	June 15, '85
3910	Dailey, John	200	Private	Va. Cont. Line	3 yrs.	June 21, '85
3915	Davis, Thomas (George Wilke, assee.)	400	Corporal	Va. Cont. Line	war	June 21, '85
3943	Dent, John	2000	Lieutenant	Va. Cont. Line	3 yrs.	Aug. 9, 1785
3944	Dent, John	666⅔	Lieutenant	Va. Cont. Line	3 yrs.	Aug. 9, 1785
3981	Davis, William	400	Corporal	Va. Cont. Line	war	Oct. 18, '85
4019	Davenport, William	4000	Captain	Va. Cont. Line	3 yrs.	
4060	Dennis, William	200	Private	Va. Cont. Line	war	Dec. 31, '85
4073	Dicks, George	200	Private	Va. Cont. Line	war	Jan. 13, '86
4075	Davis, Arthur (Elizabeth Davis, rep.)	200	Private	Va. Cont. Line	war	Jan. 13, '86
4135	Davis, Thompson	200	Private	Va. Cont. Line	war	Mch. 23, '86
4138	Delozier, Richard D. (Daniel Delozier, rep.)	200	Private	Va. St. Line	3 yrs.	Mch. 31, '86
4231	Davis, Jeduthin (Douther Davis, heir at law)	100	Sailor	Va. St. Navy	3 yrs.	Nov. 16, '86
4243	Day, Westerbrook	100	Private	Va. Cont. Line	3 yrs.	Dec. 21, '86
4284	Diskin, Daniel	100	Private	Va. Cont. Line	3 yrs.	Apr. 16, '86
4319	Davis, Henry	100	Private	Va. Cont. Line	3 yrs.	Oct. 23, '87
4327	Drake, Thomas (Thomas Drake, rep.)	2666⅔	Lieutenant	Va. Cont. Line	3 yrs.	Nov. 3, 1787
4363	Davis, William (Parker Bailey, assee.)	100	Private	Va. St. Line	3 yrs.	Jan. 14, '88
4376	Darvill, William (Wm. Reynolds, assee. of Jno. Depriest, assee. of)	2666⅔	Lieutenant	Va. Cont. Line	3 yrs.	Jan. 23, '88
4432	Diven, William	200	Sergeant	Va. Cont. Line	3 yrs.	Sept. 5, 1788
4433	Diven, Robert	100	Private	Va. Cont. Line	3 yrs.	Sept. 5, 1788
4434	Derossett, Samuel	200	Private	Va. Cont. Line	war	Sept. 13, '88
4441	Duncan, John (William Duncan, heir at law)	100	Private	Va. St. Line	3 yrs.	Nov. 1, 1788
4445	Dikes, Henry (Edward Mitchell, assee.)	100	Sailor	Va. St. Line	3 yrs.	Dec. 24, '88
4486	Dyer, Francis	100	Private	Va. Cont. Line	3 yrs.	Dec. 29, '89
4490	Dark, William	1111½	Lieutenant	Va. Cont. Line	7 yrs.	Mch. 5, 1790
4493	Daniel, Christopher (Geo. Rice, assee. of Charles Lewis, assee. of)	100	Private	Va. Cont. Line	3 yrs.	May 12, '90
4497	Davenport, Moses (the rep. of)	100	Private	Va. Cont. Line	3 yrs.	June 24, '90

LAND BOUNTY WARRANTS. 25

Warrant.	Name.	Acres	Rank.	Department.	Term	Date.
4499	DAVENPORT, Moses (Thos. Murry, assee.)	100	Private	Va. Cont. Line	3 yrs.	June 24, '90
4504	DASHPER, John (Sam'l Paine, assee. of Angel George, assee. of Thos. Dashper, heir at law to)	100	Private	Va. Cont. Line	3 yrs.	Nov. 13, '90
4507	DARING, Henry	3110⅔	Ensign	Va. St. Line	war	Nov. 27, '90
4508	DENTON, Thomas	400	Sergeant	Va. St. Line	war	Nov. 27, '90
4521	DALBY, William	200	Sergeant	Cont. Line	3 yrs.	Apr. 21, '91
4575	DIDLAKE, James (Robert Means, assee.)	200	Sergeant	Cont. Line	3 yrs.	May 7, 1792
4593	DUDLEY, Robert	100	Private	Cont. Line	3 yrs.	Nov. 15, '92
4597	DESHAZO, William	100	Private	Va. St. Line	3 yrs.	Dec. 8, 1792
4617	DOREN, James (Francis Graves, assee. of Edward Davis, assee. of Robert Nash, assee. of James Doren)	200	Corporal	Cont. Line	3 yrs.	June 29, '93

E

Warrant.	Name.	Acres	Rank.	Department.	Term	Date.
6	EWING, Alexander	2666⅔	Lieutenant	Va. Cont. Line	3 yrs.	Sept. 3, 1782
40	EDMUNDS, Thomas	4000	Captain	Service of U. S.	3 yrs.	Dec. 11, '82
166	EDMONDS, Elias	6000	Lieut.-Col.	Art. in St. Line	3 yrs.	Mch. 9, 1783
206	EDDENS, Samuel	4000	Captain	Artillery	3 yrs.	Mch. 27, '83
247	EVANS, William	1000	Lieutenant	Va. Cont. Line	3 yrs.	Apr. 2, 1783
248	EVANS, William	1666⅔	Lieutenant	Va. Cont. Line	3 yrs.	Apr. 2, 1783
253	ENGLISH, Charles (Rev. Robert Andrews, assee.)	100	Private	St. Line	3 yrs.	Apr. 3, 1783
294	EASTEN, Richard	2666⅔	Lieutenant	Va. Cont. Line	3 yrs.	Apr. 5, 1783
295	ESKRIDGE, William	1000	Lieutenant	Cont. Line	7 yrs.	Apr. 5, 1783
296	ESKRIDGE, William	2110⅔	Lieutenant	Cont. Line	7 yrs.	Apr. 5, 1783
302	EASTIN, Phillip	3110⅔	Lieutenant	Va. Cont. Line	7 yrs.	Apr. 8, 1783
339	EMRY, Thomas	200	Private	St. Line	war	Apr. 15, '83
412	EVANS, Thomas	200	Private	Va. St. Line	war	Apr. 25, '83
518	EDWARDS, Benjamin	200	Private	St. Line	war	May 1, 1783
534	ELLIOTT, Jeremiah	200	Private	St. Line	war	May 2, 1783
554	ELLMORE, Daniel (William Ellmore, heir at law)	200	Private	Va. St. Line		May 7, 1783
570	ELLMORE, William	400	Sergeant	Va. St. Line	3 yrs.	May 12, '83
575	ELZEY, Edward	100	Private	Va. St. Line	3 yrs.	May 15, '83
583	EWELL, Charles	4000	Captain	St. Line	3 yrs.	May 15, '83
648	EDWARDS, Thomas	100	Private	Va. St. Line	3 yrs.	May 27, '83
674	EPPS, William	4000	Captain	Va. Cont. Line	3 yrs.	May 29, '83
703	ELZY, Edward	200	Private	Va. St. Line	war	May 31, '83
718	EMMINS, William	200	Sergeant	Va. Cont. Art	3 yrs.	June 3, 1783
721	EDWARDS, Richard	100	Private	Va. Cont. Line	3 yrs.	June 3, 1783
747	EVANS, Charles	100	Private	Va. St. Line		
781	ELLIOTT, Wyatt	200	Private	Va. St. Line	3 yrs.	June 10, '83
837	ESTIS, Elisha	200	Sergeant	Va. Cont. Line	3 yrs.	June 16, '83
875	EUBANK, Royal	100	Private	Va. Cav. on Cont. Estab.	3 yrs.	June 19, '83
1030	EDMONSON, William	200	Sergeant	Va. Cont. Line	3 yrs.	June 23, '83
1081	EARLYWINE, Daniel	200	Private	Va. Cont. Line	war	June 24, '83
1106	ENGLISH, John	200	Private	Va. Cont. Line	war	June 24, '83
1269	EASTEN, William	200	Sergeant	Va. St. Line	3 yrs.	June 28, '83
1292	ENGLISH, Charles	200	Private	Va. St. Line	3 yrs.	June 28, '83
1303	EASTWOOD, Demsy	100	Private	Va. Cont. Line	3 yrs.	June 30, '83
1329	EWELL, Thomas	4000	Captain	St. Line	3 yrs.	July 5, 1783
1339	EDWARD, John	200	Private	Cont. Line	war	July 9, 1783
1386	EGGLESTON, Joseph	5333⅓	Major	Cont. Line	3 yrs.	July 17, '83
1406	EVANS, Philip	100	Private	Cont. Line	3 yrs.	July 21, '83
1407	ELMORE, George	100	Private	Cont. Line	3 yrs.	July 21, '83
1475	EPPS, William	4000	Capt.-Lieut	Cont. Line	3 yrs.	Aug. 1, 1783
1476	EDWARDS, Leroy	4000	Captain	Cont. Line	3 yrs.	Aug. 2, 1783
1481	EVANS, William	100	Private	Cont. Line	3 yrs.	Aug. 2, 1783
1573	EDWARDS, John	100	Private	St. Line	3 yrs.	Aug. 15, '83
1578	ELDER, Ephraim	200	Private	Cont. Line	war	Aug. 18, '83
1675	EMANUEL, Henry	200	Private	Va. Cont. Line	war	Aug. 27, '83
1818	ELAM, Lodwick	100	Private	Va. St. Line	3 yrs.	Oct. 3, 1783
1860	EPPES, Richard	200	Sergeant	Va. Cont. Line	3 yrs.	Oct. 14, '83
1864	EATON, Joseph	100	Private	Va. Cont. Line	3 yrs.	Oct. 14, '83
1929	ELLIOTT, William	200	Corporal	Va. Cont. Line	3 yrs.	Oct. 22, '83
1940	EDWARDS, Enoch	100	Seaman	Va. St. Navy	3 yrs.	Nov. 22, '83
1962	EDMUNDSON, Richard (John Deperest, assee.)	200	Sergeant	Va. Cont. Line	3 yrs.	Nov. 24, '83
2022	EDWARDS, William	100	Sailor	Va. St. Navy	3 yrs.	Dec. 6, 1783

LAND BOUNTY WARRANTS.

War-rant.	Name.	Acres	Rank.	Department.	Term	Date.
2092	EAKIN, Samuel	200	Sergeant	Va. Cont. Line	3 yrs.	Dec. 10, '83
2096	EDWARDS, Rodham	100	Sailor	Va. St. Navy	3 yrs.	Dec. 10, '83
2130	EDWARDS, Edmund	200	Private	Va. Cont. Line	war	Dec. 15, '83
2157	EUSTACE, John (William Eustace, heir at law)	4000	Captain	Va. Cont. Line	3 yrs.	Dec. 19, '83
2198	EVANS, John	200	Private	Va. Cont. Line	war	Dec. 22, '83
2293	EDGE, John	100	Private	Va. Cont. Line	3 yrs.	Jan. 26, '84
2366	EGGLESTON, William (Richard Eggleston, heir at law)	2666⅔	Lieutenant	Va. Cont. Line	3 yrs.	Feb. 2, 1784
2406	EMERSON, Henry	200	Sergeant	Va. Cont. Line	3 yrs.	Feb. 4, 1784
2420	ELLIS, James	100	Drummer	Va. St. Line	3 yrs.	Feb. 6, 1784
2450	EVANS, George	6000	Surgeon	Va. Cont. Line	3 yrs.	Feb. 10, '84
2493	EVANS, Henry	100	Private	Va. Cont. Line	3 yrs.	Feb. 14, '84
2505	ERSKINE, Charles	2666⅔	Subaltern	Va. Cont. Line	3 yrs.	Feb. 17, '84
2561	ELLIS, John (Jacob Goulden, assee.)	200	Sergeant	Va. Cont. Line	3 yrs.	Feb. 20, '84
2566	ELLIS, William (William Reynolds, assee.)	100	Private	Va. Cont. Line	3 yrs.	Feb. 20, '84
2585	ELLIOTT, James (Farrell O'Neal assee.)	200	Private	Va. Cont. Line	war	Feb. 23, '84
2637	EUSTACE, John	2666⅔	Lieutenant	Va. Cont. Line	war	Feb. 26, '84
2673	ELMORE, John	200	Sergeant	Va. Cont. Line	3 yrs.	Feb. 11, '84
2706	EPPES, Wyatt (John Depriest, assee. of Thomas Eppes, legal rep.)	100	Private	Va. Cont. Line	3 yrs.	Mch. 4, 1784
2723	EDMUNDSON, Benjamin	2666⅔	Lieutenant	Va. St. Line	3 yrs.	Mch. 6, 1784
2798	EDWARDS, James (Alexander Roan, assee.)	100	Private	Va. Cont. Line	3 yrs.	Mch. 20, '84
2847	EDMONDS, Daniel (John Stockdell, assee.)	200	Private	Va. St. Line	war	Mch. 30, '84
2924	ELLIOTT, Jidethan (William Reynolds, assee.)	100	Carpenter	Va. St. Navy	3 yrs.	Apr. 13, '84
2949	EATON, Micajah (Richard Claibourne and John Hawkins, assees.)	100	Private	Va. Cont. Line	3 yrs.	Apr. 17, '84
3158	EDWARDS, LE ROY	666⅔	Captain	Va. Cont. Line	7 yrs.	June 14, '84
3280	EDWARDS, Ellis (Samuel Blackwell, assee.)	100	Sailor	Va. St. Navy	3 yrs.	July 1, 1784
3344	ELMS, James	100	Private	Va. St. Line	3 yrs.	July 19, '84
3399	EVANS, Thomas	100	Private	Va. St. Line	3 yrs.	Aug. 17, '84
3491	ESKRIDGE, George	200	Sergeant	Va. Cont. Line	3 yrs.	Oct. 29, '84
3501	EVERHART, Laurence	200	Sergeant	Va. Cont. Line	3 yrs.	Apr. 25, '84
3679	EATON, William	100	Private	Va. Cont. Line	3 yrs.	Jan. 8, 1785
3723	EDWARDS, Spencer (James Thompson, assee.)	100	Private	Va. Cont. Line	3 yrs.	Jan. 28, '85
3762	EMMONS, John	200	Private	Va. Cont. Line	war	Feb. 28, '85
3812	EUBANK, John	200	Corporal	Va. Cont. Line	3 yrs.	Apr. 20, '85
3822	ETHEL, Benjamin (Henry Ethel, assee.)	100	Private	Va. Cont. Line	3 yrs.	Apr. 22, '85
3887	EPPERSON, Samuel (Thomas Richardson, assee.)	200	Private	Va. Cont. Line	war	June 6, 1785
3895	EBB, William	100	Private	Va. Cont. Line	3 yrs.	June 16, '85
3933	ELDRIDGE, Christopher (William Reynolds, assee.)	100	Private	Va. Cont. Line	3 yrs.	Aug. 1, 1785
3941	EVANS, William (Phillis Evans, legal rep.)	200	Private	Va. Cont. Line	war	Aug. 3, 1785
3986	ETHERINGTON, John	100	Private	Va. Cont. Line	3 yrs.	Oct. 21, '85
3988	EBBS, John (Jas. Ebbs, legal rep.)	200	Private	Va. Cont. Line	war	Oct. 28, '85
4043	EVANS, Stephen (Sam McCraw, assee.)	400	Corporal	Va. Cont. Line	war	Dec. 17, '85
4069	EWING, Edward (James Ewing, Jr., heir at law)	100	Private	Va. Cont. Line	war	Jan. 6, 1786
4072	ESKRIDGE, Edwin (Thomas Hobson, heir at law)	2666⅔	Midshipman	Va. St. Navy	3 yrs.	Jan. 13, '86
ⓐ 4083	ETTER, John	200	Private	Va. Cont. Line	war	Jan. 18, '86
4105	ESTIS, George	100	Private	Va. Cont. Line	3 yrs.	Feb. 7, 1786
4106	ESTIS, Rowland	100	Private	Va. Cont. Line	3 yrs.	Feb. 7, 1786
4122	ELWELL, Thomas	400	Corporal	Va. Cont. Line	war	Mch. 7, 1786
4126	ERMIN, Thomas	100	Private	Va. Cont. Line	3 yrs.	Mch. 11, '86
4266	ESKRIDGE, Samuel	2666⅔	Lieutenant	Va. St. Navy	3 yrs.	Mch. 28, '87
4282	EAGLE, William	100	Private	Va. Cont. Line	3 yrs	Apr. 11, '87
4331	EVANS, Philip	2666⅔	Carpenter (Gunner)	Va. St. Navy	3 yrs.	Nov. 9, 1787

LAND BOUNTY WARRANTS. 27

Warrant.	Name.	Acres	Rank.	Department.	Term	Date.
4396	Ellis, Matthew (Jas. Hines, assee. of Jno. Sims, assee. of Jno. Courtney, assee. of Thos. Armistead, assee. of)..	100	Private	Va. Cont. Line....	3 yrs.	Apr. 3, 1788
4398	Edward, George (Isaac Sims, assee. of the rep.)	100	Private	Va. St. Navy......	3 yrs.	Apr. 16, '88
4402	Elliotte, Alexander	2666⅔	Midshipman.	Va. St. Navy......	3 yrs.	June 1, 1788
4403	Elliotte, George	4000	Captain	Va. St. Navy......	3 yrs.	June 1, 1788
4475	Engel, Windel (Robt. Williams, assee.).....	200	Private	Va. Cont. Line....	war	Nov. 3, 1789
4512	Evans, Joseph	200	Sergeant . ..	Va. Cont. Line....	3 yrs.	Dec. 9, 1790
4539	Elms, James	100	Private	St. Line	3 yrs.	Nov. 10, '91
4540	Elms, William	200	Sergeant . ..	St. Line	3 yrs.	Nov. 10, '91

F

125	Fenn, Thomas	4000	Capt.-Lieut	Art. in Va. Line...	3 yrs.	Feb. 13, '83
145	Fowler, William	4000	Captain . . .	Va. Line	3 yrs.	Feb. 24, '83
244	Field, Reuben	4000	Captain . . .	Va. Cont. Line....	3 yrs.	Apr. 1, 1783
284	Fortune, Gardner	100	Private	St. Line	3 yrs.	Apr. 3, 1783
335	Franklin, James	100	Private	Va. Line	3 yrs.	Apr. 14, '83
373	Fletcher, Thomas	200	Private	St. Line	war	Apr. 19, '83
383	Fling, Philip (Philip Daw, assee.).....	100	Private	Va. Cont. Line....	3 yrs.	Apr. 23, '83
465	Finch, James	200	Private	St. Legion	war	Apr. 28, '83
468	Feagon, John	200	Private	St. Line	war	Apr. 29, '83
469	Fleet, John	2666⅔	Lieutenant .	St. Line	3 yrs.	Apr. 29, '83
485	Falvey, Patrick	200	Private	St. Line	war	Apr. 30, '83
493	Frogett, William	200	Private	St. Line	war	Apr. 30, '83
510	Farrow, Robert	200	Private	St. Line	war	May 1, 1783
520	Fears, Thomas	200	Private	St. Cav	war	May 1, 1783
537	Forrest, George	100	Private . ..	Cont. Line	3 yrs.	May 2, 1783
546	Fair, James (John Lyne, assee.)	200	Sergeant . ..	St. Line	3 yrs.	May 5, 1783
550	Flax, John	200	Private	St. Line	war	May 6, 1783
599	Fox, Thomas	4000	Captain . . .	Va. Cont. Line....	3 yrs.	May 20, '83
624	Foster, Robert	2666⅔	Lieutenant .	Va. Cont. Line....	3 yrs.	May 23, '83
655	Fisher, John	100	Private . ..	Va. St. Line.......	3 yrs.	May 27, '83
686	Fox, Lewis	100	Services ...	Va. Cont. Line....	3 yrs.	May 30, '83
696	Flournoy, Jacob	100	Private	Va. St. Art.......	3 yrs.	May 31, '83
707	Fox, Nathaniel	4000	Captain . . .	Va. Cont. Line....	3 yrs.	May 31, '83
867	Floyd, Thomas	200	Private	Va. St. Art.......	3 yrs	June 19, '83
881	French, Thomas	200	Private	Va. Cont. Line....	war	June 20, '83
885	Farrell, John	200	Drummer ..	Va. Cont. Line....	3 yrs.	June 20, '83
886	Farrell, John	100	Drummer ..	Va. Cont. Line....	3 yrs.	June 20, '83
918	Flaugherty, James	200	Sergeant . ..	Va. Cont. Line....	3 yrs.	June 20, '83
944	France, Peter	100	Private . ..	Va. Cont. Line....	3 yrs.	June 20, '83
980	France, Lewis	100	Private . ..	Va. Cont. Line....	3 yrs.	June 20, '83
982	Finley, Archibald	100	Private	Va. Cont. Line....	3 yrs.	June 20, '83
1001	Fantz, Valentine	100	Private	Va. Cont. Line....	3 yrs.	June 21, '83
1047	Finnegan, Patrick	200	Private	Va. Cont. Line....	war	June 24, '83
1077	Finney, John	200	Private	Va. Cont. Line....	war	June 24, '83
1096	Frazer, Alexander	400	Sergeant . ..	Va. Cont. Line....	war	June 24, '83
1112	Fowler, Joseph	200	Private	Va. Cont. Line....	war	June 24, '83
1257	Fromaget, Daniel	200	Private	Va. Cont. Line....	war	June 27, 83
1305	Field, William	100	Private	Va. Cont. Line....	3 yrs.	June 30, '83
1358	Fitzgerald, James	100	Private	St. Line	3 yrs.	July 12, '83
1377	Foster, John	200	Sergeant . ..	St. Line	3 yrs.	July 15, '83
1440	Foster, Peter	200	Sergeant . ..	St. Line	3 yrs.	July 28, '83
1442	Fall, Henry	100	Private ..	St. Line	3 yrs.	July 30, '83
1450	Finley, Samuel	6222	Major	Cont. Line	war	July 31, '83
1488	Flippin, Robert	100	Private	Cont. Line	3 yrs.	Aug. 4, 1783
1574	Flournoy, Samuel	200	Sergeant . ..	Cont. Line	3 yrs.	Aug. 15, '83
1582	Flemister, Lewis	233⅓	Private . ..	Cont. Line	7 yrs	Aug. 18, '83
1596	Fisher, Thomas	200	Private	Cont. Line	war	Aug. 20, '83
1605	Fletcher, Stephen	200	Private . ..	Cont. Line	war	Aug. 20, '83
1650	Fleming, William	400	Corporal . .	Va. Cont. Line....	war	Aug. 23, '83
1659	Fortune, Nathan	200	Private	Va. Cont. Line....	war	Aug. 25, '83
1701	Flatford, Robert	400	Sergeant . ..	Va. St. Line.......	war	Sept. 1, 1783
1731	Farenholtz, David	100	Private	Va. Cont. Line....	3 yrs.	Sept. 8, 1783
1758	Fleming, John	200	Sergeant . ..	Va. St. Line.......	3 yrs.	Sept. 12, '83
1829	Fitzsimmons, Nicholas	100	Private	Va. Cont. Line....	3 yrs.	Oct. 7, 1783
1861	Faris, William	100	Private	Va. Cont. Line....	3 yrs.	Oct. 14, '83
1863	Foster, William	200	Private	Va. Cont. Line....	war	Oct. 14, '83
1870	Foster, George	200	Private	Va. Cont. Line...	war	Oct. 15, '83
ⓐ 1880	Fleming, Charles	6000	Lieut.-Col .	Va. Cont. Line....	3 yrs.	Nov. 8, 1783
ⓐ 1910	Fennell, Reuben	100	Private	Va. Cont. Line....	3 yrs.	Nov. 19, '83

LAND BOUNTY WARRANTS.

Warrant.	Name.	Acres	Rank.	Department.	Term	Date.
⑨1912	Foster, John	100	Private	Va. Cont. Line	3 yrs.	Nov. 20, '83
⑤1935	Fitzgerald, James	200	Private	Va. Cont. Line	war	Nov. 22, '83
1966	Furbush, William	200	Sergeant	Va. Cont. Line	3 yrs.	Nov. 25, '83
1967	Faintleroy, Henry (William Moore, John Griffin, Joseph and Robert Faintleroy, heirs at law to)	4000	Captain	Va. Cont. Line	3 yrs.	Nov. 26, '83
1988	Fleet, Henry	2666⅔	Midshipman.	Va. St. Navy	3 yrs.	Nov. 28, '83
1994	Foster, William	200	Private	Va. Cont. Line	war	Nov. 29, '83
2009	Franklin, Joseph	200	Corporal	Va. Cont. Line	3 yrs.	Dec. 3, 1783
2046	Floyd, William	200	Private	Va. Cont. Line	war	Dec. 9, 1783
2048	Fear, Jacob	200	Private	Va. Cont. Line	war	Dec. 9, 1783
2049	Feggins, James	200	Private	Va. Cont. Line	war	Dec. 9, 1783
2067	Flint, John	100	Carpenter	Va. St. Navy	3 yrs.	Dec. 10, '83
2210	Foster, Peter	100	Sailor	Va. St. Line	3 yrs.	Dec. 23, '83
2232	Farmer, Jesse	100	Private	Va. Cont. Line	3 yrs.	Jan. 12, '84
2253	French, Richard	100	Private	Va. St. Line	3 yrs.	Jan. 21, '84
2279	Febiger, Christian	7777⅞	Colonel	Va. Cont. Line	7 yrs.	Jan. 24, '84
2288	Frowman, Elijah	100	Private	Va. St. Art	3 yrs.	Jan. 26, '84
2295	Fathorn, Edward	200	Private	Va. Cont. Line	war	Jan. 26, '84
2309	Fitzgerald, John	4666⅔	Captain	Va. Cont. Line	7 yrs.	Jan. 29, '84
2354	Flin, Thomas (Martin Hawkins, assee.)	100	Private	Va. Cont. Line	3 yrs.	Jan. 31, '84
2397	Fowler, Anderson (Thomas Aslin, assee.)	100	Private	Va. Cont. Line	3 yrs.	Feb. 3, 1784
2430	Fleetwood, Isaac	100	Seaman	St. Navy	3 yrs.	Feb. 9, 1784
2437	Forrest, Zach (Lewis Ford, assee.)	200	Sergeant	Va. Cont. Line	3 yrs.	Feb. 9, 1784
2492	Freeman, Hezekiah	100	Private	Va. St. Line	3 yrs.	Feb. 14, '84
2545	Fox, Nathaniel	666⅔	Captain	Va. Cont. Line	7 yrs.	Feb. 19, '84
2547	Fitzhugh, William	2666⅔	Lieutenant	Va. Cont. Line	war	Feb. 20, '84
2558	Fitzpatrick, Solomon (James Fitzpatrick, heir at law)	400	Sergeant	Va. Cont. Line	war	Feb. 20, '84
2602	Flowers, John (John Depriest, assee.)	200	Sergeant	Va. Cont. Line	3 yrs.	Feb. 24, '84
2610	Foster, John	2666⅔	Subaltern	Va. Cont. Line	war	Feb. 24, '84
2633	Foster, James (Robert Foster, heir at law)	4000	Captain	Va. Cont. Line	3 yrs.	Feb. 25, '84
2645	Fraser, Roderick	200	Sergeant	Va. St. Line	3 yrs.	Feb. 26, '84
2699	Fry, Joseph (George Fry, heir at law)	100	Private	Va. Cont. Line	3 yrs.	Mch. 3, 1784
2713	Fukeway, Joseph (Thomas Aselin, assee.)	100	Private	Va. Cont. Line	3 yrs.	Mch. 5, 1784
2733	Ferguson, John (Moses Ferguson, heir to)	100	Private	St. Art	3 yrs.	Mch. 6, 1784
2763	Fleming, Thomas (Warner Lewis and Mary, his wife; Addision Lewis and Susannah, his wife, legal reps.)	6666⅔	Colonel	Va. Cont. Line	3 yrs.	Mch. 16, '84
2764	Fleming, John (Warner Lewis and Mary, his wife; Addison Lewis and Susannah, his wife, legal reps.)	5333⅓	Major	Va. Cont. Line	3 yrs.	Mch. 16, '84
2767	Foster, Cosby	200	Private	Va. Cont. Line	war	Mch. 17, '84
2817	Farmer, Lodwick (Patrick Wright, assee.)	100	Private	Va. St. Line	3 yrs.	Mch. 25, '84
2831	Freeman, Anderson (John Depriest, assee.)	200	Sergeant	Va. Cont. Line	3 yrs.	Mch. 26, '84
2839	Frazer, Falvey (Thomas Frazier, heir at law)	2666⅔	Lieutenant	Va. Cont. Line	3 yrs.	Mch. 29, '84
2840	Furguson, Larkin	100	Private	Va. St. Line	3 yrs.	Mch. 29, '84
2851	Foster, William	100	Private	Va. Cont. Line	3 yrs.	Apr. 1, 1784
2868	Fitzgerald, John	5333⅓	Major	Va. Cont. Line	3 yrs.	Apr. 2, 1784
2931	Foster, John (Edward Valentine, assee.)	100	Private	Va. Cont. Line	3 yrs.	Apr. 15, '84
3012	Fleming, Bernard	100	Private	Va. St. Line	3 yrs.	Apr. 24, '84
3025	Ferguson, John	100	Fifer	Va. St. Line	3 yrs.	Apr. 27, '84
3038	Forehand, John	100	Private	Va. Cont. Line	3 yrs.	May 3, 1784
3066	Fleming, Ludwell C. (Edward Valentine, assee.)	100	Private	Va. St. Line	3 yrs.	May 10, '84
3090	Franklin, Henry	100	Private	Va. St. Line	3 yrs.	May 22, '84
3113	Ferrol, John	100	Private	Va. Cont. Line	3 yrs.	May 29, '84
3144	Frazer, James	400	Sergeant	Va. Cont. Line	war	June 10, '84
3221	Fauntleroy, Griffin (Wm. Reynolds, assee. of Jno. Fauntleroy, who was heir at law)	4000	Captain	Va. Cont. Line	3 yrs.	June 26, '84

LAND BOUNTY WARRANTS.

Warrant.	Name.	Acres	Rank.	Department.	Term	Date.
3395	FARGUSON, William	100	Private	Va. St. Line	3 yrs.	Aug. 16, '84
3404	FERGUSON, Robert	2666⅔	Surg's Mate.	Va. St. Navy	3 yrs.	Aug. 20, '84
3455	FITZHUGH, Perregrine	2666⅔	Lieutenant	Va. Cont. Line	5 yrs.	Oct. 6, 1784
3465	FIGG, Thomas	100	Private	Va. Cont. Line	3 yrs.	Oct. 15, '84
3468	FRANCIS, Christopher	100	Private	Va. Cont. Line	3 yrs.	Oct. 18, '84
3514	FREELAND, Isaac	100	Private	Va. Cont. Line	3 yrs.	Nov. 9, 1784
3526	FINNIE, William (per Res. of Gen. Assby., 10th Nov., 1784)	2000	Colonel	Va. Cont. Line	3 yrs.	Nov. 20, '84
3527	FINNIE, William (per Res. of Gen. Assby., 10th Nov., 1784)	2000	Colonel	Va. Cont. Line	3 yrs.	Nov. 20, '84
3528	FINNIE, William (per Res. of Gen. Assby., 10th Nov., 1784)	2000	Colonel	Va. Cont. Line	3 yrs.	Nov. 20, '84
3529	FINNIE, William (per Res. of Gen. Assby., 10th Nov., 1784)	666⅔	Colonel	Va. Cont. Line	3 yrs.	Nov. 20, '84
3531	FRYER, Richard	100	Private	Va. Cont. Line	3 yrs.	Nov. 22, '84
3543	FLEMING, John	200	Private	Va. Cont. Line	war	Nov. 27, '84
3545	FITZPATRICK, James	200	Private	Va. Cont. Line	war	Nov. 29, '84
3652	FARMER, John	200	Private	Va. Cont. Line	war	Dec. 31, '84
3710	FINN, Philip	100	Private	Va. Cont. Line	3 yrs.	Jan. 20, '85
3712	FITZHUGH, Wm. B.	100	Private	Va. Cont. Line	3 yrs.	Jan. 20, '85
3727	FEAGLE, Michael	100	Private	Va. Cont. Line	3 yrs.	Jan. 31, '85
3735	FLINN, Osburn	400	Sergeant	Va. Cont. Line	war	Feb. 7, 1785
3740	FAENT, Philip	200	Private	Va. Cont. Line	war	Feb. 7, 1785
3742	FEANT, George	100	Private	Va. Cont. Line	3 yrs.	Feb. 7, 1785
3757	FOSTER, Edmund	200	Corporal	Va. Cont. Line	3 yrs.	Feb. 19, '85
3863	FILBURY, George	200	Private	Va. Cont. Line	war	May 7, 1785
3879	FICKLIN, Charles (Thos. Ficklin, heir at law)	100	Private	Va. Cont. Line	3 yrs.	May 20, '85
3885	FOREHAND, Darby (John Forehand, legal rep.)	100	Private	Va. Cont. Line	3 yrs.	June 1, 1785
3900	FISHER, William (William Reynolds, assee.)	200	Private	Va. Cont. Line	war	June 21, '85
3901	FRANKLIN, John (William Reynolds, assee.)	200	Private	Va. Cont. Line	war	June 21, '85
4008	FITZHUGH, Peregrine	1333⅓	Captain	Va. Cont. Line	3 yrs.	Nov. 25, '85
4017	FINNY, Reuben	200	Private	Va. Cont. Line	3 yrs.	Dec. 3, 1785
4037	FOLEY, Enock	100	Private	St. Line	3 yrs.	Dec. 15, '85
4076	FREEMAN, Coldrop	200	Private	Va. Cont. Line	war	Jan. 14, '86
4078	FOSSIE, Christopher	200	Private	Va. St. Line	war	Jan. 14, '86
4080	FULLIN, William (Thos. Hughes, assee.)	100	Private	Va. St. Line	3 yrs.	Jan. 16, '86
4086	FOSTER, Thomas	100	Private	Va. Cont. Line	3 yrs.	Jan. 21, '86
4112	FOWLER, Jo (Joseph Fowler, rep.)	100	Private	Va. Cont. Line	3 yrs.	Mch. 2, 1786
4152	FOX, John	100	Private	Va. Cont. Line	3 yrs.	May 6, 1786
4172	FRITTS, George	100	Private	Va. Cont. Line	3 yrs.	June 14, '86
4193	FRISKETT, George	200	Private	Va. Cont. Line	war	Aug. 9, 1786
4222	FEAR, Edmond (John Overstreet, assee.)	100	Private	Va. Cont. Line	3 yrs.	Oct. 28, '86
4235	FURLEY, James (John Callaway, assee.)	100	Private	Va. St. Line	3 yrs.	Dec. 11, '86
4308	FREND, James	100	Private	Va. St. Line	3 yrs.	Sept. 22, '87
4371	FREEMAN, John (Wm. Reynolds, assee. of the rep. of)	200	Private	Va. Cont. Line	war	Jan. 23, '88
4410	FLING, Edward (Thomas Hopkins, assee. of James Shepherd, rep. A duplicate issued 1st February, 1792)	200	Private	Va. Cont. Line	war	July 11, '88
4427	FEELY, Timothy (Michael Feeley, rep. of)	2666⅔	Lieutenant	Va. Cont. Line	3 yrs.	July 29, '88
4463	FIELDER, George (Patrick Lockhart, assee.)	100	Private	Va. Cont. Line	3 yrs.	Sept. 18, '89
4494	FOUNTLEROY, Moore	6222	Major	Va. Cont. Line	war	May 25, '90
4498	FOWLER, Robert Martin	100	Private	Va. Cont. Line	3 yrs.	June 24, '90
4503	FERGUSON, Robert	200	Private	Va. Cont. Line	war	Nov. 10, '90
4534	FISHBACK, Jacob	200	Private	Cont. Line	war	Oct. 26, '91
4554	FRAILS, Charles (Wm. Bigger, assee. of Sally Frailes, legal assee. of Sally Frails, legal	100	Private	Cont. Line	3 yrs.	Nov. 29, '91

G

67	GILES, John (William Giles, Jr., heir at law)	2666⅔	Ensign	Va. Cont. Line		Dec. 21, '82
85	GARY, John	200	Sergeant	Art. in St. Line	3 yrs.	Dec. 31, '82

LAND BOUNTY WARRANTS.

Warrant	Name	Acres	Rank	Department	Term	Date
107	Green, John	7777½	Colonel	Va. Line	7 yrs.	Feb. 1, 1783
108	Green, John (William Green, heir at law)	2666⅔	Lieutenant			Feb. 1, 1783
119	Graves, William	2666⅔	Cornet	Cav. in St. Line	3 yrs.	Feb. 8, 1783
129	Gordan, Alben	200	Sergeant	Cav. in Cont. Line	3 yrs.	Feb. 15, '83
147	Gist, Nathaniel	6666⅔	Colonel	Va. Cont. Line	3 yrs.	Feb. 25, '83
194	Galt, Patrick (James Galt, heir at law)	6000	Surgeon	9th Va. Reg.		Mch. 24, '83
218	Gibson, John	1000	Colonel	Va. Cont. Line	3 yrs.	Apr. 1, 1783
219	Gibson, John	1000	Colonel	Va. Cont. Line	3 yrs.	Apr. 1, 1783
200	Gibson, John	1000	Colonel	Va. Cont. Line	3 yrs.	Apr. 1, 1783
221	Gibson, John	3666⅔	Colonel	Va. Cont. Line	3 yrs.	Apr. 1, 1783
242	Gray, George	4000	Captain	Drag. in Cont. Line	3 yrs.	Apr. 1, 1783
243	Gray, William	2666⅔	Lieutenant	Va. Line	3 yrs.	Apr. 1, 1783
287	Guthrie, John	100	Fifer	Va. Line	3 yrs.	Apr. 1, 1783
323	Green, Robert	2666⅔	Lieutenant	Va. Cont. Line	3 yrs.	Apr. 4, 1783
349	Graham, Arthur	400	Sergeant	St. Line		Apr. 12, '83
352	Griffith, the Rev'd David	6666⅔	Brig. Chapl.	Va. Cont. Line	3 yrs.	Apr. 16, '83
370	Goldman, Daniel	200	Private	St. Line		Apr. 17, '83
377	Griffith, David	6000	Surgeon	Va. Line	3 yrs.	Apr. 19, '83
400	Gasky, Richard	200	Private	Va. St. Line		Apr. 19, '83
428	Granger, William	200	Private	Va. Line	war	Apr. 25, '83
456	Gaines, William Fleming	4000	Capt.-Lieut.	Va. Art.	6 yrs.	Apr. 26, '83
475	Garrett, Mark	200	Sergeant	St. Line	3 yrs.	Apr. 28, '83
501	Gardner, George	400	Corporal	St. Line	war	Apr. 29, '83
503	Gellen, Casper	200	Private	St. Line	war	May 1, 1783
545	Gunnell, Joseph	200	Private	St. Line	war	May 1, 1783
560	Garland, Peter	4000	Captain	Cont. Line	3 yrs.	May 5, 1783
561	Gentry, James	200	Corporal	Va. Cont. Line	3 yrs.	May 8, 1783
565	Graves, William	100	Private	St. Line	3 yrs.	May 8, 1783
588	Gillison, John	4000	Captain	Va. Cont. Line	3 yrs.	May 16, '83
613	Gates, John	100	Private	Va. Cont. Line	3 yrs.	May 21, '83
654	Goff, Samuel (Abraham Goff, heir and legal rep.)	200	Private	Va. Cont. Line	war	May 27, '83
690	Graham, Walter	4000	Capt.-Lieut.	Va. St. Art.	3 yrs.	May 30, '83
700	Green, Jessee	100	Private	Va. Cont. Cav.	3 yrs.	May 31, '83
705	Guthrie, John	100	Private	Va. St. Line	3 yrs.	May 31, '83
706	Guthrie, James	200	Sergeant	Va. St. Line	3 yrs.	May 31, '83
708	Gammells, Nathan	200	Sergeant	Va. St. Line	3 yrs.	May 31, '83
724	Gibson, John	2666⅔	Sail'g Mast'r	Va. St. Navy	3 yrs.	June 3, 1783
765	Gaskins, Thomas	6000	Lieut.-Col.	Va. Cont. Line	3 yrs.	June 7, 1783
772	Gresham, John	100	Private	Va. Cont. Line	3 yrs.	June 9, 1783
778	Gibson, Robert	200	Corporal	Va. St. Line	3 yrs.	June 10, '83
791	Gilchrist, George	5333⅓	Major	Va. Cont. Line	3 yrs.	June 12, '83
802	Gates, Horatio	2000	Maj. Gen.	Va. Line	7 yrs.	June 13, '83
803	Gates, Horatio	2000	Maj. Gen.	St. Line	7 yrs.	June 13, '83
804	Gates, Horatio	2000	Maj. Gen.	St. Line	7 yrs.	June 13, '83
805	Gates, Horatio	2000	Maj. Gen.	St. Line	7 yrs.	June 13, '83
806	Gates, Horatio	2000	Maj. Gen.	St. Line	7 yrs.	June 13, '83
807	Gates, Horatio	2000	Maj. Gen.	St. Line	7 yrs.	June 13, '83
808	Gates, Horatio	1500	Maj. Gen.	St. Line	7 yrs.	June 13, '83
809	Gates, Horatio	1500	Maj. Gen.	St. Line	7 yrs.	June 13, '83
810	Gates, Horatio	2500	Maj. Gen.	St. Line	7 yrs.	June 13, '83
883	Glass, Isaac	200	Private	Va. Cont. Line	war	June 20, '83
884	Glass, Isaac	100	Private	Va. Cont. Line	war	June 20, '83
913	Gassaway, James	100	Private	Va. Cont. Line	war	June 20, '83
916	Green, John	100	Private	Va. Cont. Line	3 yrs.	June 20, '83
936	Glass, Hugh	100	Private	Va. Cont. Line	3 yrs.	June 20, '83
957	Gassaway, John	100	Private	Va. Cont. Line	3 yrs.	June 20, '83
963	Grove, Anthony	100	Private	Cont. Line	3 yrs.	June 20, '83
971	Gray, Benjamin	100	Private	Cont. Line	3 yrs.	June 20, '83
975	Ginomon, Henry	100	Private	Cont. Line	3 yrs.	June 20, '83
985	Gibbs, William	100	Private	Cont. Line	3 yrs.	June 20, '83
987	Giles, James	100	Private	Cont. Line	3 yrs.	June 20, '83
1005	Grayson, William	6666⅔	Colonel	Va. Cont. Line	3 yrs.	June 23, '83
1048	Gowan, Bryan	200	Private	Va. Cont. Line	war	June 24, '83
1071	Gossett, John	200	Private	Va. Cont. Line	war	June 24, '83
1117	Gilleham, Clem	200	Private	Va. Cont. Line	war	June 24, '83
1140	Guthrey, John	200	Private	Cont. Line		June 24, '83
1164	Greer, Charles	2000	Surgeon	Va. Cont. Line	3 yrs.	June 24, '83
1165	Greer, Charles	1000	Surgeon	Va. Cont. Line	3 yrs.	June 24, '83
1166	Greer, Charles	1000	Surgeon	Va. Cont. Line	3 yrs.	June 24, '83
1167	Greer, Charles	2000	Surgeon	Va. Cont. Line	3 yrs.	June 24, '83
1175	Gloucester, James	200	Private	Va. St. Line	war	June 25, '83

LAND BOUNTY WARRANTS. 31

Warrant.	Name.	Acres	Rank.	Department.	Term	Date.
1182	Guille, John	100	Private	Va. Cont. Line	3 yrs.	June 25, '83
1231	Grig, George	233½	Private	Va. Cont. Line	7 yrs.	June 27, '83
1263	George, Francis	200	Private	Va. Cont. Line	war	June 27, '83
1267	George, James Mayo	100	Private	Va. St. Line	3 yrs.	June 28, '83
1288	Groves, Thomas	200	Drummer	Va. Cont. Line	war	June 28, '83
1314	Griffin, Reuben	100	Private	Va. Cav	3 yrs.	June 30, '83
1325	Gill, Erasmus	4666⅔	Captain	Va. Cav	7 yrs.	July 4, 1783
1362	Grant, Daniel	100	Private	Cont. Line	3 yrs.	July 12, '83
1368	Grymes, William	200	Corporal	St. Line	3 yrs.	July 12, '83
1388	Grinstead, James	100	Private	St. Art	3 yrs.	July 17, '83
1418	Goodall, John	200	Sergeant	Cont. Line	3 yrs.	July 22, '83
1433	Gilbert, Joseph	200	Private	St. Line	war	July 27, '83
1437	Gregory, William	100	Private	Cont. Line	3 yrs.	July 28, '83
1444	Goff, Phillip	200	Musician	Cont. Line	war	July 30, '83
1472	Green, William	200	Private	Cont. Line	war	Aug. 1, 1783
1491	Grafton, John	100	Private	St. Line	3 yrs.	Aug. 4, 1783
1494	Gamble, Robert	4000	Captain	Cont. Line	3 yrs.	Aug. 4, 1783
1495	Gratton, John, Sr., (John Gratton, heir at law)	2666⅔	Lieutenant	Cont. Line	3 yrs.	Aug. 4, 1783
1589	Grymes, George	200	Sergeant	Cont. Line	3 yrs.	Aug. 20, '83
1590	Gary, John	200	Sergeant	St. Line	3 yrs.	Aug. 20, '83
1600	Green, John	200	Private	Cont. Line	war	Aug. 20, '83
1662	Gressell, John	100	Private	Va. Cont. Line	3 yrs.	Aug. 25, '83
1702	Galbreath, Robert	200	Sergeant	Va. Cont. Line	3 yrs.	Sept. 1, 1783
1704	Gregory, Charles (Walter Gregory, heir at law of)	200	Sergeant	Va. Cont. Line	3 yrs.	Sept. 1, 1783
1703	Gregory, William (Walter Gregory, heir at law of)	100	Private	Va. Cont. Line	3 yrs.	Sept. 1, 1783
1725	Griffin, Robert	100	Private	Va. St. Line	3 yrs.	Sept. 4, 1783
1741	Gray, James	400	Sergeant	Va. Cont. Line	war	Sept. 11, '83
1752	Gregg, Lewis	100	Private	Va. St. Line	3 yrs.	Sept. 11, '83
1753	Grigg, Abner	100	Private	Va. St. Line	3 yrs.	Sept. 11, '83
1757	Grant, William	100	Private	Va. Cont. Line	3 yrs.	Sept. 12, '83
1764	Gardner, John	200	Sergeant	Va. Cont. Line	3 yrs.	Sept. 13, '83
1771	Gentry, William	100	Private	Va. Cont. Art	3 yrs.	Sept. 17, '83
1772	Garner, William	200	Private	Va. St. Cav	war	Sept. 18, '83
1773	Garner, John	200	Private	Va. St. Cav	war	Sept. 18, '83
1794	Garner, Presly	100	Seaman	Va. St. Navy	3 yrs.	Sept. 26, '83
1855	Grimsley, James	100	Private	Va. Cont. Line	3 yrs.	Oct. 13, '83
1872	Grey, William	100	Private	Va. Cont. Line	3 yrs.	Oct. 15, '83
1892	Guthery, George	2666⅔	Lieutenant	Va. Cont. Line	3 yrs.	Oct. 18, '83
②1841	Gibson, John, Jr	2666⅔	Ensign	Va. Cont. Line	3 yrs.	Oct. 31, '83
1853	Grant, Daniel	100	Gun'r's Mate	Va. St. Navy	3 yrs.	Nov. 4, 1783
②1869	Gray, Daniel	200	Private	Va. Cont. Line	war	Nov. 6, 1783
②1872	Gaines, John	100	Private	Va. St. Navy	3 yrs.	Nov. 7, 1783
1903	Grant, John	100	Private	Va. Cont. Line	3 yrs.	Oct. 22, '83
1905	Goulding, Jesse	100	Private	Va. St. Line	3 yrs.	Oct. 23, '83
1925	Gray, Francis	2666⅔	Lieutenant	Va. Cont. Line	3 yrs.	Oct. 28, '83
1939	Green, Gabriel	2666⅔	Lieutenant	Va. Cont. Line	3 yrs.	Oct. 31, '83
②1900	Gold, Michael	233½	Private	Va. Cont. Line	7 yrs.	Oct. 17, '83
②1903	Goodwin, Sherod	100	Private	Va. Cont. Line	3 yrs.	Nov. 17, '83
②1930	Goodrum, Thomas	200	Corporal	Va. Cont. Line	3 yrs.	Nov. 22, '83
1984	George, William	4000	Captain	Va. Cont. Line	3 yrs.	Nov. 28, '83
2004	Griffin, Thompson (John Griffin, heir at law)	100	Private	Va. Cont. Line	3 yrs.	Dec. 2, 1783
2018	Grissel, Joel	200	Sergeant	Va. Cont. Line	3 yrs.	Dec. 5, 1783
2064	Graham, Arthur (Samuel Griffin, assee.)	100	Private	Va. St. Line	3 yrs.	Dec. 9, 1783
2077	Green, William	100	Private	Va. Cont. Line	3 yrs.	Dec. 10, '83
2083	Gray, David	200	Sergeant	Va. Line	3 yrs.	Dec. 10, '83
2100	Glason, Patrick	200	Private	Va. Cont. Line	war	Dec. 11, '83
2119	Guilliams, William	200	Private	Va. Cont. Line	3 yrs.	Dec. 13, '83
2150	Gimbo, William	200	Sergeant	Va. Cont. Line	3 yrs.	Dec. 17, '83
2166	Gunter, Charles	100	Private	Va. Cont. Line	3 yrs.	Dec. 20, '83
2174	Gray, George	100	Private	Va. Cont. Line	3 yrs.	Dec. 20, '83
2209	Griffin, Thomas, Jr	100	Private	Va. St. Line	3 yrs.	Dec. 23, '83
2226	Galloway, Terry (Richard Taylor, Jr., assee. of)	100	Private	Va. Cont. Line	3 yrs.	Jan. 10, '84
2262	Gordon, Ambrose	2666⅔	Lieutenant	Va. Cont. Line	3 yrs.	Jan. 21, '84
2343	Grubbs, Hensley (William Reynolds, assee.)	200	Private	Va. Cont. Line	war	Jan. 31, '84
2412	Graves, Francis	100	Private	Va. Cont. Line	3 yrs.	Feb. 5, 1784
2461	Gregory, Obadiah (Lewis Ford, assee. of)	200	Sergeant	Va. Cont. Line	3 yrs.	Feb. 11, '84
2530	Gaines, Thomas	200	Sergeant	Va. Cont. Line	3 yrs.	Feb. 19, '84

LAND BOUNTY WARRANTS.

Warrant.	Name.	Acres	Rank.	Department.	Term	Date.
2590	Graves, William (Francis Graves, assee.)	100	Artificer . ..	Va. St. Line.......	3 yrs.	Feb. 23, '84
2626	Gibson, Jacob (Daniel Flowerree, assee.)	1C0	Private	Va. St. Line.......	3 yrs.	Feb. 24, '84
2631	Gray, James	4000	Captain	Va. Cont. Line....	3 yrs.	Feb. 25, '84
2641	Gaskins, Thomas	1000	Lieut.-Col. .	Va. Cont. Line....	7 yrs.	Feb. 26, '84
2646	Garner, or Gardner, John....	100	Private	Va. Cont. Line....	3 yrs.	Feb. 26, '84
2678	Geraull, John	4000	Captain ...	Va. St. Line.......	3 yrs.	Mch. 3, 1784
2715	Gibson, Aaron (Thomas Aselin, assee.)	200	Sergeant ...	Va. Cont. Line....	3 yrs.	Mch. 5, 1784
2717	Gray, Robert	100	Private	Va. Cont. Line....	3 yrs.	Mch. 5, 1784
2718	Graham, Williamson (Francis Graves. of John Booker, assee. of)	100	Private	Va. Cont. Line....	3 yrs.	Mch. 5, 1784
2743	Gressitt, Thomas	100	Private	Va. Cont. Line....	3 yrs.	Mch. 9, 1784
2752	Gordon, Arthur	2666⅔	Lieutenant .	Va. Cont. Line....	3 yrs.	Mch. 11, '84
2806	Gowden, William	100	Private	Va. Cont. Line....	3 yrs.	Mch. 22, '84
2885	Goodin, Benjamin	200	Sergeant ...	Va. Cont. Line....	3 yrs.	Apr. 5, 1785
2907	Griffith, Michael (William McIntosh, assee.)	200	Private	Va. Cont. Line....	war	Apr. 8, 1785
2938	Glascock, Thomas	2666⅔	Lieutenant .	Va. Cont. Line....	3 yrs.	Apr. 17, '85
2967	Gilmore, Robert	100	Private ...	Va. St. Line.......	3 yrs.	Apr. 20, '85
3007	Gillon, Hugh	200	Private .. .	Va. Cont. Line....	war	Apr. 23, '85
3032	George, Robert	4000	Captain .. .	Va. St. Line.......	3 yrs.	Apr. 29, '85
3033	Gill, Samuel	4000	Captain .. .	Va. Cont. Line....	3 yrs.	Apr. 30, '85
3078	Grinter, John	200	Sergeant ...	Va. Cont. Line....	3 yrs.	May 14, '84
3102	Griffin, Peter (William Reynolds, assee.)	200	Private	Va. Cont. Line....	war	Apr. 26, '84
3103	Gibbs, Churchill	2666⅔	Lieutenant .	Va. St. Line.......	3 yrs.	May 26, '84
3104	Golson, William (Francis Graves, assee.)	400	Sergeant ...	Cont. Line	war	May 27, '84
3107	Graves, John	200	Private	Va. Cont. Line....	war	May 28, '84
3110	Gray, John (Thomas McGlenn, heir and legal rep.)	200	Private	Va. Cont. Line....	war	May 29, '84
3202	Galaspy, Thomas (John Rice, assee.)	100	Private	Va. Cont. Line....	3 yrs.	June 24, '84
3214	Galley, William	200	Private	Va. Cont. Line....	war	June 26, '84
3331	Gagney, Lewis	200	Private	Va. St. Line.......	war	July 19, '84
3368	Goatley, John	233½	Private	Va. Cont. Line....	7 yrs.	July 31, '84
3408	Goran, Henry	200	Private	Va. Cont. Line....	war	Aug. 23, '84
3425	Green, Moses (William Reynolds, assee.)	100	Private	Va. St. Line.......	3 yrs.	Aug. 28, '84
3432	Galt, John Minson (Res. of Gen. Assby., Nov. 29, 1783).	6000	Surgeon .. .	Services		Sept. 2, 1784
3451	Green, Samuel B	2666⅔	Ensign	Va. Cont. Line....	3 yrs.	Sept. 25, '84
3486	Gunnett, William (Lindsey Arnold, assee.)	200	Private	Va. Cont. Line....	war	Oct. 26, '84
3494	Gollaspy, George	100	Private	Va. Cont. Line....	3 yrs.	Nov. 3, 1784
3520	Grigsby, Moses (Francis Graves, assee.)	100	Private	Va. Cont. Line....	3 yrs.	Nov. 12, '84
3530	Goodwin, Dinwiddi (Stephen Goodwin, heir at law)	2666⅔	Subaltern ..	Va. Cont. Line....	3 yrs.	Nov. 20, '84
3562	Garnett, Anthony	100	Private	Va. Cont. Line....	3 yrs.	Dec. 8, 1784
3571	Graves, William	200	Private	Va. Cont. Line....	war	Dec. 14, '84
3574	Garner, William	100	Private	Va. St Line.......	3 yrs.	Dec. 15, '84
3587	Gardner, Thomas	200	Sergeant ...	Va. St. Line.......	3 yrs.	Dec. 18, '84
3633	Goff, Adam (Francis Peyton, assee.)	200	Sergeant ...	Va. Cont. Line....	3 yrs.	Dec. 29, '84
3635	Green, Thomas (John Green, heir at law)	100	Private	Va. Cont. Line....	3 yrs.	Dec. 29, '84
3645	Graves, Jeremiah (Major Graves, rep.)	100	Private	Va. St. Line.......	3 yrs.	Dec. 30, '84
3747	Gesnor, John	200	Private	Va. Cont. Line....	war	Dec. 31, '84
3768	Guner, James	100	Private	Va. Cont. Line....	3 yrs.	Mch. 5, 1785
3832	Gibbs, Joseph	200	Private	Va. Cont. Line....	war	Apr. 29, '85
3853	George, John	100	Private	Va. Cont. Line....	3 yrs.	May 6, 1785
3860	Gester, John	100	Private	Va. St. Line.......	3 yrs.	May 7, 1785
3868	Gillaspy, William	100	Private	Va. Cont. Line....	3 yrs.	May 10, '85
3922	Gold, James	100	Private	Va. Cont. Line....	3 yrs.	June 21, '85
3923	Griffin, James	200	Private	Va. Cont. Line....	war	June 21, '85
3924	Garrett, John	100	Private	Va. Cont. Line....	3 yrs.	June 21, '85
3966	Gunnell, John	200	Private	Va. Cont. Line....	war	Aug. 26, '85
3990	Grymes, William (Nancy Grymes, daughter and legal rep.)	4000	Captain .. .	Va. Cont. Line....	3 yrs.	Nov. 2, 1785

LAND BOUNTY WARRANTS. 33

Warrant.	Name.	Acres	Rank.	Department.	Term	Date.
4077	Grady, Jonathan	100	Private	Va. Cont. Line	3 yrs.	Jan. 14, '86
4087	Gallahue, Charles (Walter Ashman, devisee)	4000	Captain	Va. Cont. Line	3 yrs.	Jan. 21, '86
4095	Gehegan, John (William Gehegan, heir at law)	200	Private	Va. Cont. Line	war	Jan. 25, '86
4115	Gibson, George	6666⅔	Colonel	Va. Cont. Line	3 yrs.	Mch. 4, 1786
4121	Gallady, Joseph	400	Corporal	Va. Cont. Line	war	Mch. 7, '86
4142	Gore, Jacob	400	Sergeant	Va. Cont. Line	war	Apr. 6, 1786
4188	Gordon, John	100	Private	Va. Cont. Line	3 yrs.	July 18, '86
4233	Garbon, Benjamin	100	Sailor	Va. St. Navy	3 yrs.	Nov. 16, '86
4250	Gist, Thomas	100	Private	Va. Cont. Line	3 yrs.	Jan. 12, '87
4297	Gray, David	100	Private	Va. Cont. Line	3 yrs.	June 14, '87
4302	Gully, Richard	100	Private	Va. Cont. Line	3 yrs.	July 27, '87
4307	Guilder, Daniel	100	Private	Va. Cont. Line	3 yrs.	Sept. 22, '87
4315	Gardner, Caswell	200	Sergeant	Va. Cont. Line	3 yrs.	Oct. 23, '87
4345	Grass, Frederick	100	Private	Va. Cont. Line	3 yrs.	Nov. 30, '87
4346	Garvin, Benjamin	100	Private	Va. Cont. Line	3 yrs.	Nov. 30, '87
4362	Grey, Sabred (John Grey, heir at law)	100	Private	Va. Cont. Line	3 yrs.	Jan. 12, '88
4370	Glascock, Robert (Wm. Reynolds, assee. of Jas. Hodges, assee.)	100	Private	Va. Cont. Line	war	Jan. 23, '88
4384	Golden, Jesse (Abraham Golden, heir at law)	100	Private	Va. St. Line	3 yrs.	Feb. 2, 1788
4390	Griffith, David	400	Corporal	Va. Cont. Line	war	Mch. 12, '88
4422	Green, William (Jeremiah Munday, assee.)	1400	Gunner	Va. St. Navy	3 yrs.	July 17, '88
4423	Green, William (Jeremiah-Munday, assee.)	1266⅔	Gunner	Va. St. Navy	3 yrs.	July 17, '88
4438	Gwinn, Jacob (Sarah Gwinn, heiress)	200	Private	Va. St. Line	war	Oct. 22, '88
4462	Glenn, Bernard (who served the term by Act of Assby.)	2666⅔		Crockett's Reg		Aug. 10, '89
4469	George, Benjamin (William Reynolds, assee. of Sam'l McCraw, assee. of Wm. Bigger, assee. of the rep.)	100	Sailor	Va. St. Navy	3 yrs.	Oct. 22, '89
4524	Givin, Willis	100	Private	Cont. Line	3 yrs.	May 30, 1791
4526	Gilliam, John (James) (Hincha Gilliam, heir at law)	2666⅔	Lieutenant	Cont. Line	war	June 30, '91
4542	Goodman, Thomas	200	Private	Cont. Line	war	Nov. 11, '91
4553	Gabriel, James (Wm. Bigger, assee. of Jno. Langston and Mary, his wife, she being heiress of)	100	Private	Cont. Line	3 yrs.	Nov. 29, '91
4594	Gregory, John (Murford Gregory, heir at law)	2666⅔	Lieutenant	Cont. Line	war	Nov. 19, '92
4615	Gray, Wilson	100	Private	Cont. Line	3 yrs.	May 27, '93
4618	Gunn, James	4666⅔	Captain	Cont. Line	7 yrs.	July 17, '93

H

3	Hendricks, Elijah	200	Sergeant	Va. Cont. Line	3 yrs.	Aug. 25, '82
8	Holmes, Benjamin, Esq.	4000	Captain	Va. Cont. Line	3 yrs.	Sept. 17, '82
12	Hoomes, Thomas Claiborn (Joseph Hoomes, heir at law)	2666⅔	Lieutenant	Va. Cont. Line	3 yrs.	Nov. 4, 1782
34	Holt, John Hunter	4000	Captain	Va. St. Line	3 yrs.	Dec. 5, 1782
38	Hall, John	100	Private	St. Art	3 yrs.	Dec. 11, '82
73	Hogg, Samuel	4000	Captain	Va. Cont. Reg.	3 yrs.	Dec. 24, '82
76	Hill, Thomas	5333⅓	Major	Cont. Army	3 yrs.	Dec. 27, '82
96	Hill, Baylor	4000	Captain	Lt. Drag. Cont. Line	3 yrs.	Jan. 21, '83
109	Hall, William (David Clark, assee.)	100	Private	2d St. Reg	3 yrs.	Feb. 2, 1783
112	Hoffler, William	4000	Captain	St. Line	3 yrs.	Feb. 5, 1783
123	Hardyman, John	2666⅔	Lieutenant	St. Line	3 yrs.	Feb. 12, '83
171	Harrison, John Peyton	4000	Captain	Va. Cont. Line	3 yrs.	Mch. 10, '83
177	Huffman, Lud. Philip (Christian Huffman, heir at law)	2666⅔	Lieutenant	Va. Cont. Line	3 yrs.	Mch. 13, '83
186	Humphreys, Reuben	100	Private	St. Cav	3 yrs.	Mch. 20, '83
204	Hays, John	5333⅓	Major	Va. Line	3 yrs.	Mch. 27, '83
214	Holmes, David	3000	Surgeon	Va. Cont. Line	3 yrs.	Apr. 1, 1783
215	Holmes, David	3000	Surgeon	Va. Cont. Line	3 yrs.	Apr. 1, 1783
236	Harrison, John	1333⅓	Lieutenant	Va. Cont. Line	3 yrs.	Apr. 1, 1783
237	Harrison, John	1333⅓	Lieutenant	Va. Cont. Line	3 yrs.	Apr. 1, 1783

34   LAND BOUNTY WARRANTS.

Warrant.	Name.	Acres	Rank.	Department.	Term	Date.
267	HAMPTON, William (Dr. James McClung, assee.)	100	Private	St. Line	3 yrs.	Apr. 3, 1783
271	HEAKEN, William (Dr. James McClung, assee.)	100	Private	St. Line	3 yrs.	Apr. 3, 1783
300	HITE, Abraham	2000	Captain	Va. Cont. Line	3 yrs.	Apr. 7, 1783
301	HITE, Abraham	2000	Captain	Va. Cont. Line	3 yrs.	Apr. 7, 1783
316	HARPER, James	2666⅔	Lieutenant	Va. St. Line	3 yrs.	Apr. 12, '83
338	HEBRON, John	200	Private	Va. St. Line	war	Apr. 15, '83
355	HOWELL, Phillison	400	Corporal	St. Line	war	Apr. 17, '83
356	HIGHLAND, William	200	Private	St. Line	war	Apr. 17, '83
358	HOBBS, Thomas	200	Private	St. Line	war	Apr. 17, '83
361	HENDRIN, Ephraim	200	Private	Va. St. Line	war	Apr. 18, '83
362	HILL, Amos (Nancy Hill, widow)	200	Private	St. Line		Apr. 18, '83
394	HUGHES, Nathan	100	Private	Va. Cont. Line	3 yrs.	Apr. 24, '83
402	HIGHLAND, Robert	200	Drummer	Va. St. Line	war	Apr. 25, '83
407	HADLEY, Isaac	200	Private	Va. St. Line	war	Apr. 25, '83
451	HAYES, Joseph	200	Private	St. Line	war	Apr. 28, '83
487	HAIT, Leonard	200	Private	St. Line	war	Apr. 30, '83
490	HODGINS, Joseph	200	Private	St. Line	war	Apr. 30, '83
508	HUDDLESTON, John	200	Private	St. Line	war	May 1, 1783
524	HAYWORD, John Hale	200	Private	St. Line	war	May 2, 1783
539	HILL, James	200	Sergeant	St. Line	3 yrs.	May 2, 1783
548	HENRYES, Christopher	200	Private	St. Line	war	May 5, 1783
552	HARDY, Rhodius	200	Private	St. Line	war	May 6, 1783
581	HARDYMAN, John	200	Sergeant	St. Line	3 yrs.	May 15, '83
582	HART, James	100	Private	St. Line	3 yrs.	May 15, '83
593	HUDGINS, Moses	100	Private	Va. Cont. Line	3 yrs.	May 17, '83
595	HARWOOD, Littleberry	200	Sergeant	Va. St. Line	3 yrs.	May 19, '83
596	HACKLEY, John	2666⅔	Lieutenant	Va. Cont. Line	3 yrs.	May 20, '83
600	HORD, Thomas	4666⅔	Captain	Va. Cont. Line	7 yrs.	May 20, '83
633	HOLT, Thomas	4000	Captain	Va. Cont. Line	3 yrs.	May 24, '83
640	HARDAWAY, Joseph	200	Private	St. Cav	war	May 26, '83
652	HIX, William	100	Private	Va. St. Line	3 yrs.	May 27, '83
687	HAMILTON, James	2666⅔	Lieutenant	Va. Cont. Line	3 yrs.	May 30, '83
688	HOPKINS, Samuel	7000	Lieut.-Col	Va. Cont. Line	3 yrs.	May 24, '83
716	HARPER, John	200	Corporal	Va. St. Line	3 yrs.	June 2, 1783
720	HARDEN, James	100	Private	Va. Cont. Line	3 yrs.	June 3, 1783
759	HIGDEN, John	100	Sailor	Va. St. Navy	3 yrs.	June 6, 1783
760	HUGHES, Pratt	3110⅔	Lieutenant	Va. St. Line	7 yrs.	June 6, 1783
771	HIGGINS, Peter	2666⅔	Lieutenant	Va. Cont. Line	3 yrs.	June 9, 1783
817	HINES, James	200	Corporal	Va. Cont. Art	3 yrs.	June 14, '83
821	HARVES, Samuel	7000	Lieut.-Col	Va. Cont. Line	7 yrs.	June 14, '83
827	HALCOMB, John	4000	Captain	Va. Cont. Line	3 yrs.	June 14, '83
835	HUNT, James	100	Private	Va. Cont. Line	3 yrs.	June 16, '83
844	HALLOBY, Thomas	400	Sergeant	Va. Cont. Line	war	June 16, '83
870	HEALTY, William (Robert Flatford, assee.)	100	Private	Va. Cont. Line	3 yrs.	June 19, '83
874	HUNNY, Calis	100	Private	Va. Cav. on Cont. Establishment	3 yrs.	June 19, '83
890	HEADEN, Anthony	200	Private	Va. Cont. Line	war	June 20, '83
906	HALFPENNY, John	200	Private	Va. Cont. Line	war	June 20, '83
941	HICKS, William	100	Private	Va. Cont. Line	3 yrs.	June 20, '83
942	HALL, Thomas	200	Sergeant	Va. Cont. Line	3 yrs.	June 20, '83
958	HAINES, Peter	100	Private	Va. Cont. Line	3 yrs.	June 20, '83
997	HOWARD, Robert	100	Private	Va. Cont. Line	3 yrs.	June 21, '83
1008	HOOD, John	100	Private	Va. Cav	3 yrs.	June 23, '83
1038	HOSFIELD, Thomas	400	Sergeant	Va. Cont. Line	war	June 24, '83
1040	HAGERLY, Nicholas	400	Corporal	Va. Cont. Line	war	June 24, '83
1043	HINDS, John	200	Fifer	Va. Cont. Line	war	June 24, '83
1051	HARVEY, Michael	200	Private	Va. Cont. Line	war	June 24, '83
1053	HERBERT, William	200	Private	Va. Cont. Line	war	June 24, '83
1060	HEATHORN, Philip	200	Private	Va. Cont. Line	war	June 24, '83
1079	HINLEY, Matthew	200	Private	Va. Cont. Line	war	June 24, '83
1080	HANSFORD, William	200	Private	Va. Cont. Line	war	June 24, '83
1090	HULLING, James	200	Private	Va. Cont. Line	war	June 24, '83
1091	HALEY, Thomas	200	Private	Va. Cont. Line	war	June 24, '83
1095	HULL, John	400	Sergeant	Va. Cont. Line	war	June 24, '83
1135	HALFPENNY, Isaac	200	Private	Va. Cont. Line	war	June 24, '83
1170	HACKETT, John	233⅓	Private	Va. Cont. Line	7 yrs.	June 25, '83
1184	HURT, West	100	Private	Va. Cont. Line	war	June 25, '83
1191	HUTSON, William	100	Private	Va. Cont. Line	3 yrs.	June 26, '83
1254	HAINES, George	400	Sergeant	Va. Cont. Line	war	June 28, '83
1272	HACKETT, James	200	Private	Va. Cont. Line	war	June 28, '83
1275	HOBBS, Frederick	233⅓	Private	Va. Cont. Line	war	June 28, '83
1277	HODGES, William	233⅓	Private	Va. Cont. Line	war	June 28, '83
1316	HARDEN, John	100	Private	Va. Cont. Line	war	July 1, 1783

LAND BOUNTY WARRANTS. 35

Warrant.	Name.	Acres	Rank.	Department.	Term	Date.
1328	Harris, Edward	400	Drum Major	Va. Cont. Line	war	July 5, 1783
1351	Harrison, Joseph	200	Sergeant	Cont. Line	3 yrs.	July 10, '83
1354	Hagerty, Patrick	400	Sergeant	Cont. Line	war	July 11, '83
1378	Hudson, John	4000	Captain	St. Line	3 yrs.	July 15, '83
1381	Hutchings, Charles (John Kay, assee.)	200	Private	Cont. Line	war	July 17, '83
1404	Harris, William	400	Drum Major	Cont. Line	war	July 21, '83
1417	Hayes, Thomas	2666⅔	Lieutenant	St. Line	3 yrs.	July 22, '83
1426	Hutts, Leonard	200	Private	Cont. Line	war	July 25, '83
1427	Hutts, Jacob	200	Private	Cont. Line	war	July 25, '83
1434	Hutt, Read	100	Private	Cont. Line	3 yrs.	July 28, '83
1435	Hutt, Read	200	Private	Cont. Line	war	July 28, '83
1470	Hodge, James	200	Sergeant	Cont. Line	3 yrs.	Aug. 1, 1783
1503	Ham, William	100	Seaman	St. Navy	3 yrs.	Aug. 5, 1783
1517	Hudson, John	200	Private	Cont. Line	war	Aug. 7, 1783
1538	Hill, John	100	Private	St. Art	3 yrs.	Aug. 9, 1783
1540	Hix, Edward	100	Private	Cont. Line	3 yrs.	Aug. 9, 1783
1546	Harris, Walter	100	Private	Cont. Line	3 yrs.	Aug. 11, '83
1571	Haly, William	233½	Private	Cont. Line	war	Aug. 14, '83
1580	Harrison, Valentine	4000	Captain	Cont. Line	3 yrs.	Aug. 18, '83
1597	Hunt, William	200	Private	Cont. Line	war	Aug. 20, '83
1604	Hatton, William	200	Private	Cont. Line	war	Aug. 20, '83
1608	Haynes, William	200	Private	Cont. Line	war	Aug. 20, '83
1643	Hopkinstock, Christopher	200	Private	Va. Cont. Line	war	Aug. 23, '83
1645	Hill, Thomas	200	Private	Va. Cont. Line	war	Aug. 23, '83
1647	Hillard, Joseph	200	Private	Va. Cont. Line	war	Aug. 23, '83
1664	Haynes, James	200	Private	Va. Cont. Line	war	Aug. 25, '83
1665	Hart, Robert	400	Drum Major	Va. Cont. Line	3 yrs.	Aug. 26, '83
1668	Hart, Robert	200	Drum Major	Va. Cont. Line	3 yrs.	Aug. 26, '83
1678	Holmes, Lewis	100	Private	Va. Cont. Line	3 yrs.	Aug. 27, '83
1693	Higgins, Robert	4000	Captain	Va. Cont. Line	3 yrs.	Aug. 30, '83
1709	Hewell, Thomas	200	Private	Va. St. Line	war	Sept. 2, 1783
1720	Helms, Meredith	100	Seaman	Va. St. Navy	3 yrs.	Sept. 2, 1783
1723	Hundley, Joshua	100	Private	Va. Cont. Line	3 yrs.	Sept. 3, 1783
1738	Hull, David	100	Private	Va. Cont. Line	3 yrs.	Sept. 10, '83
1740	Hughes, James	400	Sergeant	Va. St. Line	war	Sept. 10, '83
1750	Holmes, Isaac	2666⅔	Lieutenant	Va. St. Line	3 yrs.	Sept. 11, '83
1754	Huts, James	100	Private	Va. Cont. Line	3 yrs.	Sept. 12, '83
1760	Hughes, Jesse	100	Private	Va. Cont. Line	3 yrs.	Sept. 13, '83
1774	Harrison, William Butler	2666⅔	Cornet	Va. Cont. Line	war	Sept. 19, '83
1776	Hooper, John	200	Private	Va. St. Line	3 yrs.	Sept. 19, '83
1777	Hobdy, William	100	Private	Va. St. Line	3 yrs.	Sept. 20, '83
1797	Holt, James	2666⅔	Lieutenant	Va. Cont. Line	3 yrs.	Sept. 27, '83
1802	Hays, John	200	Private	Va. Cont. Line	war	Sept. 30, '83
1812	Howard, John	100	Private	Va. Cont. Line	3 yrs.	Oct. 1, 1783
1821	Heth, John	1000	Lieutenant	Va. Cont. Line	3 yrs.	Oct. 4, 1783
1822	Heth, John	1666⅔	Lieutenant	Va. Cont. Line	3 yrs.	Oct. 4, 1783
1827	Hawley, Rawleigh	200	Private	Va. Cont. Line	war	Oct. 6, 1783
1841	Harris, John	100	Private	Va. Cont. Line	3 yrs.	Oct. 9, '83
1842	Hampton, Thomas	100	Private	Va. St. Line	3 yrs.	Oct. 10, '83
1885	Hoofman, Joseph	100	Private	St. Line	3 yrs.	Oct. 16, '83
1886	Hoofman, Reuben	100	Private	St. Line	3 yrs.	Oct. 16, '83
1891	Hood, Thomas	400	Sergeant	Va. Cont. Line	3 yrs.	Oct. 18, '83
1894	Heth, Henry	200	Captain	Cont. Line	3 yrs.	Oct. 20, '83
ⓑ1851	Henderson, David	2666⅔	Midshipman.	Va. St. Navy	3 yrs.	Nov. 4, 1783
ⓑ1871	Henshaw, William	200	Private	Va. Cont. Line	war	Nov. 7, 1783
ⓑ1875	Hopkins, Patrick	100	Private	Va. St. Navy	3 yrs.	Nov. 7, 1783
ⓑ1883	Hannah, Robert	100	Private	Va. Cont. Line	3 yrs.	Nov. 11, '83
ⓑ1885	Haley, William	233½	Private	Va. Cont. Line	7 yrs.	Nov. 11, '83
ⓑ1898	Hughes, Joseph	100	Private	Va. Cont. Line	3 yrs.	Nov. 14, '83
1902	Harriss, William	100	Private	Va. Cont. Line	3 yrs.	Oct. 22, '83
1913	Hogland, Evert	200	Corporal	Va. Cont. Line	3 yrs.	Oct. 25, '83
1914	Hughs, Benjamin	100	Private	Va. Cont. Line	3 yrs.	Oct. 25, '83
1917	Hulse, William	200	Sergeant	Va. Cont. Line	3 yrs.	Oct. 25, '83
1920	Hutcheson, Thomas	200	Sergeant	Va. Cont. Line	3 yrs.	Oct. 25, '83
1926	Hudson, Rush	400	Corporal	Va. Cont. Line	3 yrs.	Oct. 28, '83
1933	Hearn, Daniel	200	Sergeant	Va. Cont. Line	3 yrs.	Oct. 29, '83
ⓐ1907	Hill, Henry	100	Private	Va. St. Line	3 yrs.	Nov. 18, '83
ⓑ1925	Hawkins, James	100	Private	Va. Cont. Line	3 yrs.	Nov. 21, '83
ⓑ1932	Hazlewood, William	400	Sergeant	Va. St. Line	war	Nov. 22, '83
1959	Humphlett, William	100	Seaman	Va. St. Navy	3 yrs.	Nov. 22, '83
2000	Hockaday, Philip	2666⅔	Lieutenant	Va. Cont. Line	3 yrs.	Nov. 29, '83
2005	Humphreys, Samuel	100	Seaman	Va. St. Navy	3 yrs.	Dec. 2, 1783
2029	Humphreys, John	100	Private	Va. Cont. Line	3 yrs.	Dec. 6, 1783
2062	Huey, John (Samuel Griffin, assee.)	100	Private	Va. St. Line	3 yrs.	Dec. 9, 1783

LAND BOUNTY WARRANTS.

Warrant.	Name.	Acres	Rank.	Department.	Term	Date.
2068	Huse, William	200	Gunner	Va. St. Navy	3 yrs.	Dec. 10, '83
2072	Harrup, Arthur	400	Sergeant	Va. Cont. Line	war	Dec. 10, '83
2073	Hancock, Henry	100	Private	Va. Cont. Line	3 yrs.	Dec. 10, '83
2082	Haynes, Gabriel	200	Sergeant	Va. Cont. Line	3 yrs.	Dec. 10, '83
2098	Harcum, Rodham	2666⅔	Midshipman	Va. St. Navy	3 yrs.	Dec. 10, '83
2102	Hooper, Walter	200	Private	Va. Cont. Line	war	Dec. 12, '83
2106	Humphries, John (Sarah Humphries, widow and legal heir)	2666⅔	Lieutenant	Va. Cont. Line	3 yrs.	Dec. 12, '83
2110	Honey, Elias (John Depriest, assee.)	200	Private	Va. Cont. Line	war	Dec. 12, '83
2148	Hudson, John	100	Private	Va. St. Line	3 yrs.	Dec. 18, '83
2161	Heth, William	1000	Colonel	Va. Cont. Line	7 yrs.	Dec. 20, '83
2162	Heth, William	6777	Colonel	Va. Cont. Line	7 yrs.	Dec. 20, '83
2177	Henry, James	100	Private	Va. St. Line	3 yrs.	Dec. 20, '83
2186	Hogings, Isham	200	Sergeant	Va. Cont. Line	3 yrs.	Dec. 22, '83
2190	Hodgins, Samuel	233⅓	Private	Va. Cont. Line	7 yrs.	Dec. 22, '83
2192	Holliday, James	100	Private	Va. Cont. Line	3 yrs.	Dec. 22, '83
2241	Hunt, Samuel	233⅓	Private	Va. Cont. Line	7 yrs.	Jan. 12, '84
2247	Hurt, John	7000	Chaplain	Va. Cont. Line	7 yrs.	Jan. 15, '84
2252	Harris, John	2666⅔	Lieutenant	Va. Cont. Line	war	Jan. 21, '84
2318	Harris, Thomas	100	Private	Va. Cont. Line	3 yrs.	Jan. 30, '84
2333	Hubbard, Elias	100	Private	Va. Cont. Line	3 yrs.	Jan. 31, '84
2346	Hailey, Daniel (William Reynolds, assee. of John Hailey, rep. of Daniel Hailey)	200	Private	Va. Cont. Line	war	Jan. 31, '84
2351	Haldrop, Thomas (Martin Hawkins, assee.)	100	Private	Va. Cont. Line	3 yrs.	Jan. 31, '84
2356	Humphries, John (Martin Hawkins, assee.)	100	Private	Va. Cont. Line	3 yrs.	Jan. 31, '84
2360	Harrison, Charles	6666⅔	Colonel	Va. Cont. Line	3 yrs.	Feb. 2, 1784
2365	Hall, John	533	Sergeant	Va. Cont. Line	8 yrs.	Feb. 2, 1784
2369	Hazlewood, Richard	100	Private	Va. Cont. Line	3 yrs.	Feb. 2, 1784
2373	Holland, George	500	Lieutenant	Va. Cont. Line	3 yrs.	Feb. 3, 1784
2374	Holland, George	2166⅔	Lieutenant	Va. Cont. Line	3 yrs.	Feb. 3, 1784
2384	Haldrop, Thomas (Martin Hawkins, assee.)	100	Fifer	Va. Cont. Line	3 yrs.	Feb. 3, 1784
2402	Harris, Jordon	2666⅔	Lieutenant	Va. Cont. Line	war	Feb. 4, 1784
2428	Hinton, William	100	Sailor	St. Navy	3 yrs.	Feb. 9, 1784
2456	Hancock, Bennett (Robert Brison, assee.)	200	Private	Va. Cont. Line	war	Feb. 11, '84
2459	Hill, Gideon (Milton Ford, assee. of	100	Private	Va. Cont. Line	3 yrs.	Feb. 11, '84
2474	Hopper, John (Daniel Feagan, assee.)	100	Private	Va. Cont. Line	3 yrs.	Feb. 11, '84
2475	Higgins, John (Daniel Feagan, assee. of)	100	Private	Va. St. Line	3 yrs.	Feb. 11, '84
2517	Hart, Thomas	100	Private	Va. St. Line	3 yrs.	Feb. 19, '84
2519	Heaby, James	200	Sergeant	Va. St. Line	3 yrs.	Feb. 19, '84
2525	Howell, Vincent	100	Private	Va. Cont. Line	3 yrs.	Feb. 19, '84
2527	Harris, James	100	Private	Va. Cont. Line	3 yrs.	Feb. 19, '84
2540	Hawkins, John	2666⅔	Lieutenant	Va. Cont. Line	3 yrs.	Feb. 19, '84
2565	Harris, Robert (Daniel Perryman, assee.)	100	Private	Va. Cont. Line	3 yrs.	Feb. 20, '84
2582	Hubbard, James (Lewis Ford, assee.)	200	Private	Va. Cont. Line	war	Feb. 21, '84
2589	Hines, John	100	Private	Va. Cont. Line	3 yrs.	Feb. 23, '84
2598	Halbert, William	233⅓	Private	Va. Cont. Line	7 yrs.	Feb. 23, '84
2608	Hill, George	2666⅔	Subaltern	Va. Cont. Line	war	Feb. 24, '84
2613	Hambrick, David (Daniel Flowerree, assee.)	200	Corporal	Va. Cont. Line	3 yrs.	Feb. 24, '84
2622	Hammond, John (Daniel Flowerree, assee.)	100	Private	Va. St. Line	3 yrs.	Feb. 24, '84
2691	Head, Benjamin (Martin Hawkins, assee.)	100	Private	Va. Cont. Line	3 yrs.	Mch. 3, 1784
2714	Hendrake, Moses (Thos. Aselin, assee.)	100	Private	Va. Cont. Line	3 yrs.	Mch. 5, 1784
2731	Hay, Mourning (Wm. Reynolds, assee; Samuel Hay, heir at law)	100	Private	Va. St. Line	3 yrs.	Mch. 6, 1784
2741	Hughes, John	4666⅔	Captain	Va. Cont. Line	3 yrs.	Mch. 9, 1784
2742	Hughes, Jasper	2666⅔	Cornet	Va. Cont. Line	3 yrs.	Mch. 9, 1784
2744	Holmes, Christian (Anthony Singleton, attorney in fact for)	5333⅓	Major	Va. Cont. Line	3 yrs.	Mch. 9, 1784
2751	Houragen, Patrick	100	Private	Va. Cont. Line	3 yrs.	Mch. 11, '84
2756	Hood, William	100	Private	Va. Cont. Line	3 yrs.	Mch. 11, '84

LAND BOUNTY WARRANTS. 37

Warrant.	Name.	Acres	Rank.	Department.	Term	Date.
2766	Harrell, James	200	Private	Va. Cont. Line	war	Mch. 16, '84
2793	Hagard, Baker	200	Private	Va. Cont. Line	war	Mch. 19, '84
2800	Harris, John (William Plume, executor)	5333⅓	Captain	Va. St. Navy	3 yrs.	Mch. 20, '84
2804	Haney, Holland	2666⅔	Lieutenant	Va. Cont. Line	3 yrs.	Mch. 22, '84
2807	Haynes, Griffith	200	Private	Va. Cont. Line	war	Mch. 22, '84
2811	Hughes, Reuben	100	Private	Va. Cont. Art	3 yrs.	Mch. 24, '84
2812	Hubbard, Eppa	200	Sergeant	Va. Cont. Art	3 yrs.	Mch. 24, '84
2823	Haild, Caleb	100	Private	Va. Cont. Line	3 yrs.	Mch. 26, '84
2829	Harrison, James (Richard Harrison, legal rep.)	2666⅔	Lieutenant	Va. Cont. Line	3 yrs.	Mch. 26, '84
2834	Horn, Ralph	100	Private	Va. St. Line	3 yrs.	Mch. 27, '84
2878	Hagan, Barney (Arthur Hagan, heir at law)	200	Sergeant	Va. Cont. Line	war	Apr. 5, 1784
2880	Howard, Peter	200	Private	Va. Cont. Line	war	Apr. 5, 1784
2887	Hamilton, John	100	Private	Va. Cont. Line	3 yrs.	Apr. 5, 1784
2893	Hutcheson, Charles	200	Sergeant	Va. St. Line	3 yrs.	Apr. 5, 1784
2897	Hupp, Philip	100	Private	Va. Cont. Line	3 yrs.	Apr. 6, 1784
2908	Howell, Abner	100	Private	Va. Cont. Line	3 yrs.	Apr. 8, 1784
2912	Hendren, William	400	Sergeant	Va. Cont. Line	war	Apr. 10, '84
2925	Hill, James (William Reynolds, assee.)	100	Sailor	Va. St. Navy	3 yrs.	Apr. 13, '84
2961	Haley, George (Milton Ford, assee.)	200	Private	Va. Cont. Line	war	Apr. 19, '84
2973	Haley, Peter	100	Private	Va. St. Line	3 yrs.	Apr. 20, '84
2976	Haley, William	100	Private	Va. Cont. Line	3 yrs.	Apr. 20, '84
2992	Howell, David (John Pannell, assee.)	100	Private	Va. Cont. Line	3 yrs.	Apr. 21, '84
2998	Hawkins, Joseph (William Jenkins, assee.)	100	Private	Va. Cont. Line	3 yrs.	Apr. 21, '84
3031	Harrison, Richard	2666⅔	Lieutenant	V. St. Line	3 yrs.	Apr. 29, '84
3037	Hall, John (Thomas Hall, heir at law)	200	Corporal	Va. Cont. Line	3 yrs.	May 3, 1784
3047	Hite, Julius	400	Corporal	Va. Cont. Line	war	May 5, 1784
3059	Humphries, Robert	100	Private	Va. St. Line	3 yrs.	May 8, 1784
3072	Humphries, Ralph (William Reynolds, assee.)	100	Private	Va. St. Line	3 yrs.	May 11, '84
3076	Hanson, Thomas	100	Private	Va. Cont. Line	3 yrs.	May 13, '84
3094	Haley, Daniel	100	Private	Va. Cont. Line	3 yrs.	May 22, '84
3096	Hasty, John	100	Private	Va. Cont. Line	3 yrs.	May 24, '84
3123	Hite, Isaac	2666⅔	Lieutenant	Va. Cont. Line	3 yrs.	June 5, 1784
3125	Harrison, John	100	Private	Va. Cont. Line	3 yrs.	June 5, 1784
3135	Hatcher, William (James Fear, assee.)	400	Corporal	Va. Cont. Line	war	June 8, 1784
3153	Humphries, Thomas	200	Sergeant	Va. St. Line	3 yrs.	June 12, '84
3169	Haley, Martin	4000	Captain	Va. St. Line	3 yrs.	June 17, '84
3208	Hopkins, Thomas	200	Private	Va. St. Cav.	war	June 24, '84
3213	Hackney, William	100	Private	Va. Cont. Line	3 yrs.	June 26, '84
3215	Hudgins, Samuel	100	Private	Va. Cont. Line	3 yrs.	June 26, '84
3226	Hopewell, Thomas	100	Private	Va. Cont. Line	3 yrs.	June 28, '84
3244	Hogan, Francis	100	Private	Va. Cont. Line	3 yrs.	June 29, '84
3248	Hutchinson, Thomas	200	Corporal	Va. St. Line	3 yrs.	June 29, '84
3262	Hix, James	100	Private	Va. Cont. Line	3 yrs.	June 30, '84
3264	Harrison, Richard	100	Private	Va. Cont. Line	3 yrs.	June 30, '84
3269	Hammontree, John (Sam'l Blackwell, assee.)	100	Sailor	Va. St. Navy	3 yrs.	July 1, 1784
3299	Hight, George	100	Private	Va. Cont. Line	3 yrs.	July 1, 1784
3316	Herbert, Thomas	4000	Captain	Va. St. Navy	3 yrs.	July 5, '84
3325	Hocker, John (Byrd Hocker, assee.)	100	Private	Va. St. Line	3 yrs.	July 15, '84
3326	Hawkins, Moses (William Strother, heir at law)	4000	Captain	Va. Cont. Line	3 yrs.	July 17, '84
3357	Holloway, George (Elizabeth Clark, assee. of Elizabeth Dickenson, rep.)	200	Private	Va. Cont. Line	war	July 23, '84
3363	Henley, Henry	200	Sergeant	Va. Cont. Line	3 yrs	July 28, '84
3370	Harris, James (Henry Pendleton, assee.)	200	Private	Va. Cont. Line	war	Aug. 2, 1784
3372	Haley, Peter	100	Sailor	Va. St. Line	3 yrs.	Aug. 3, 1784
3381	Holback, Eddy	100	Private	Va. Cont. Line	3 yrs.	Aug. 5, 1784
3409	Holbrook, Jessee (Mathew Pate, assee.)	100	Private	Va. Cont. Line	war	Aug. 25, '84
3419	Hawkins, Benjamin	200	Private	Va. Cont. Line	war	Aug. 27, '84
3424	Hannam, John (William Reynolds, assee.)	100	Private	Va. St. Line	3 yrs.	Aug. 28, '84
3430	Harvey, Richard	100	Private	Va. Cont. Line	3 yrs.	Aug. 31, '84

LAND BOUNTY WARRANTS.

Warrant.	Name.	Acres	Rank.	Department.	Term	Date.
3452	Harper, David	200	Sergeant	Va. St. Line	3 yrs.	Sept. 30, '84
3460	Hubbard, Charles	100	Sailor	Va. St. Navy	3 yrs.	Oct. 13, '84
3461	Holland, Drury	100	Private	Va. Cont. Line	3 yrs.	Oct. 13, '84
3469	Hensley, William (Richard Hensley, heir at law)	100	Private	Va. Cont. Line	3 yrs.	Oct. 18, '84
3487	Hughes, Henry	2666⅔	Lieutenant	Va. Cont. Line	war	Oct. 27, '84
3489	Hudnall, Thomas (Eppa Hubbard, assee.)	200	Private	Va. Cont. Line	war	Oct. 29, '84
3496	Hutchinson, James	200	Private	Va. Cont. Line	war	Nov. 3, 1784
3500	Hiller, John	100	Private	Va. Cont. Line	3 yrs.	Nov. 4, 1784
3502	Hughes, Thomas	100	Private	Va. Cont. Line	3 yrs.	Nov. 4, 1784
3521	Hunt, Thomas	200	Private	Va. St. Line	war	Nov. 12, '84
3558	Hopper, Samuel	100	Private	Va. Cont. Line	3 yrs.	Dec. 7, 1784
3568	Hughes, George (Charles Lewis, assee.)	400	Sergeant	Va. Cont. Line	war	Dec. 9, 1784
3595	Hefferlin, John	100	Private	Va. Cont. Line	3 yrs.	Dec. 21, '84
3596	Hennage, George	100	Private	Va. St. Line	3 yrs.	Dec. 21, '84
3622	Howell, Vincent (James Howell, heir at law)	2666⅔	Lieutenant	Va. Cont. Line	3 yrs.	Dec. 27, '84
3627	Hatton, Samuel	100	Private	Va. St. Line	3 yrs.	Dec. 29, '84
3639	Harrison, John	100	Private	Va. Cont. Line	3 yrs.	Dec. 30, '84
3651	Haynice, William	100	Private	Va. St. Line	3 yrs.	Dec. 31, '84
3653	Hopper, John	400	Corporal	Va. Cont. Line	3 yrs.	Dec. 31, '84
3655	Hawkins, Benjamin	100	Private	Va. Cont. Line	3 yrs.	Dec. 31, '84
3677	Hoskins, Joseph	100	Private	Va. St. Line	3 yrs.	Jan. 5, 1785
3690	Hays, John	200	Sergeant	Va. Cont. Line	3 yrs.	Jan. 20, '85
3695	Holloway, Thomas	200	Sergeant	Va. Cont. Line	3 yrs.	Jan. 20, '85
3721	Heirs, Henry (James Thompson, assee.)	100	Private	Va. St. Line	3 yrs.	Jan. 28, '85
3744	Hooks, William	100	Private	Va. Cont. Line	3 yrs.	Feb. 7, 1785
3755	Henderson, John (David Henderson, heir at law)	100	Private	Va. Cont. Line	3 yrs.	Feb. 17, '85
3759	Hipkenstall, James	200	Private	Va. Cont. Line	war	Feb. 24, '85
3772	Hunter, William (Alexander Machir, assee.)	100	Private	Va. Cont. Line	3 yrs.	Mch. 9, 1785
3777	Hardy, John	100	Private	Va. St. Line	3 yrs.	Mch. 12, '85
3784	Hughes, John (George Burroughs, assee.)	200	Private	Va. Cont. Line	war	Mch. 22, '85
3794	Hardy, John	200	Private	Va. Cont. Line	war	Apr. 2, 1785
3825	Hart, William (Joseph Herill, assee.)	100	Private	Va. Art. on Cont. Establishment	3 yrs.	Apr. 23, '85
3827	Harvey, Edward	100	Private	Va. Cont. Line	3 yrs.	Apr. 27, '85
3828	Hopper, John	400	Corporal	Va. Cont. Line	war	Apr. 27, '85
3829	Hawkins, John	1333⅓	Captain	Va. Cont. Line	3 yrs.	Apr. 28, '85
3838	Helm, Leonard	200	Private	Va. Cont. Line	war	Apr. 29, '85
3880	Hendren, Robert	100	Private	Va. St. Line	3 yrs.	May 23, '85
3882	Hill, Spencer	100	Private	Va. Cont. Line	3 yrs.	May 25, '85
3893	Hunt, Munacan (Robert Rankins, assee.)	100	Private	Va. Cont. Line	3 yrs.	June 15, '85
3960	Hays, John M. (Wm. Reynolds, assee. of Wm. Bigger, assee. of Dimack Hay, executor)	100	Private	Va. St. Line	3 yrs.	Aug. 12, '85
3983	Hubbert, Isaac (Jno. W. Johnson, assee. of Jas. Roan, who was assee. of)	100	Private	Va. St. Line	3 yrs.	Oct. 18, '85
4025	Hughes, Jacob (Wm. Pettyjohn, assee. of Joshua Humphreys, who was assee. of)	200	Sergeant	Va. Cont. Line	3 yrs.	Dec. 5, 1785
4026	Horsley, James (William Reynolds, assee.)	200	Private	Va. Cont. Line	war	Dec. 5, 1785
4030	Hill, Abraham	100	Private	Va. Cont. Line	3 yrs.	Dec. 9, 1785
4039	Hull, Thomas	100	Private	Va. Cont. Line	3 yrs.	Dec. 15, '85
4040	Hull, Hopewell	100	Private	Va. Cont. Line	3 yrs.	Dec. 15, '85
4048	Hagerty, John	100	Private	Va. Cont. Line	3 yrs.	Dec. 20, '85
4049	Hill, James (Thos. Hill, heir at law)	100	Private	Cont. Line	3 yrs.	Dec. 21, '85
4057	Hays, William	200	Private	Va. Cont. Line	war	Dec. 31, '85
4059	Hull, Bucham	200	Private	Va. Cont. Line	war	Dec. 31, '85
4068	Henson, Shadrack (William Henson, heir at law)	200	Private	Va. Cont. Line	war	Jan. 6, 1786
4070	Halks, James	100	Private	Va. St. Line	3 yrs.	Jan. 10, '86
4090	Hammilton, John (Patsey Hamilton, daughter and heir at law)	2666⅔	Lieutenant	Va. St. Navy	3 yrs.	Jan. 23, '86

LAND BOUNTY WARRANTS. 39

Warrant.	Name.	Acres	Rank.	Department.	Term	Date.
①4100	Holderley, William (John Kerney, assee. of Wm. Reynolds, assee.)	400	Sergeant	Va. St. Line	war	Jan. 30, '86
4125	Howard, Charles (Edward Howard, heir at law)	200	Private	Va. Cont. Line	war	Mch. 10, '86
4141	Hoop, James	400	Corporal	Va. Cont. Line	war	Apr. 6, 1786
4164	Hampton, John (Richard Booker, assee.)	200	Private	Va. Cont. Line	war	June 1, 1786
4167	Harris, David	100	Private	Va. Cont. Line	3 yrs.	June 5, 1786
4184	Hall, George	100	Sailor	Va. St. Navy	3 yrs.	July 5, 1786
4185	Hoye, Alexander (Elizabeth and Mary Hoye, reps.)	200	Private	Va. Cont. Line	war	July 11, '86
4192	Hackworth, William	200	Corporal	Va. Cont. Line	3 yrs.	Aug. 5, 1786
4199	Henderson, Sampson	100	Private	Va. Cont. Line	3 yrs.	July 26, '86
4200	Hamilton, Robert (James Hamilton, heir at law)	400	Sergeant	Va. Cont. Line	war	Aug. 28, '86
①4204	Hanson, John	100	Private	Va. Cont. Line	3 yrs.	Aug. 31, '86
4212	Higden, Charles (Sam'l Lamm, assee. of Wm. Reynolds, assee. of)	100	Sailor	Va. St. Navy	3 yrs.	Oct. 4, 1786
①4237	Hagin, John (John Hagin, heir at law)	100	Private	Va. Cont. Line	3 yrs.	Dec. 16, '86
4268	Howard, James	200	Private	Va. Cont. Line	war	Apr. 5, 1787
4273	Harlen, George	100	Private	Va. Cont. Line	3 yrs.	Apr. 7, 1787
4281	Hutchison, John	100	Private	Va. St. Line	3 yrs.	Apr. 9, 1787
4289	Hefferling, John	200	Private	Va. Cont. Line	war	May 31, '87
4300	Hendrick, Benjamin (Zachariah Hendrick, heir at law)	100	Private	Va. Cont. Line	3 yrs.	July 2, 1787
4304	Hooly, Clem (Philip Paker, alias, "Baker," assee)	100	Private	Va. Cont. Line	3 yrs.	Aug. 15, '87
4311	Hall, Robert (Wm. Reynolds, assee. of Thos. Hall, rep.)	2666⅔	Master	Va. St. Navy	3 yrs.	Oct. 6, 1787
4320	Hatcher, William	400	Corporal	Va. Cont. Line	war	Oct. 23, '87
4364	Harris, Richard	200	Sergeant	Va. Cont. Line	3 yrs.	Dec. 14, '87
4386	Hubbard, John (Jos. Saunders, assee. of Thos. Pollard, assee. of the rep.)	2666⅔	Midshipman	Va. St. Navy	3 yrs.	Feb. 6, 1788
4388	Hamilton, Thomas (Hans Hamilton, legal rep.)	4000	Captain	Va. St. Line	3 yrs.	Mch. 4, 1788
4399	Harcum, Lot	2666⅔	Midshipman	Va. St. Navy	3 yrs.	May 1, 1788
4412	Holmes, Bartlett	200	Private	Va. Cont. Line	war	July 17, '88
4420	Harrison, Robert (Wm. Reynolds, assee. of Jno. Vaughan, assee. of the rep.)	200	Private	Va. Cont. Line	war	July 17, '88
4428	Hughlate, John (Jos. Saunders, assee. of Garrett Hughlett, rep.)	2666⅔	Midshipman	Va. St. Navy	3 yrs.	Aug. 2, 1788
4435	Hicks, William	100	Private	Va. Cont. Line	3 yrs.	Oct. 20, '88
4436	Holman, Tandy (Wm. Reynolds, assee. of Richard Burnett, assee. of)	200	Private	Va. Cont. Line	war	Oct. 22, '88
4448	Hill, John	200	Private	Va. Cont. Line	war	Jan. 29, '89
4457	Holt, Samuel (John Carter, assee.)	100	Private	Va. St. Line	3 yrs.	May 14, '89
4472	Hubbard, William (Wm. Reynolds, assee. of Sam'l McCraw, assee. of Wm. Bigger, assee. of)	100	Private	Va. St. Navy	3 yrs.	Oct. 22, '89
4506	Harris, John	100	Private	Va. Cont. Line	3 yrs.	Nov. 25, '90
4546	Hollyday, William	100	Fifer	Cont. Line	3 yrs.	Nov. 14, '91
4547	Hollyday, Henry (the rep. of)	200	Drummer	Cont. Line	war	Nov. 14, '91
4549	Hamilton, John	100	Private	Cont. Line	3 yrs.	Nov. 18, '91
4570	Harris, John	100	Private	Cont. Line	3 yrs.	Feb. 21, '92
①4571	Hines, James	100	Private	Cont. Line	3 yrs.	No date to the Original.
4576	Hurt, John	777⅔	Captain	Cont. Line	7 yrs.	May 22, '92
4582	Hill, Caleb (William Bigger, assee.)	100	Private	Cont. Line	3 yrs.	June 21, '92
4583	Hopkins, David (Peter Mansfield, assee.)	5333⅓	Major	Cont. Line	war	July 6, 1792
4588	Hogan, Michael (Hannah Hawkins, rep.)	200	Private	Cont. Line	war	Oct. 17, '92
4589	Harrison, Philip (Wm. Biggers, assee. of Wm. Reynolds, assee. of James Thomas, admr.)	400	Sergeant	Cont. Line	war	Oct. 19, '92
4596	Hay, Joseph	6000	Surgeon	Va. St. Line	3 yrs.	Nov. 27, '92

40 LAND BOUNTY WARRANTS.

Warrant	Name	Acres	Rank	Department	Term	Date
4606	HIGGINBOTHAM, William	400	Sergeant	Cont. Line	war	Mch. 9, 1793
4620	HORTON, Samuel	200	Private	Cont. Line	war	Aug. 12, '93
4456	HUTCHINSON, Joseph (John Carter, assee.)	200	Sergeant	Va. St. Line	3 yrs.	May 14, '89

I

869	IRONMONGER, Robert	200	Fife Major	Va. Cont. Line	3 yrs.	June 19, '83
1395	IRBY, Hardyman (Andrew Nicholson, assee.)	200	Sergeant	St. Line	3 yrs.	July 19, '83
2352	IRVING, William (Martin Hawkins, assee.)	200	Sergeant	Va. Cont. Line	3 yrs.	Jan. 31, '84
2494	ISDELL, Thomas (Francis Graves, assee.)	100	Private	Va. St. Line	3 yrs.	Feb. 14, '84
3011	IRESON, George	100	Private	Va. St. Line	3 yrs.	Apr. 24, '84
3230	ISBELL, Daniel	100	Private	Va. St. Line	3 yrs.	June 29, '84
3928	ISBELL, Thomas (William Reynolds, assee.)	100	Private	Va. St. Line	3 yrs.	Aug. 1, 1785
4292	IRBY, William	100	Private	Va. Cont. Line	3 yrs.	June 14, '87
4293	ISAACS, John (John Isaacs, heir at law)	200	Private	Va. St. Line	war	June 14, '87
4407	IRVIN, John	100	Private	Va. Cont. Line	3 yrs.	June 20, '88
4571	INLOE, Thomas	100	Private	St. Line	3 yrs.	Apr. 28, '92

J

60	JONES, Samuel	4000	Captain	Va. Cont. Line	3 yrs.	Dec. 19, '82
88	JONES, Strother	4000	Captain	Cont. Line	3 yrs.	Jan. 3, 1783
192	JAMESON, John	6000	Lieut.-Col.	Cav. in Cont. Line.	3 yrs.	Mch. 20, '83
390	JONES, William	200	Private	Va. St. Line	war	Apr. 24, '83
416	JEFFERS, Thomas	200	Sergeant	St. Line	3 yrs.	Apr. 26, '83
463	JOUETT, Matthew (John Jouett, legal heir)	4000	Captain	Va. Line	3 yrs.	Apr. 28, '83
499	JOHNSON, Joseph	200	Private	St. Line	war	May 1, 1783
525	JOURDEN, Michael	200	Private	St. Line	war	May 2, 1783
658	JOHNSTON, Edward	200	Private	Va. St. Line	war	May 27, '83
669	JOHNSTON, Gideon	4000	Captain	Va. State Art.	3 yrs.	May 27, '83
680	JETT, John	100	Seaman	St. Navy	3 yrs.	May 29, '83
766	JONES, Alexander	200	Private	Va. St. Line	war	June 7, 1783
825	JOLLIFFE, John (John Jolliffe, eldest son and heir to)	2666⅔	Lieutenant	Va. Cont. Line	3 yrs.	June 14, '83
919	JENKINS, William	200	Sergeant	Va. Cont. Line	3 yrs.	June 20, '83
923	JACOBS, Raley	100	Private	Va. Cont. Line	3 yrs.	June 20, '83
935	JACOBS, William	100	Private	Va. Cont. Line	3 yrs.	June 20, '83
956	JOHNSON, Moses	100	Private	Va. Cont. Line	3 yrs.	June 20, '83
973	JOHNSTON, John	100	Private	Va. Cont. Line	3 yrs.	June 20, '83
1102	JOHNSTON, James	200	Private	Va. Cont. Line	war	June 24, '83
1126	JACKSON, Thomas	200	Private	Va. Cont. Line	war	June 24, '83
1134	JONES, Thomas	200	Private	Va. Cont. Line	war	June 24, '83
1178	JONES, Zachariah	100	Private	Va. Cont. Line	3 yrs.	June 25, '83
1200	JONES, Lewis	2666⅔	Lieutenant	Va. St. Navy	3 yrs.	June 26, '83
1201	JONES, Lewis	2666⅔	Master's Mate	Va. St. Navy	3 yrs.	June 26, '83
1230	JONES, Edward	200	Private	Va. St. Line	war	June 27, '83
1233	JONES, Jessee	100	Private	Va. Cont. Line	3 yrs.	June 27, '83
1318	JAMES, Elisha	100	Private	Va. St. Line	3 yrs.	July 2, 1783
1327	JAMES, Peter	100	Private	St. Line	3 yrs.	July 4, 1783
1359	JONES, William	200	Private	Cont. Line	3 yrs.	July 12, '83
1360	JONES, John	200	Private	Cont. Line	war	July 12, '83
1451	JONES, Charles	2666⅔	Lieutenant	Cont. Line	3 yrs.	July 31, '83
1609	JONES, Richard	400	Sergeant	Va. Cont. Line	war	Aug. 27, '83
1680	JONES, John	200	Private	Va. Cont. Line	war	Aug. 27, '83
1706	JONES, Peter	200	Corporal	Va. Cont. Line	3 yrs.	Sept. 2, 1783
1732	JONES, Robert	200	Sergeant	Va. Cont. Line	3 yrs.	Sept. 8, 1783
1815	JENKINS, Richard	200	Sergeant	Va. Cont. Line	3 yrs.	Oct. 2, 1783
1825	JOHNSTON, William	2000	Captain	Va. Cont. Line	3 yrs.	Oct. 6, 1783
1826	JOHNSTON, William	2000	Captain	Va. Cont. Line	3 yrs.	Oct. 6, 1783
1853	JEROW, Jacob	100	Private	Va. St. Line	3 yrs.	Oct. 13, '83
1867	JACO, William	100	Private	Va. Cont. Line	3 yrs.	Oct. 18, '83
1889	JONES, Peter	4000	Captain	Va. Cont. Line	3 yrs.	Oct. 18, '83
ⓓ1842	JONES, William	400	Corporal	Va. Cont. Line	war	Oct. 31, '83
ⓔ1867	JORDAIN, John	100	Private	Va. Cont. Line	3 yrs.	Nov. 6, 1783
ⓕ1895	JONES, Samuel	200	Corporal	Va. Cont. Line	war	Nov. 12, '83
1877	JENNINGS, John	2666⅔	Sail'g Master	Va. St. Navy	3 yrs.	Oct. 15, '83
ⓖ1905	JOHNSON, Thomas	200	Private	Va. Cont. Line	war	Nov. 18, '83
1948	JENNINGS, Thomas	100	Sailor	Va. St. Navy	3 yrs.	Nov. 22, '83
1949	JENNINGS, William	100	Sailor	Va. St. Navy	3 yrs.	Nov. 22, '83

LAND BOUNTY WARRANTS. 41

Warrant	Name	Acres	Rank	Department	Term	Date
1950	JENKINS, Richard	100	Private	Va. Cont. Line	3 yrs.	Nov. 22, '83
2032	JEFFRIES, Elisha	100	Private	Va. Cont. Line	3 yrs.	Dec. 6, 1783
2045	JACKSON, Isaac	200	Private	Va. Cont. Line	war	Dec. 9, 1783
2080	JACKSON, John	200	Private	Va. Cont. Line	war	Dec. 10, '83
2081	JONES, Godfrey	100	Private	Va. Cont. Line	3 yrs.	Dec. 10, '83
2111	JONES, Solomon	200	Private	Va. Cont. Line	war	Dec. 13, '83
2117	JOHNSTON, John B.	4000	Captain	Va. Cont. Line	3 yrs.	Dec. 13, '83
2125	JOHNSON, Richard	200	Corporal	Va. Cont. Line	3 yrs.	Dec. 15, '83
2126	JONES, Albridgton	2666⅔	Lieutenant	Va. Cont. Line	3 yrs.	Dec. 15, '83
2135	JOHNSON, Stephen	2000	Private	Va. Cont. Line	war	Dec. 15, '83
2152	JENNINGS, Solomon (Miles Jennings, heir to)	200	Sergeant	Va. Cont. Line	3 yrs.	Dec. 19, '83
2160	JOY, Richard	200	Private	Va. Cont. Line	war	Dec. 19, '83
2173	JACKSON, Samuel	100	Private	Va. St. Line	3 yrs.	Dec. 20, '83
2178	JOHNSON, William	100	Sailor	Va. St. Navy	3 yrs.	Dec. 20, '83
2199	JOHNSON, William	4666⅔	Captain	Va. Cont. Line	7 yrs.	Dec. 23, '83
2214	JONES (Junes), James	6666⅔	Colonel	Va. Cont. Line	3 yrs.	Dec. 27, '83
2258	JONES, Richard	100	Private	Va. Cont. Line	3 yrs.	Jan. 21, '84
2264	JONES, Thomas	100	Private	Va. Cont. Line	3 yrs.	Jan. 21, '84
2269	JONES, Richard	200	Private	Va. Cont. Line	war	Jan. 21, '84
2303	JARRELL, Solomon	100	Private	Va. St. Line	3 yrs.	Jan. 28, '84
2311	JONES, Churchill	4000	Captain	Va. Cont. Line	3 yrs.	Jan. 29, '84
2313	JACKSON, William (Charles Clay, assee.)	200	Private	Va. Cont. Line	war	Jan. 29, '84
2408	JONES, John (B)	200	Private	Va. Cont. Line	war	Feb. 5, 1784
2467	JESSEE, Turner (Lewis Ford, assee.)	200	Sergeant	Va. Cont. Line	3 yrs.	Feb. 11, '84
2500	JONES, William	200	Sergeant	Va. Cont. Line	3 yrs.	Feb. 16, '84
2509	JORDAN, John	4666⅔	Captain	Va. Cont. Line	7 yrs.	Feb. 18, '84
2576	JONES, Cadwallader	2000	Captain	Va. Cont. Line	3 yrs.	Feb. 21, '84
2577	JONES, Cadwallader	1000	Captain	Va. Cont. Line	3 yrs.	Feb. 21, '84
2578	JONES, Cadwallader	1000	Captain	Va. Cont. Line	3 yrs.	Feb. 21, '84
2586	JOHNSTONE, Peter	2666⅔	Lieutenant	Va. Cont. Line	war	Feb. 23, '84
2593	JACKSON, William (William Reynolds, assee.)	100	Private	Va. St. Line	3 yrs.	Feb. 23, '84
2596	JACKSON, Michael (William Reynolds, assee.)	100	Private	Va. St. Line	3 yrs.	Feb. 23, '84
2675	JOUITT, Robert	2666⅔	Lieutenant	Va. Cont. Line	3 yrs.	Mch. 3, 1784
2721	JONES, Charles	444	Lieutenant	Va. Cont. Line	7th yr.	Mch. 6, 1784
2754	JONES, James	200	Private	Va. Cont. Line	war	Apr. 11, '84
2755	JONES, George	200	Private	Va. Cont. Line	war	Apr. 11, '84
2920	JONES, Gabriel (Robert Jones, heir at law)	4000	Captain	Va. St. Line	3 yrs.	Apr. 12, '84
2922	JOHNSON, John (Nicholas Payne, assee.)	100	Private	Va. Cont. Line	3 yrs.	Apr. 12, '84
3003	JONES, Ambrose	100	Private	Va. Cont. Line	3 yrs.	Apr. 22, '84
3014	JOINES, Leven	3000	Lieut.-Col.	Va. Cont. Line	3 yrs.	Apr. 24, '84
3015	JOINES, Leven	1000	Lieut.-Col.	Va. Cont. Line	3 yrs.	Apr. 24, '84
3016	JOINES, Leven	1000	Lieut.-Col.	Va. Cont. Line	3 yrs.	Apr. 24, '84
3017	JOINES, Leven	1000	Lieut.-Col.	Va. Cont. Line	3 yrs.	Apr. 24, '84
3036	JONES, Thomas	100	Private	Va. Cont. Line	3 yrs.	May 3, 1784
3080	JOHNSON, William	200	Non-com. Officer	Va. Cont. Line	3 yrs.	May 17, '84
3173	JACOBS, Samuel	100	Private	Va. St. Line	3 yrs.	June 19, '84
3174	JAMESON, John	1000	Lieut.-Col.	Va. Cont. Line	7 yrs.	June 19, '84
3252	JACKSON, John	200	Sergeant	Va. Cont. Line	3 yrs.	June 30, '84
3329	JOHNSON, Edward	100	Private	Va. St. Line	3 yrs.	July 19, '84
3340	JOINES, John	400	Sergeant	Va. St. Line	war	July 19, '84
3365	JONES, Joel	200	Private	Va. Cont. Line	war	July 29, '84
3373	JONES, William	400	Sergeant	Va. Cont. Line	war	Aug. 3, 1784
3375	JAMES, Michael	2666⅔	Lieutenant	Va. St. Navy	3 yrs.	Aug. 3, 1784
3421	JONES, Thomas	200	Private	Va. Cont. Line	war	Aug. 28, '84
3433	JOHNSTON, Thomas	100	Private	Va. Cont. Line	3 yrs.	Sept. 2, 1784
3439	JONES, Elisha (Samuel Couch, assee.)	100	Private	Va. St. Line	3 yrs.	Sept. 11, '84
3479	JOHNSON, Phillip	200	Sergeant	Va. Cont. Line	3 yrs.	Oct. 23, '84
3498	JACKSON, James	400	Sergeant	Va. Cont. Line	war	Nov. 4, 1784
3524	JONES, Richard	100	Private	Va. Cont. Line	3 yrs.	Nov. 16, '84
3570	JEFFRIES, James (Edmond Jeffries, heir at law)	100	Private	Va. Cont. Line	3 yrs.	Dec. 14, '84
3576	JAMES, William	100	Private	Va. St. Line	3 yrs.	Dec. 15, '84
3617	JACOBS, John	200	Private	Va. Cont. Line	war	Dec. 23, '84
3662	JOHNSON, William	100	Private	Va. Cont. Line	3 yrs.	Dec. 31, '84
3681	JACKSON, Nathaniel (William Reynolds, assee.)	200	Private	Va. Cont. Line	war	Jan. 11, '85

LAND BOUNTY WARRANTS.

War-rant.	Name.	Acres	Rank.	Department.	Term	Date.
3687	Jones, William (William Reynolds, assee.)	100	Private	Va. Cont. Line	3 yrs.	Jan. 11, '85
3703	Jenkins, William	100	Private	Va. Cont. Line	3 yrs.	Jan. 20, '85
3716	Johnston, Richard	100	Private	Va. Cont. Line	3 yrs.	Jan. 21, '85
3767	Johnson, Cornelius	100	Private	Va. Cont. Line	3 yrs.	Mch. 8, 1785
3782	Johnson, James	200	Private	Va. Cont. Line	war	Mch. 19, '85
3818	Johnson, Silas	100	Private	Va. Cont. Line	3 yrs.	Apr. 21, '85
3848	Jones, John	100	Private	Va. Cont. Line	3 yrs.	May 5, 1785
3903	Jenkins, John (William Reynolds, assee.)	200	Private	Va. Cont. Line	war	June 21, '85
3953	Jenkins, Job	100	Private	Va. Cont. Line	3 yrs.	Aug. 12, '85
3964	Junial, Anthony	100	Private	Va. Cont. Line	3 yrs.	Aug. 13, '85
4002	Jeffries, Wm. (Wm. Pettyjohn, assee. of Joshua Humphreys, who was assee. of)	200	Private	Va. Cont. Line	war	Nov. 19, '85
4012	Jones, Peter (Henry Banks, assee.)	100	Private	Va. Cont. Line	3 yrs.	Dec. 2, 1785
4014	Jones, Thomas	100	Private	Va. Cont. Line	3 yrs.	Dec. 2, 1785
4024	Jacobs, Benjamin (Wm. Reynolds, assee. of Jacob Jacobs, rep. of)	100	Private	Va. Cont. Line	3 yrs.	Dec. 5, 1785
4029	Jackson, William	100	Private	Va. St. Line	3 yrs.	Dec. 9, 1785
4053	Jeffcoat, John	100	Private	Va. Cont. Line	3 yrs.	Dec. 21, '85
4118	Jones, Samuel	200	Private	Va. Cont. Line	war	Mch. 7, 1786
4160	Johnson, James	100	Private	Va. Cont. Line	3 yrs.	May 26, '86
4168	Jordan, James (Fleming Jordan, heir to)	100	Private	Va. Cont. Line	3 yrs.	June 9, 1786
4179	Jones, John	100	Private	Va. Cont. Line	3 yrs.	June 22, '86
4189	Johnston, George (Archibald Johnston, Patrick Moore and Betty, his wife, devisees)	6000	Lieut.-Col.	Va. Cont. Line	3 yrs.	July 20, '86
4237	Jackson, Edward	100	Private	Va. Cont. Line	3 yrs.	Dec. 13, '86
4246	Jackson, Hezekiah (John Schartell, assee.)	100	Private	Va. Cont. Line	3 yrs.	Dec. 30, '86
4290	Johnson, Edward (Daniel Johnson, heir at law)	100	Private	Va. St. Line	3 yrs.	June 5, 1787
4349	Jenkins, Abraham (Jeremiah Jenkins, heir at law)	100	Private	Va. Cont. Line	3 yrs.	Dec. 5, 1787
4350	Jenkins, Isaac (Jeremiah Jenkins, heir at law)	100	Private	Va. Cont. Line	3 yrs.	Dec. 5, 1787
4450	Jenkins, William (William Reynolds, assee. of the rep.)	200	Private	Va. Cont. Line	war	Feb. 26, '89
4470	Jones, Benjamin (Wm. Reynolds, assee. of Sam'l McCraw, assee. of Jno. Jones, rep.)	100	Private	Va. St. Line	3 yrs.	Oct. 22, '89
4476	Johnson, Ellis	100	Private	Va. St. Line	3 yrs.	Oct. 13, '89
4543	Jones, James	100	Bombardier	St. Art	3 yrs.	Nov. 11, '91
4557	Jones, Charles	200	Sergeant	Cont. Line	3 yrs.	Dec. 3, 1791
4562	Jones, James (Jno. Jones, heir at law)	100	Private	Cont. Line	3 yrs.	Dec. 22, '91
4563	Jones, Richard (Jno. Jones, heir at law)	100	Private	Cont. Line	3 yrs.	Dec. 22, '91
4568	Johns, James (Thomas Hopkins, assee. of Jno. Johns, heir at law to)	100	Private	Cont. Line	3 yrs.	Feb. 1, 1792
4598	Jeffries, Isaac (the rep. or reps. of)	2666⅔	Ensign	Cont. Line	war	Dec. 12, '92
4612	Johnston, Jacob	100	Private	Cont. Line	3 yrs.	May 27, '93
4613	Johnston, Benjamin (the rep. or reps. of)	200	Private	Cont. Line	war	May 27, '93

K

66	Kennedy, James	2666⅔	Lieutenant	St. Gar. Reg.	3 yrs.	Dec. 20, '82
169	King, John	100	Private	Va. Cont. Line	3 yrs.	Mch. 10, '83
170	Kelly, Thaddely	4000	Captain	St. Line	3 yrs.	Mch. 10, '83
190	Kirby, John	200	Drummer	Va. Cont. Line	war	Mch. 20, '83
191	Kemp, Peter	4000	Captain	Art. in St. Line	3 yrs.	Mch. 20, '83
216	Knight, John	2000	Surg.'s Mate	Va. Cont. Line	3 yrs.	Apr. 1, 1783
217	Knight, John	2000	Surg.'s Mate	Va. Cont. Line	3 yrs.	Apr. 1, 1783
268	King, Francis (Doctor James McClung, assee.)	100	Private	St. Line	3 yrs.	Apr. 3, 1783
280	Kelly, John	100	Private	Va. St. Line	3 yrs.	Apr. 3, 1783
379	Kelly, Benjamin	200	Private	Va. St. Line	3 yrs.	Apr. 22, '83
421	Kennady, Moses	200	Private	Va. St. Line	war	Apr. 26, '83

LAND BOUNTY WARRANTS. 43

War-rant.	Name.	Acres	Rank.	Department.	Term	Date.
528	Kendall, George	200	Private	St. Line	war	May 2, 1783
556	Kays, Robert	2666⅔	Lieutenant	Va. Cont. Line	3 yrs.	May 7, 1783
578	Kelly, Benjamin	100	Private	Va. Cont. Line		May 14, '83
922	Kelly, John	100	Private	Va. Cont. Line	3 yrs.	June 20, '83
928	Knight, James	100	Private	Va. Cont. Line	3 yrs.	June 20, '83
949	Kingore, William	100	Private	Va. Cont. Line	3 yrs.	June 20, '83
986	Kerford, William	200	Sergeant	Cont. Line	3 yrs.	June 20, '83
1146	Karr, James	200	Private	Va. Cont. Line	war	June 24, '83
1161	Kerney, John	1000	Captain	Va. St. Line	3 yrs	June 24, '83
1162	Kerney, John	1500	Captain	Va. St. Line	3 yrs.	June 24, '83
1163	Kerney, John	1500	Captain	Va. St. Line	3 yrs.	June 24, '83
1188	Kindrick, Daniel	100	Private	Va. Cont. Line	3 yrs.	June 26, '83
1262	Kairns, John	400	Corporal	Va. Cont. Line	war	June 27, '63
1270	Kidd, Benjamin	100	Private	Va. Cont. Line	3 yrs.	June 28, '83
1274	Keen, Thomas	233⅓	Private	Va. Cont. Line	7 yrs.	June 28, '83
1278	Kouts, Jacob	233⅓	Private	Va. Cont. Line	war	June 28, '83
1287	Klung, Henry	200	Private	Va. Cont. Line	war	June 28, '83
1298	Keep, James	200	Private	Va. Cont. Line	war	June 30, '83
1383	Kirk, Robert	2666⅔	Lieutenant	Cont. Line	3 yrs.	July 17, '83
1424	Knight, John	100	Private	St. Line	3 yrs.	July 25, '83
1425	Knight, John	100	Private	St. Line	3 yrs.	July 25, '83
1636	Kirkpatrick, James	200	Private	Va. Cont. Line	war	Aug. 23, '83
1830	Kenney, Richard	233⅓	Private	Cont. Line	8 yrs.	Oct. 7, 1783
1856	Kimble, Robert	100	Private	Va. Cont. Line	3 yrs.	Oct. 13, '83
②1866	Kenton, Mark	233⅓	Private	Va. Cont. Line	7 yrs.	Nov. 6, 1783
①1894	Kennedy, William	100	Private	Va. Cont. Line	3 yrs.	Nov. 12, '83
1910	Kent, Smith	200	Sergeant	Va. Cont. Line	3 yrs.	Oct. 24, '83
1929	King, Francis	200	Private	Va. Cont. Line	war	Oct. 28, '83
②1911	King, Elisha	2666⅔	Lieutenant	Va. Cont. Line	3 yrs.	Nov. 19, '83
②1915	Kelly, Jesse	200	Private	Va. Cont. Line	war	Nov. 20, '83
2025	Knox, James	5333⅓	Major	Va. Cont. Line	3 yrs.	Dec. 6, 1783
2052	Kirkpatrick, Abraham	4666⅔	Captain	Va. Cont. Line	7 yrs.	Dec. 9, 1783
2122	Keith, Daniel	200	Private	Va. Cont. Line	war	Dec. 13, '83
2143	Kenny, Joseph (James Kenny, heir at law)	100	Private	Va. Cont. Line	3 yrs.	Dec. 16, '83
2145	King, John	100	Private	Va. Cont. Line	3 yrs.	Dec. 17, '84
2154	Knight, Andrew	100	Private	Va. Cont. Line	3 yrs.	Dec. 19, '83
2388	Kelley, Andrew (Martin Hawkins, assee.)	200	Corporal	Va. Cont. Line	3 yrs.	Feb. 3, 1784
2477	Kibble, William (Daniel Feagan, assee.)	200	Corporal	Va. St. Line	3 yrs.	Feb. 11, '84
2512	King, Zachariah (James Hawkins, assee.)	100	Private	Va. St. Line	3 yrs.	Feb. 18, '84
2614	Kanard, Joshua (Daniel Flowerree, assee.)	100	Private	Va. St. Line	3 yrs.	Feb. 24, '84
2615	Kanard, James (Daniel Flowerree, assee.)	100	Private	Va. St. Line	3 yrs.	Feb. 24, '84
2700	King, Miles	2666⅔	Surg.'s Mate	Va. Cont. Line	3 yrs.	Mch. 4, 1784
2711	Kinley, Benjamin (Benjamin Berry, heir at law)	4000	Captain	Va. St. Line	3 yrs.	Mch. 5, 1784
2727	Kemp, Peter (Henrick Finch, assee.)	100	Private	Va. St. Line	3 yrs.	Mch. 6, 1784
2769	King, William	100	Private	Va. St. Line	3 yrs.	Mch. 17, '84
2860	Knox, Thomas	100	Private	Va. Cont. Line	3 yrs.	Apr. 2, 1784
2926	Kendall, Custus	4666⅔	Captain	Va. Cont. Line	7 yrs.	Apr. 13, '84
2933	Kemp, James	2666⅔	Ensign	Va. St. Line	3 yrs.	Apr. 15, '84
2990	Kent, Alexander (William Reynolds, assee.)	100	Private	Va. Cont. Line	3 yrs.	Apr. 21, '84
3043	Kenner, Rodham	100	Sailor	Va. St. Navy	3 yrs.	May 4, 1784
3054	Kantzman, John	2666⅔	Lieutenant	Va. St. Navy	3 yrs.	May 7, 1784
3069	Kennon, John (William Randolph, rep.)	2666⅔	Lieutenant	Va. Cont. Line	3 yrs.	May 11, '84
3074	Keysar, William	100	Private	Va. St. Line	3 yrs.	May 12, '84
3087	Kennady, John	200	Private	Va. Cont. Line	war	May 22, '84
3133	Kennon, John (William Randolph, rep.)	1333⅓	Captain	Va. Cont. Line		June 7, 1784
3152	Kertiller, Abraham	100	Private	Va. Cont. Line	3 yrs.	June 11, '84
3204	King, James	200	Sergeant	Va. Cont. Line	3 yrs.	June 24, '84
3320	Keeth, Isham (Res. Gen. Assby., June 28, 1784)	2666⅔	Lieutenant	Services		July 9, 1784
3321	Keller, Abraham (Mary Keller, rep.)	4000	Captain	Va. St. Line	3 yrs.	July 12, '84
3330	King, Nicholas	200	Private	Va. St. Line	war	July 19, '84
3382	Key, George	100	Private	Va. St. Line	3 yrs.	Aug. 5, 1784
3387	King, John (Jacob Lockhard and Casper Kersman, assees.)	200	Private	Va. Cont. Line	war	Aug. 10, '84

LAND BOUNTY WARRANTS.

Warrant.	Name.	Acres	Rank.	Department.	Term	Date.
3392	Kemp, William (Thomas B. Adams, assee.)	200	Private	Va. Cont. Line	war	Aug. 13, '84
3445	Kersey, William	100	Private	Va. Cont. Line	3 yrs.	Sept. 20, '84
3511	Kelly, William	200	Private	Va. Cont. Line	war	Nov. 8, 1784
3534	Keen, John	200	Private	Va. Cont. Line	war	Nov. 23, '84
3564	Knight, James	200	Sergeant	Va. St. Line	3 yrs.	Dec. 9, 1784
3590	Kearnes, John	100	Private	Va. Cont. Line	3 yrs.	Dec. 21, '84
3606	Knight, William (John Knight, heir at law)	100	Private			
3644	Keeton, William and Edmund (John Keeton, Jr., heir at law)	200	Privates	Va. Cont. Line	3 yrs.	Dec. 22, '84
3722	Kurns, John (Elizabeth Stadler, heir at law)	200	Private	Va. Cont. Line	war	Dec. 30, '84
3725	Kelly, Timothy	100	Private	Va. Cont. Line	3 yrs.	Jan. 28, '85
3780	Kenner, Rodham	100	Private	Va. St. Line	3 yrs.	Jan. 31, '85
3783	Kenner, Howson	2666⅔	Midshipman	Va. St. Navy	3 yrs.	Mch. 17, '85
4194	Kent, Jesse (Thos. Kent, heir at law)	2666⅔	Lieutenant	Va. St. Navy	3 yrs.	Mch. 21, '85
4211	Kendall, Jesse (Sam'l Lamm, assee. of Wm. Reynolds, assee. of)	100	Private	Va. St. Line	3 yrs.	Aug. 9, 1786
4232	Kent, Thomas	100	Sailor	Va. St. Navy	3 yrs.	Oct. 4, 1786
4234	Kent, William	100	Sailor	Va. St. Navy	3 yrs.	Nov. 16, '86
4336	King, Charles	200	Sergeant	Va. Cont. Line	3 yrs.	Nov. 13, '87
4343	Kelly, Gordon	100	Private	Va. Cont. Line	3 yrs.	Nov. 28, '87
4348	Knox, George	100	Private	Va. Cont. Line	3 yrs.	Dec. 5, 1787
4365	Kennady, Andrew (Wm. Reynolds, assee. of Benj. Kennady, rep. of)	100	Private	Va. St. Line	3 yrs.	Jan. 17, '88
4391	Kemp, James	100	Private	Va. Cont. Line	3 yrs.	Mch. 12, '88
4609	Kilty, John	4000	Captain	Cont. Line	war	Apr. 11, '93

L

65	Lincoln, Michael	100	Private	1st Va. Reg.	3 yrs.	Dec. 20, '82
72	Lewis, William	6222	Major	Va. Cont. Line	7 yrs.	Dec. 24, '82
60	Lipscomb, Bernard	4000	Capt.-Lieut	Art.	3 yrs.	Dec. 31, '82
81	Lipscomb, Reuben (Berna. Lipscomb, heir at law)	4000	Captain	Cont. Line	3 yrs.	Dec. 31, '82
82	Lipscomb, Yancy	4000	Capt.-Lieut	Art. of St. Line	3 yrs.	Feb. 20, '83
138	Leigh, John	200	Sergeant	Va. Line		
288	Lovely, William L.	4000	Captain	4th Va. Cont. Reg.	3 yrs.	Apr. 4, 1783
320	Lock, William	200	Private	St. Cav	war	Apr. 12, '83
324	Lepling, Joseph	400	Corporal	St. Cav		Apr. 12, '83
345	Lina, Arthur	4000	Captain	Va. Cont. Line	war	Apr. 15, '83
367	Lewis, George	4000	Captain	Va. Cav	3 yrs.	Apr. 19, '83
372	Loden, Jesse	200	Private	Va. St. Line	war	Apr. 19, '83
387	Lapsley, Samuel	4000	Captain	Va. Line	3 yrs.	Apr. 23, '83
389	Lapsley, John	2666⅔	Lieutenant	Va. Cont. Line	3 yrs.	Apr. 23, '83
395	Locke, Joseph	100	Private	Va. Art	3 yrs.	Apr. 25, '83
396	Lewis, Addison	4000	Captain	Va. Cont. Cav	3 yrs.	Apr. 25, '83
408	Lyon, Thomas	400	Sergeant	Va. Line	war	Apr. 25, '83
420	Love, John	400	Sergeant	Va. St. Line	war	Apr. 26, '83
439	Lee, Edward	200	Private	Va. St. Line	war	Apr. 26, '83
454	Lambert, John	400	Sergeant	St. Line	war	Apr. 28, '83
474	Lee, John	5333⅓	Major	Va. St. Line	3 yrs.	Apr. 29, '83
477	Lynch, Timothy	200	Private	St. Line	war	Apr. 30, '83
513	Lucas, Samuel	400	Fife Major	St. Line	war	May 1, 1783
514	Leggit, Owen	200	Private	St. Line	war	May 1, 1783
521	Lorde, John	400	Sergeant	St. Line	war	May 1, 1783
551	Lucas, Thomas	200	Private	St. Line	war	May 6, 1783
609	Link, John	100	Private	Va. Cont. Line	3 yrs.	May 21, '83
617	Lawrence, Thomas	200	Sergeant	Va. Cont. Line	3 yrs.	May 21, '83
634	Langford, Euclid	100	Private	Va. Line	3 yrs.	May 24, '83
647	Legg, John	100	Private	Va. Line	3 yrs.	May 27, '83
656	Landrum, Thomas	100	Private	Va. St. Line	3 yrs.	May 27, '83
683	Lipscomb, John	200	Corporal	Va. Cav	3 yrs.	May 30, '83
728	Lewis, Andrew	2666⅔	Lieutenant	Va. Cont. Line	3 yrs.	June 3, 1783
731	Long, William	4000	Captain	Va. Cont. Line	3 yrs.	June 3, 1783
746	Lord, Roberson	200	Private	Va. St. Line	war	June 5, 1783
761	Lawson, Benjamin	2666⅔	Lieutenant	Va. Cont. Line	3 yrs.	June 6, 1783
786	Lynch, Patrick	100	Private	Va. Cont. Line	3 yrs.	June 11, '83
818	Ludman, J. William	2666⅔	Lieutenant	Va. Cont. Line	3 yrs.	June 14, '83
876	Lightfoot, Philip	200	Corporal	Va. St. Line	3 yrs.	June 19, '83
961	Lahaw, Jeremiah	100	Private	Cont. Line		June 20, '83

LAND BOUNTY WARRANTS. 45

Warrant.	Name.	Acres	Rank.	Department.	Term	Date.
972	Lahaw, David	100	Private	Cont. Line		June 20, '83
1011	Lawson, Andrew	100	Private	Va. Line	3 yrs.	June 23, '83
1028	Lindsay, Hezekiah	100	Private	Va. Cont. Line	3 yrs.	June 23, '83
1045	Lockart, John	200	Private	Va. Cont. Line	war	June 24, '83
1063	Loveall, James	200	Private	Va. Cont. Line	war	June 24, '83
1094	Lane, James	400	Q. M. Serg.	Va. Cont. Line	war	June 24, '83
1116	Lemmon, Samuel	200	Private	Va. Cont. Line	war	June 24, '83
1124	Low, James	200	Private	Va. Cont. Line	war	June 24, '83
1199	Lindsay, William	4000	Captain	Va. Cav	3 yrs.	June 26, '83
1202	Lightburn, Richard	2666⅔	Lieutenant	Va. St. Navy	3 yrs.	June 26, '83
1219	Lyle, Charles	100	Private	Va. Cont. Line	3 yrs.	June 26, '83
1221	London, William	100	Private	Va. St. Line	3 yrs.	June 26, '83
1234	Lipscomb, Henry	200	Fifer	Cont. Line	war	June 27, '83
1285	Layne, John	200	Private	Va. St. Line	war	June 28, '83
1286	Lewis, John	200	Private	Va. Cont. Line	war	June 28, '83
1397	Lynch, James	200	Private	Cont. Line	war	July 19, '83
1400	Langham, Elias	2666⅔	Lieutenant	Va. Cont. Line	3 yrs.	July 21, '83
1408	Levingston, Justice	2000	Surgeon	St. Navy	3 yrs.	July 22, '83
1409	Levingston, Justice	2000	Surgeon	St. Navy	3 yrs.	July 22, '83
1410	Levingston, Justice	1000	Surgeon	St. Navy	3 yrs.	July 22, '83
1411	Levingston, Justice	1000	Surgeon	St. Navy	3 yrs.	July 22, '83
1465	Lipscomb, Mourning	100	Private	Cont. Line	3 yrs.	Aug. 1, 1783
1466	Lipscomb, Thomas	100	Private	Cont. Line	3 yrs.	Aug. 1, 1783
1525	Loaden, William	200	Private	St. Line	war	Aug. 7, 1783
1541	Lawe, John	100	Private	Cont. Line	3 yrs.	Aug. 9, 1783
1542	Lowe, Thomas	200	Sergeant	Cont. Line	3 yrs.	Aug. 9, 1783
1551	Learwood, Josiah	100	Private	Cont. Line	3 yrs.	Aug. 11, '83
1570	Long, Reuben	2666⅔	Lieutenant	Cont. Line	3 yrs.	Aug. 14, '83
1588	League, James	200	Private	Cont. Line	war	Aug. 20, '83
1603	Lee, James	100	Private	Cont. Line	3 yrs.	Aug. 20, '83
1669	Lawless, Austin	100	Private	Va. Cont. Line	3 yrs.	Aug. 26, '83
1781	Leftwich, Joel	100	Private	Va. Cont. Line	3 yrs.	Sept. 22, '83
1786	Leitch, James	400	Corporal	Va. Cont. Line	war	Sept. 24, '83
1906	Langpitt, Francis	100	Private	Va. Cont. Line	3 yrs.	Oct. 23, '83
1908	Lee, Richard	200	Corporal	Va. St. Line	3 yrs.	Oct. 23, '83
1909	Langpitt, Philip	100	Private	Va. Cont. Line	3 yrs.	Oct. 24, '83
1911	Lee, Richard	200	Private	Cont. Line	war	Oct. 25, '83
1937	Lee, Henry	7777⅞	Lieut.-Col.	Va. Cont. Line	7 yrs.	Oct. 31, '83
(3) 1847	Lewis, Ambrose	100	Sailor	St. Navy	3 yrs.	Nov. 1, 1783
(3) 1897	Lee, Randolph	100	Private	Va. St. Line	3 yrs.	Nov. 14, '83
(2) 1901	Leonard, Robert	233⅓	Private	Va. Cont. Line	war	Nov. 17, '83
(2) 1921	Lawson, Robert	10,000	Brig. Gen.	Va. Cont. Line	3 yrs.	Nov. 21, '83
1942	Lane, Zachariah	100	Private	Va. St. Line	3 yrs.	Nov. 22, '83
1946	Lewis, Matthew	100	Seaman	Va. St. Navy	3 yrs.	Nov. 22, '83
1951	Leonard, William	100	Sailor	Va. St. Navy	3 yrs.	Nov. 22, '83
1964	Loyd, George	200	Sergeant	Va. Cont. Line	3 yrs.	Nov. 25, '83
2002	Lewis, William	200	Private	Va. Cont. Line	war	Dec. 1, 1783
2037	Lindsey, Peter	200	Private	Va. Cont. Line	war	Dec. 6, 1783
2041	Leman, Dedrick	100	Private	Va. Cont. Line	3 yrs.	Dec. 9, 1783
2042	Lowe, John	200	Private	Va. Cont. Line	war	Dec. 9, 1783
2055	Lucas, Samuel (Samuel Griffin, assee.)	100	Private	Va. St. Line	3 yrs.	Dec. 9, 1783
2057	Little, Moses (Samuel Griffin, assee.)	100	Private	Va. St. Line	3 yrs.	Dec. 9, 1783
2063	Lank, John (Samuel Griffin, assee.)	100	Private	Va. St. Line	3 yrs.	Dec. 9, 1783
2116	Lipscomb, Archibald	100	Private	Va. St. Line	3 yrs.	Dec. 9, 1783
2144	Lockhart, James (James Johnson, assee.)	100	Private	Va. St. Line	3 yrs.	Dec. 16, '83
2164	Lewis, John	100	Private	Va. Cont. Line	3 yrs.	Dec. 20, '83
2202	Long, Gabriel	4000	Captain	Va. Cont. Line	3 yrs.	Dec. 22, '83
2282	Larty, John	4000	Captain	Va. St. Navy	3 yrs.	Jan. 24, '84
2305	Linton, John	2666⅔	Lieutenant	Va. Cont. Line	3 yrs.	Jan. 28, '83
2362	Lear, John	200	Private	Va. Cont. Line	war	Feb. 2, 1784
2371	Lewis, Zachariah	200	Sergeant	Va. Cont. Line	3 yrs.	Feb. 3, 1784
2385	Lyne, Nabas (Martin Hawkins, assee.)	100	Private	Va. Cont. Line	3 yrs.	Feb. 3, 1784
2392	Lambs, Joseph (Martin Hawkins, assee.)	100	Private	Va. Cont. Line	war	Feb. 3, 1784
2411	Linton, John	444	Lieutenant	Va. Cont. Line	7 yrs.	Feb. 5, 1784
2438	Lyon, William	100	Private	Va. St. Line	3 yrs.	Feb. 9, 1784
2460	Lenwick, Samuel (Lewis Ford, assee. of)	200	Corporal	Va. Cont. Line	3 yrs.	Feb. 11, '84
2476	Leech, George (Francis Peyton, assee. of)	100	Private	Va. St. Line	3 yrs.	Feb. 11, '84
2487	Longwith, John	100	Seaman	Va. St. Navy	3 yrs.	Feb. 13, '84

LAND BOUNTY WARRANTS.

Warrant.	Name.	Acres	Rank.	Department.	Term	Date.
2488	LUNCIFORD, Elias	100	Sailor	Va. St. Navy	3 yrs.	Feb. 13, '84
2496	LAYNE, Josiah (Francis Graves, assee.)	100	Private	Va. St. Line	3 yrs.	Feb. 14, '84
2503	LACY, Henry R.	100	Private	Va. Cont. Line	3 yrs.	Feb. 17, '84
2521	LONG, Evans	200	Sergeant	Va. Cont. Line	3 yrs.	Feb. 19, '84
2522	LONG, Nicholas	200	Sergeant	Va. Cont. Line	3 yrs.	Feb. 19, '84
2533	LOYD, William	100	Private	Va. Cont. Line	3 yrs.	Feb. 19, '84
2553	LUCAS, James	5333⅓	Major	Va. Cont. Line	3 yrs.	Feb. 19, '84
2555	LEIGH, John ("to complete with a warrant that has already issued to him as a Sergeant, his Bounty")	2466⅔	Lieutenant	Va. Cont. Line	3 yrs.	Feb. 20, '84
2655	LAWSON, Claiborne (William Lawson, heir at law)	4000	Captain	Va. Cont. Line	3 yrs.	Mch. 1, 1784
2680	LAWSON, John (Edmund Clarke, assee.)	200	Private	Va. Cont. Line	war	Mch. 3, 1784
2690	LOYD, Thomas (Martin Hawkins, assee.)	100	Private	Va. Cont. Line	3 yrs.	Mch. 3, 1784
2694	LANDWICK, William (Martin Hawkins, assee.)	200	Corporal	Va. Cont. Line	3 yrs.	Mch. 3, 1784
2735	LEWIS, John	100	Private	Va. Cont. Line	3 yrs.	Mch. 6, 1784
2760	LAWSON, Benjamin	100	Private	Va. Cont. Line	3 yrs.	Mch. 12, '84
2777	LYLES, Elijah (James Jenkins, assee.)	100	Private	Va. Cont. Line	3 yrs.	Mch. 18, '84
2801	LOCKET, Jacob	100	Private	Va. Cont. Line	3 yrs.	Mch. 22, '84
2818	LONGWITH, Burgess	2666⅔	Gunner	Va. St. Line	3 yrs.	Mch. 25, '84
2837	LYON, James (John Lyon, heir at law)	100	Private	Va. St. Line	3 yrs.	Mch. 27, '84
2854	LEMASTERS, James	100	Private	Va. Cont. Line	3 yrs.	Apr. 1, 1784
2863	LONDON, Adam	200	Private	Va. Cont. Line	war	Apr. 2, 1784
2867	LINDSEY, David	100	Private	Va. Cont. Line	3 yrs.	Apr. 2, 1784
2898	LEWIS, Stephen (Thomas Lewis, legal rep.)	2666⅔	Lieutenant	Va. Cont. Line	3 yrs.	Apr. 6, 1784
2910	LUCAS, William	100	Private	Va. St. Line	3 yrs.	Apr. 8, 1784
2965	LIPSCOMB, Benjamin	100	Private	Va. Cont. Line	3 yrs.	Apr. 19, '84
2971	LAYTON, Reuben	100	Private	Va. Cont. Line	3 yrs.	Apr. 20, '84
3009	LEWIS, James	200	Private	Va. Cont. Line	war	Apr. 23, '84
3019	LILLY, Thomas	5333⅓	Captain	Va. St. Navy	3 yrs.	Apr. 26, '84
3035	LEWIS, Joseph (Martha Lewis, legal rep.)	200	Private	Va. Cont. Line	war	May 3, 1784
3060	LONG, Andrew (Jas. Fair, assee. of David Frainam, who was assee. of)	100	Private	Va. St. Line	3 yrs.	May 8, 1784
3068	LAWSON, John (Edward Valentine, assee.)	100	Private	Va. St. Line	3 yrs.	May 10, '84
3091	LEE, John (Richard Edwards, assee.)	100	Private	Va. Cont. Line	3 yrs.	May 22, '84
3112	LEFTWICH, John (James Turner, assee.)	200	Sergeant	Va. Cont. Line	3 yrs.	May 29, '84
3129	LONG, Daniel	100	Private	Va. Cont. Line	3 yrs.	June 5, 1784
3175	LEE, Richard Francis (Richard Lee, Esq., heir at law)	4000	Captain	Va. Cont. Line	3 yrs.	June 21, '84
3233	LODEN, Benjamin (John Brent, assee.)	200	Private	Va. Cont. Line	war	June 29, '84
3255	LONG, Richard	200	Corporal	Va. St. Line	3 yrs.	June 30, '84
3263	LUCAS, Nathaniel (Res. Gen. Assby., June 23, 1784)	4000	Captain	Services		June 30, '84
3285	LOWRY, William	100	Sailor	Va. St. Navy	3 yrs.	July 1, 1784
3288	LUNSFORD, William (Lewis Lunsford, heir at law)	2666⅔	Cornet	Va. Cont. Line	3 yrs.	July 1, 1784
3290	LEE, Simmons	100	Private	Va. Cont. Line	3 yrs.	July 1, 1784
3294	LEE, Jesse	100	Private	Va. St. Line	3 yrs.	July 1, 1784
3327	LOVEL, Richard	200	Private	Va. St. Line	war	July 19, '84
3385	LEMMON, John (Peter Tardiveau, assee.)	200	Private	Illinois Regiment	war	Aug. 6, 1784
3390	LOCKETT, Benjamin	100	Private	Va. Cont. Line	3 yrs.	Aug. 11, '84
3394	LEITCH, Andrew (James Frisby Leitch, legal rep.)	5333⅓	Major	Va. Cont. Line	3 yrs.	Aug. 14, '84
3466	LINSEY, Edward	100	Private	Va. St. Line	3 yrs.	Oct. 16, '84
3522	LEVELL, Henry (John Thomas, assee.)	200	Private	Va. Cont. Line	war	Nov. 13, '84
3532	LAWS, John	100	Private	Va. Cont. Line	3 yrs.	Nov. 22, '84
3546	LEAR, George	200	Private	Va. Cont. Line	war	Nov. 29, '84
3557	LOCKE, John	400	Corporal	Va. Cont. Line	war	Dec. 6, 1784
3588	LOCKHART, William (Goodrich Lightfoot, assee.)	200	Private	Va. Cont. Line	war	Dec. 20, '84

LAND BOUNTY WARRANTS. 47

Warrant.	NAME.	Acres	RANK.	DEPARTMENT.	Term	DATE.
3604	LARGENT, James	100	Private	Va. Cont. Line	3 yrs.	Dec. 2,1 '84
3675	LEE, James	100	Private	Va. Cont. Line	3 yrs.	Jan. 5, 1785
3686	LOYAL, John (William Reynolds, assee.)	100	Private	Va. Cont. Line	3 yrs.	Jan. 11, '85
3708	LAWSON, Henry	100	Private	Va. Cont. Line	3 yrs.	Jan. 20, '85
3761	LAYNE, William	100	Private	Va. Cont. Line	3 yrs.	Feb. 26, '85
3559	LINTER, Edward	100	Private	Va. Cont. Line	3 yrs.	Dec. 7, 1784
3823	LAND, Lewis (William Reynolds, assee.)	100	Private	Va. St. Line	3 yrs.	Apr. 23, '85
3839	LETRELL, Joseph (John Letrell, heir at law)	200	Private	Va. Cont. Line	war	Apr. 29, 85
3840	LETRELL, James (John Letrell, heir at law)	400	Sergeant	Va. Cont. Line	war	Apr. 29, 85
3929	LEFECY, Shadrach (William Reynolds, assee.)	100	Private	Va. Cont. Line	3 yrs.	Aug. 1, 1785
3930	LUSTER, William (William Reynolds, assee.)	100	Private	Va. Cont. Line	3 yrs.	Aug. 1, 1785
3937	LYNE, John	100	Private	Va. Cont. Line	3 yrs.	Aug. 2, 1785
3965	LUCAS, Humphrey (Samuel Lucas, heir at law)	200	Private	Va. Cont. Line	war	Aug. 13, '85
3984	LEATH, Peter (Arthur Leath, rep.)	100	Private	Va. Cont. Line	3 yrs.	Oct. 19, '85
3987	LITTLEPAGE, John	200	Private	Va. Cont. Line	war	Oct. 26, '85
4001	LANGSDON, Daniel (William Pettyjohn, assee. of Joshua Humphreys, who was assee. of)	200	Private	Va. Cont. Line	war	Nov. 19, '85
4006	LANGSDON, Wm. (Joshua Humphreys, assee.)	200	Private	Va. Cont. Line	war	Nov. 24, '85
4007	LANGSDON, Charles (Joshua Humphreys, assee.)	200	Private	Va. Cont. Line	war	Nov. 24, '85
4015	LOCKETT, Benjamin	100	Private	Va. Cont. Line	war	Dec. 2, 1785
4034	LAMBER, Charles (John Stockdell, assee.)	200	Private	Va. Cont. Line	war	Dec. 10, '85
4083	LAMME, Nathan	4000	Captain	Va. Cont. Line	3 yrs.	Jan. 17, '86
4089	LIPSCOMB, Major	200	Sergeant	Va. Cont. Line	3 yrs.	Jan. 23, '86
4098	LIMAY, John	100	Private	Va. Cont. Line	3 yrs.	Jan. 27, '86
4103	LATIMER, Henry (Francis Graves, assee.)	200	Private	Va. Cont. Line	war	Feb. 1, 1786
4147	LANGSTON, William (William Biggers, assee. of George Langston, heir to)	100	Private	Va. Cont. Line	3 yrs.	Apr. 24, '86
4190	LEWIS, Thomas (Edward Lewis, heir at law)	1333⅓	Lieutenant	Va. Cont. Line	3 yrs.	July 28, '86
4191	LEWIS, Thomas (Edward Lewis, heir at law)	1333⅓	Lieutenant	Va. Cont. Line	3 yrs.	July 28, '86
4213	LYNES, John (Sam'l Lamm, assee. of Wm. Reynolds, assee. of)	100	Private	Va. St. Line	3 yrs.	Oct. 4, 1786
4225	LONG, Reuben	100	Private	Va. Cont. Line	3 yrs.	Nov. 1, 1786
4229	LONG, Levi	200	Private	Va. Cont. Line	war	Nov. 15, '86
4244	LYNER, Philip (Robert Galbreath, assee.)	100	Private	Va. St. Line	3 yrs.	Dec. 26, '86
4247	LEITH, George	200	Sergeant	Va. St. Line	3 yrs.	Jan. 1, 1787
4252	LAWLESS, Austin	100	Private	Va. Cont. Line	3 yrs.	Jan. 8, '87
4261	LARKIN, Edward	200	Private	Va. Cont. Line	war	Mch. 24, '87
4301	LEWIS, Daniel	200	Private	Va. Cont. Line	war	July 10, '87
4335	LITCHFIELD, Francis	100	Private	Va. Cont. Line	3 yrs.	Nov. 13, '87
4340	LAMKIN, John	100	Private	Va. St. Line	3 yrs.	Nov. 28, '87
4367	LOCKLEY, Daniel (Wm. Reynolds, assee. of Jas. Lockley, rep.)	100	Private	Va. St. Line	3 yrs.	Jan. 17, '88
4393	LOYD, James	100	Private	Va. Cont. Line	3 yrs.	Mch. 25, '88
4397	LOYD, George (James Loyd, heir at law)	100	Private	Va. St. Line	3 yrs.	Apr. 3, 1788
4401	LOYD, Morris	2666⅔	Gun'r's Mate	Va. St. Navy	3 yrs.	June 1, 1788
4409	LEROCHETTE, Michael	100	Private	Va. Cont. Line	3 yrs.	July 1, 1788
4452	LIPSCOMB, James	200	Sergeant	Va. St. Line	3 yrs.	Mch. 7, 1789
4455	LYON, Thomas (Jno. Carter, assee.)	100	Private	Va. St. Line	3 yrs.	May 14, '89
4465	LEE, John	200	Corporal	Va. Cont. Line	3 yrs.	Oct. 5, 1789
4477	LOVEL, Robert (John Lovel, heir at law)	2666⅔	Lieutenant	Va. St. Line	3 yrs.	Nov. 19, '89
4502	LEE, Peter	100	Private	Va. St. Line	3 yrs.	Nov. 8, '90

LAND BOUNTY WARRANTS.

Warrant.	Name	Acres	Rank	Department	Term	Date
4538	Lunsford, Moses (Jno. Rowland, assee. of Mark Lee, assee. of)	200	Private	St. Line	war	Nov. 10, '90
4587	Lee, Bart (Francis Graves, assee. of Lewis Lee, rep. of)	200	Private	Cont. Line	war	Oct. 12, '92
4602	Long, Armstead	200	Sergeant	Cont. Line	3 yrs.	Dec. 21, '92
4603	Lattimore, Matthew (John Tate, admr.)	200	Private	Cont. Line	war	Dec. 21, '92

M

Warrant.	Name	Acres	Rank	Department	Term	Date
7	Marks, John	4000	Captain	Va. Cont. Line	3 yrs.	Sept. 3, 1782
19	Morgan, Daniel	5000	Brig. Gen		7 yrs.	Nov. 24, '82
20	Morgan, Daniel	6666⅔	Brig. Gen		7 yrs.	Nov. 24, '82
22	Merewether, Thomas	5333⅓	Major	Va. St. Line		Nov. 25, '82
29	Morgan, John	200	Private	Va. Cont. Line		Nov. 30, '82
30	Marshall, John	4000	Captain	Army	3 yrs.	Nov. 30, '82
37	Moody, Edward (Elizabeth Moody, devisee)	4666⅔	Captain	St. Art	7 yrs.	Dec. 10, '82
41	Muter, George	6666⅔	Colonel	St. Gar. Reg	3 yrs.	Dec. 12, '82
61	Marshall, Thomas, Jr.	4000	Captain	St. Art	3 yrs.	Dec. 19, '82
62	Marshall, Humphrey	4000	Capt.-Lieut	St. Art	3 yrs.	Dec. 19, '82
74	Morton, James	2666⅔	Lieutenant	4th Va. Cont. Reg.	3 yrs.	Dec. 26, '82
75	Mosely, Benjamin	2666⅔	Lieutenant	Va. Line	3 yrs.	Dec. 26, '82
79	Mallory, Philip	4000	Captain	Cont. Line	3 yrs.	Dec. 31, '82
89	Maury, Abraham	2666⅔	Lieutenant	Cont. Line	3 yrs.	Jan. 3, 1783
114	Moore, Thomas	100	Private	St. Line	3 yrs.	Feb. 8, 1783
115	Moseley, William	5333⅓	Major	Cont. Line	3 yrs.	Feb. 8, 1783
141	Moore, Alexander	2000	Midshipman.	Cont. Line	3 yrs.	Feb. 21, '83
151	Miller, William	4000	Capt.-Lieut	Art. in Va. Cont. Line	3 yrs.	Feb. 27, '83
176	Muhlenberg, Peter	11,666⅔	Brig.-Gen	Va. Cont. Line	7 yrs.	Mch. 13, '83
96	Mabin, James	4000	Captain	Va. Line	3 yrs.	Mch. 25, '83
210	Moulden, Thomas	200	Corporal	St. Line	3 yrs.	Mch. 31, '83
230	Mills, John	1300	Lieutenant	Va. Cont. Line	3 yrs.	Apr. 1, 1783
231	Mills, John	1366⅔	Lieutenant	Va. Cont. Line	3 yrs.	Apr. 1, 1783
256	Mansfield, Thomas (Rev. Robert Andrews, assee.)	100	Private	St. Line	3 yrs.	Apr. 3, 1783
310	Miller, David	3110⅔	Lieutenant	Va. Cont. Line	7 yrs.	Apr. 9, 1783
314	Mann, David	2666⅔	Lieutenant	St. Gar. Reg	3 yrs.	Apr. 11, '83
317	Miller, James	200	Private	St. Cav	war	Apr. 12, '83
344	Massey, Theodorick	200	Private	St. Line	war	Apr. 15, '83
365	Morriss, John	200	Private	St. Line	war	Apr. 18, '83
409	Martin, Alexander	200	Drummer	Va. St. Line	war	Apr. 25, '83
411	Morxwell, William	200	Private	Va. St. Line	war	Apr. 25, '83
415	Moses, John	200	Private	St. Line	war	Apr. 26, '83
418	Manning, Samuel	200	Private	Va. Line	war	Apr. 26, '83
427	Moore, Lewis	200	Private	Va. St. Line	war	Apr. 26, '83
429	Miles, James	100	Private	Va. St. Line	3 yrs.	Apr. 26, '83
437	Mansfield, Thomas	200	Private	St. Line	war	Apr. 26, '83
452	Murray, Francis	200	Private	St. Line	war	Apr. 28, '83
459	Martin, James	400	Corporal	St. Line	war	Apr. 28, '83
488	Messaw, Joseph	200	Private	St. Line	war	Apr. 30, '83
495	Mitchell, James	400	Corporal	Va. St. Line	war	Apr. 30, '83
506	Marston, John	2666⅔	Lieutenant	St. Line	3 yrs.	May 1, 1783
530	Moore, William	400	Sergeant	St. Line	war	May 2, 1783
594	Manning, Jesse	200	Private	Va. Line	war	May 17, '83
614	Moss, Henry	4000	Captain	Va. Cont. Line	3 yrs.	May 21, '83
627	Murry, Duncan	200	Serv. for war	Va. Cont. Line		May 23, '83
637	Mills, Nicholas	100	Private	Va. St. Reg	3 yrs.	May 26, '83
638	Marrow, Robert	4000	Captain	Va. Cav. on Cont Establishment	3 yrs.	May 26, '83
643	Matingly, John	100	Private	Va. St. Line	3 yrs.	May 26, '83
646	Maderson, John	100	Service	Va. Cont. Line	3 yrs.	May 26, '83
657	Maccrell, James	200	Private	Va. Cont. Line	war	May 27, '83
660	Morton, Hezekiah	4000	Captain	Va. Cont. Line	5 yrs.	May 27, '83
ⓠ 647	Martin, John	200	Private	Va. St. Line		May 28, '83
ⓠ 652	Meriwether, David	2666⅔	Captain	Va. Cont. Line	3 yrs.	May 28, '83
734	Morriss, John	200	Private	Va. St. Line	war	June 4, 1783
742	Mars, Barnabas	100	Private	Va. St. Line	3 yrs.	June 5, 1783
749	Mills, John	100	Private	Va. Cont. Line	3 yrs.	June 6, 1783
754	Munden, Edward	200	Private	Va. Cont. Line	7 yrs.	June 6, 1783
769	Minnis, Francis	4666⅔	Captain	Va. Cont. Line	7 yrs.	June 7, '83
777	Moss, Henry	100	Private	Va. Cont. Line	3 yrs.	June 10, '83
788	Morriss, Robert	100	Private	Va. St. Line	3 yrs.	June 12, '83
822	Martin, John	100	Private	Va. Cont. Line	3 yrs.	June 14, '83

LAND BOUNTY WARRANTS.   49

Warrant.	Name.	Acres	Rank.	Department.	Term	Date.
849	Mitchell, William	200	Corporal	Va. Cont. Line	3 yrs.	June 17, '83
861	Meanly, Robert (Devens Gorrott Meanley, heir at law)	100	Private	Va. Cont. Line	3 yrs.	June 18, '83
877	Mead, Richard Kidder	6000	Lieut.-Col.	Va. Line	3 yrs.	June 19, '83
893	Marshall, Henry	400	Sergeant	Va. Cont. Line	war	June 20, '83
894	Marshall, Henry	200	Sergeant	Va. Cont. Line	war	June 20, '83
896	Mahoney, Joseph	200	Private	Va. Cont. Line	war	June 20, '83
900	Merryman, Francis	100	Private	Va. Cont. Line	3 yrs.	June 20, '83
934	Mead, John	100	Private	Va. Cont. Line	3 yrs.	June 20, '83
940	Mardis, William	100	Private	Va. Cont. Line	3 yrs.	June 20, '83
969	Margrove, William	100	Private	Cont. Line	3 yrs.	June 20, '83
974	Murdock, Joseph	100	Private	Cont. Line	3 yrs.	June 20, '83
988	Murgrove, William	200	Corporal	Va. St. Line	3 yrs.	June 20, '83
999	Mitchell, Thomas	100	Private	Va. Cont. Line	3 yrs.	June 21, '83
1000	Morgan, General (The voucher on which this warrant issued was for the eighth year's service only)	11,666⅔	Brig. Gen.	Va. Cont. Line	7 yrs.	June 21, '83
1006	Mallory, John (Peter Mallory, heir at law to)	200	Sergeant	Va. Cont. Line	3 yrs.	June 23, '83
1015	Murphey, John	100	Private	Va. Cont. Line	3 yrs.	June 23, '83
1017	Murphey, Owen	100	Private	Va. Cont. Line	3 yrs.	June 23, '83
1082	Maines, Francis	200	Private	Va. Cont. Line	war	June 24, '83
1087	Moore, Thomas	200	Private	Va. Cont. Line	war	June 24, '83
1127	Morgan, Charles	200	Private	Va. Cont. Line	war	June 24, '83
1139	Morrison, John	200	Private	Va. Cont. Line	war	June 24, '83
1151	Martin, William	200	Private	Va. Cont. Line	war	June 24, '83
1152	Murphey, Michael	200	Private	Va. Cont. Line	war	June 24, '83
1159	Mercer, Hugh (William Mercer, heir to H. M., dec'd)	10000	Brig. Gen.	Va. Cont. Line	3 yrs.	June 24, '83
1174	Massey, Thomas	5333⅓	Major	Va. Cont. Line	3 yrs.	June 25, '83
1185	Merritt, Archelaus	100	Private	Va. St. Line	3 yrs.	June 25, '83
1187	Miles, William	100	Private	Va. Cont. Line	3 yrs.	June 26, '83
1192	Mitchell, Mark	100	Private	Va. Cont. Line	3 yrs.	June 26, '83
1195	Miles, John	100	Private	Va. Cont. Line	3 yrs.	June 26, '83
1204	Mitchell, Reaps	400	Sergeant	Va. St. Line	war	June 26, '83
1217	Murry, William	100	Private	Va. Cont. Line	war	June 26, '83
1229	Minnes, John	200	Private	Va. Cont. Line	war	June 26, '83
1251	Murray, George	100	Private	Va. St. Art.	3 yrs.	June 27, '83
1279	Murphy, Patrick	233⅓	Private	Va. Cont. Line	7 yrs.	June 28, '83
1289	Morgan, David	200	Private	Va. Cont. Line	war	June 28, '83
1295	Macomber, John	400	Corporal	Va. St. Cav.	war	June 28, '83
1307	Martin, William	200	Private	Va. Cont. Line	3 yrs.	June 30, '83
1311	Muse, George	200	Sergeant	Va. Cav.	3 yrs.	June 30, '83
1338	Marshall, Thomas	400	Serg.-Maj.	Cont. Cav.	war	July 8, 1783
1349	Marshall, Thomas	6666⅔	Colonel	Cont. Line	3 yrs.	July 10, '83
1352	Macklin, James	100	Private	Va. Cav.	3 yrs.	July 10, '83
1366	Moore, William	100	Private	St. Line	3 yrs.	July 12, '83
1371	Murden, Peter	200	Private	St. Line	war	July 12, '83
1382	Meriwether, James	2666⅔	Lieutenant	Cont. Line	3 yrs.	July 17, '83
1402	Murrah, George	100	Private	Cont. Line	3 yrs.	July 21, '83
1432	Montague, Richard	2666⅔	Lieutenant	St. Navy	3 yrs.	July 27, '83
1441	Murphey, Martin	400	Sergeant	Cont. Line	war	July 30, '83
1460	Maddox, Notley	200	Private	Cont. Line	war	Aug. 1, 1783
1468	Moseley, Benjamin	2666⅔	Lieutenant	Cont. Art.	3 yrs.	Aug. 1, 1783
1474	Muir, Francis	4000	Capt.-Lieut.	Cont. Line	3 yrs.	Aug. 1, 1783
1480	Major, Ironmonger	100	Private	St. Line	3 yrs.	Aug. 2, 1783
1514	Mush, Robert	400	Private	Cont. Line	war	Aug. 6, 1783
1522	Mahanes, Tapley	100	Private	St. Line	3 yrs.	Aug. 7, 1783
1535	Madison, William	100	Private	St. Line	3 yrs.	Aug. 9, 1783
1555	Morgan, William	233⅓	Private	Cont. Line	war	Aug. 12, '83
1557	Moody, James	2000	Captain	St. Line	3 yrs.	Aug. 12, '83
1558	Moody, James	2000	Captain	St. Line	3 yrs.	Aug. 12, '83
1576	Marshall, David	100	Private	St. Line	3 yrs.	Aug. 18, '83
1616	Mulins, Anthony	200	Private	Cont. Line	war	Aug. 21, '83
1619	Monroe, George	6000	Surgeon	Cont. Line	3 yrs.	Aug. 22, '83
1623	Miller, Javan	3110½	Lieutenant	Cont. Line	7 yrs.	Aug. 23, '83
1663	Merritt, Samuel	100	Private	Va. Cont. Line	3 yrs.	Aug. 25, '83
1671	Moore, Ralph	400	Corporal	Va. Cont. Line	war	Aug. 27, '83
1676	Monk, Joseph	200	Sergeant	Va. Cont. Line	3 yrs.	Aug. 27, '83
1690	Murray, Ralph	100	Private	Va. Cont. Line	3 yrs.	Aug. 30, '83
1695	Marks, Isaiah	4000	Captain	Va. Cont. Line	3 yrs.	Aug. 30, '83
1724	Melton, Hardy	100	Private	Va. St. Line	3 yrs.	Sept. 3, 1783
1737	Murphy, Michael	200	Private	Va. Cont. Line	war	Sept. 10, '83
1745	Morgan, Andrew	200	Sergeant	Va. St. Line	3 yrs.	Sept. 11, '83
1756	Murray, Richard	100	Private	Va. Cont. Line	3 yrs.	Sept. 12, '83

LAND BOUNTY WARRANTS.

Warrant	Name	Acres	Rank	Department	Term	Date
1759	MILLER, John (John Miller, heir at law)	200	Private	Va. Cont. Line	war	Sept. 13, '83
1817	MORRISON, Hugh	200	Sergeant	Va. Cont. Line	3 yrs.	Oct. 3, 1783
1820	MOOR, William	2666⅔	Lieutenant	Va. Cont. Line	3 yrs.	Oct. 4, 1783
1833	MATTHEWS, William	200	Corporal	St. Line	3 yrs.	Oct. 7, 1783
1837	MITCHELL, David (Philip Duvall, assee. of John Davis, assee. of David Mitchell)	100	Private	Cont. Line	3 yrs.	Oct. 7, 1783
1869	MAHONEY, James	200	Private	Va. Cont. Line	war	Oct. 15, '83
1873	MARTIN, John	200	Private	Va. Cont. Line	war	Oct. 15, '83
1883	MASON, Thomas (William Mason, heir at law)	200	Private	Va. St. Line	war	Oct. 16, '83
1897	MOODY, William	200	Private	Va. Cont. Line	war	Oct. 21, '83
1922	MOTHERSHEAD, Nathaniel	200	Sergeant	Va. Cont. Line	3 yrs.	Oct. 27, '83
②1854	MOORE, John	2666⅔	Master	Va. St. Navy	3 yrs.	Nov. 4, 1783
②1887	MAGILL, Charles	2000	Major	Va. St. Line	3 yrs.	Oct. 12, '83
®1888	MAGILL, Charles	1000	Major	Va. St. Line	3 yrs.	Oct. 12, '83
②1889	MAGILL, Charles	1000	Major	Va. St. Line	3 yrs.	Oct. 12, '83
®1890	MAGILL, Charles	1000	Major	Va. St. Line	3 yrs.	Nov. 12, '83
②1891	MAGILL, Charles	333⅓	Major	Va. St. Line	3 yrs.	Nov. 12, '83
②1906	MORRIS, John	100	Private	Va. Cont. Line	3 yrs.	Nov. 18, '83
®1927	MELTON, Isham	100	Private	Va. St. Line	3 yrs.	Nov. 22, '83
®1928	MELTON, John	100	Private	Va. St. Line	3 yrs.	Nov. 22, '83
1934	MATTHEWS, George	7777⅞	Colonel	Va. Cont. Line	7 yrs.	Nov. 22, '83
1969	MORGAN, John (Charles Morgan, heir at law to)	200	Sergeant	Va. Cont. Line	3 yrs.	Nov. 26, '83
1971	MURPHEY, Charles	100	Private	Va. Cont. Line	3 yrs.	Nov. 26, '83
1981	MOORE, John	100	Private	Va. Cont. Line	3 yrs.	Nov. 28, '83
1987	MARSHALL, Richard	400	Corporal	Va. Cont. Line	war	Nov. 28, '83
1991	MAUGHAN, George	100	Seaman	Va. St. Navy	3 yrs.	Nov. 28, '83
2030	MOORE, Nicholas	200	Private	Va. Cont. Line	war	Dec. 6, 1783
2074	MURFREY, John	100	Private	Va. Cont. Line	3 yrs.	Dec. 10, '83
2086	MOORE, Michael	100	Private	Va. Cont. Line	3 yrs.	Dec. 10, '83
2107	MOSBY, William	200	Private	Va. Cont. Line	war	Dec. 12, '83
2114	MOLTON, James	100	Private	Va. Cont. Line	3 yrs.	Dec. 13, '83
2131	MATTHEW, Benjamin	100	Private	Va. Cont. Line	3 yrs.	Dec. 15, '83
2136	MADEN, Robert	200	Private	Va. St. Line	war	Dec. 16, '83
2142	MITCHELL, John (William Mitchell, heir at law)	400	Sergeant	Va. Cont. Line	war	Dec. 16, '83
2195	MEAD, Mahlon	100	Private	Va. Cont. Line	3 yrs.	Dec. 22, '83
2203	MITCHELL, George	200	Sergeant	Va. Cont. Line	3 yrs.	Dec. 25, '83
2215	MARKHAM, James	4000	Captain	Va. St. Navy	7 yrs.	Dec. 27, '83
2216	MARKHAM, James	2222	Captain	Va. St. Navy	7 yrs.	Dec. 27, '83
2217	MORRIS, Isaac	200	Private	Va. Cont. Line	war	Jan. 3, 1784
2219	MERCER, John F.	4000	Captain	Va. Cont. Line	3 yrs.	Jan. 5, 1784
2220	MARSHALL, John	200	Boatswain	Va. St. Navy	3 yrs.	Jan. 5, 1784
2224	MONEY, Isaac	100	Private	Va. Cont. Line	3 yrs.	Jan. 7, 1784
2244	MEATS, Samuel	100	Seaman	Va. St. Navy	3 yrs.	Jan. 12, '84
2271	MINNES, Holman	4000	Captain	Va. Cont. Line	3 yrs.	Jan. 22, '84
2272	MINNES, Callohill	4666⅔	Captain	Va. Cont. Line	7 yrs.	Jan. 22, '84
2274	MIDDLETON, Bassil	6000	Surgeon	Va. Cont. Line	3 yrs.	Jan. 23, '84
2275	MURRAY, Daniel	200	Private	Va. Cont. Line	war	Jan. 23, '84
2276	MURRAY, James	200	Private	Va. Cont. Line	war	Jan. 23, '84
2281	MADDOX, John	200	Private	Va. Cont. Line	war	Jan. 24, '84
2299	MARTIN, Patrick	200	Private	Va. Cont. Line	war	Jan. 26, '84
2307	MAYFIELD, John (Lawrence Muse, assee. of)	200	Private	Va. Cont. Line	war	Jan. 28, '84
2308	MAYFIELD, Henry (Lawrence Muse, assee. of)	200	Private	Va. Cont. Line	war	Jan. 28, '84
2310	MALLETT, Stephen	100	Private	Va. Cont. Line	3 yrs.	Jan. 29, '84
2315	MOORE, William	100	Private	Va. St. Line	3 yrs.	Jan. 29, '84
2319	MEREDITH, William	4000	Captain	Va. Cont. Line	3 yrs.	Jan. 30, '84
2324	MABON, James ("to complete his allowance for seven years, a warrant having already issued for 4,000 acres")	666⅔	Captain	Va. Cont. Line	7 yrs.	Jan. 31, '84
2326	MERIWETHER, James	2666⅔	Lieutenant	Va. St. Line	3 yrs.	Jan. 31, '84
2328	MARTIN, Thomas	1000	Lieutenant	Va. Cont. Line	3 yrs.	Jan. 31, '84
2329	MARTIN, Thomas	1666⅔	Lieutenant	Va. Cont. Line	3 yrs.	Jan. 31, '84
2368	MONROE, James	5333⅓	Major	Va. Cont. Line	3 yrs.	Feb. 2, 1784
2380	MARSHALL, Markham	2666⅔	Lieutenant	Va. St. Line	3 yrs.	Feb. 3, 1784
2440	MASH, Thomas (William Furbush, assee.)	100	Private	Va. Cont. Line	3 yrs.	Feb. 9, 1784
2449	MEED, John	400	Sergeant	Va. Cont. Line	war	Feb. 10, '84
2464	MUMPOWER, Nicholas (Daniel Perryman, assee. of)	100	Private	Va. Cont. Line	3 yrs.	Feb. 11, '84

LAND BOUNTY WARRANTS. 51

War-rant.	Name.	Acres	Rank.	Department.	Term	Date.
2465	MILLER, Robert (Daniel Perryman, assee. of)	100	Private	Va. Cont. Line	3 yrs.	Feb. 11, '84
2466	MASON, Daniel (Lewis Ford, assee.)	100	Private	Va. Cont. Line	3 yrs.	Feb. 11, '84
2468	MEREWETHER, James	2666⅔	Lieutenant	Va. St. Line	3 yrs.	Feb. 11, '84
2479	MAYNARD, Nathaniel	200	Corporal	Va. St. Line	3 yrs.	Feb. 12, '84
2480	MARTIN, John	200	Sergeant	Va. Cont. Line	3 yrs.	Feb. 12, '84
2485	MOORE, Peter (for the time prescribed by the act for raising said reg.)	2666⅔	Lieutenant	Crockett's Regiment		Feb. 13, '84
2560	MEAD, Everard	5333⅓	Major	Va. Cont. Line	3 yrs.	Feb. 20, '84
2625	MILLONS, Thomas (Daniel Flowerree, assee.)	100	Private	Va. Cont. Line	3 yrs.	Feb. 24, '84
2629	MORGAN, Simon	4666⅔	Captain	Va. Cont. Line	7 yrs.	Feb. 25, '84
2677	MONTGOMERY, James	2666⅔	Lieutenant	Va. St. Line	3 yrs.	Mch. 3, 1784
2685	MONTGOMERY, John	6000	Lieutenant	Va. St. Line	3 yrs.	Mch. 3, 1784
2698	MALLORY, John	100	Private	Va. St. Line	3 yrs.	Mch. 3, 1784
2716	MUNDEN, Thomas (Edmund Munden, heir at law)	100	Private	Va. Cont. Line	3 yrs.	Mch. 5, 1784
2745	MUIR, John	2666⅔	Midshipman	Va. St. Navy	3 yrs.	Mch. 10, '84
2768	MARTIN, Patrick	100	Private	Va. Cont. Line	3 yrs.	Mch. 17, '84
2824	MALAY, James	100	Private	Va. Cont. Line	3 yrs.	Mch. 26, '84
2827	MULLINS, David	100	Private	Va. Cont. Line	3 yrs.	Mch. 26, '84
2842	MURPHY, Leander (William King, assee.)	100	Private	Va. Cont. Line	3 yrs.	Mch. 29, '84
2845	MORGAN, Spencer	2666⅔	Ensign	Va. Cont. Line	3 yrs.	Mch. 30, '84
2862	MELCHER, John	100	Private	Va. Cont. Line	3 yrs.	Apr. 2, 1784
2871	MOREHEAD, Charles	400	Sergeant	Va. Cont. Line	war	Apr. 5, 1784
2906	MINTON, John (Edward Valentine, assee. of Mary Minton, who was heir at law to)	200	Private	Va. Cont. Line	3 yrs.	Apr. 7, 1784
2934	MOXLEY, George	400	Corporal	Va. Cont. Line	war	Apr. 15, '84
2935	MORRIS, Moses	100	Private	Va. St. Line	3 yrs.	Apr. 16, '84
2941	MILLER, Lodowick	100	Private	Va. Cont. Line	3 yrs.	Apr. 17, '84
2947	MEANS, John	200	Corporal	Va. Cont. Line	3 yrs.	Apr. 17, '84
2951	MADDEN, Thomas (Richard Claiborne and John Hopkins, assees.)	100	Private	Va. Cont. Line	3 yrs.	Apr. 17, '84
2957	MOXLEY, Rodham (William Moxley, heir at law)	2666⅔	Subaltern	Va. Cont. Line	3 yrs.	Apr. 17, '84
2986	MOUNT, Matthew	100	Private	Va. Cont. Line	3 yrs.	Apr. 21, '84
3005	MADISON, William (William Bigger, assee.)	100	Private	Va. Cont. Line	3 yrs.	Apr. 22, '84
3082	MAY, William (Benjamin May, heir at law)	200	Private	Va. Cont. Line	war	May 20, '84
3105	MILLER, Thomas	2666⅔	Lieutenant	Va. Cont. Line	3 yrs.	May 27, '84
3106	MOORE, Peter (Sarah Moore, mother and legal rep.)	200	Private	Va. Cont. Line	war	May 28, '84
3109	MARTIN, Josiah	200	Private	Va. Cont. Line	war	May 29, '84
3137	MORRISS, Reuben (Robert Pollard, assee.)	100	Private	Va. Cont. Line	3 yrs.	June 9, 1784
3139	MORRIS, Gilson (Robert Pollard, assee.)	100	Private	Va. Cont. Line	3 yrs.	June 9, 1784
3148	MONROE, William	100	Private	Va. St. Line	3 yrs.	June 11, '84
3164	MURPHEY, Lemuel	100	Private	Va. Cont. Line	3 yrs.	June 16, '84
3166	MEACHAM, William	200	Sergeant	Va. Cont. Line	3 yrs.	June 17, '84
3168	MASON, John	200	Private	Va. Cont. Line	war	June 17, '84
3183	MASSEY, Taliaferro	100	Private	Va. St. Line	3 yrs.	June 22, '84
3184	MASSEY, Dade (Taliaferro Massey, heir at law)	100	Private	Va. St. Line	3 yrs.	June 22, '84
3199	MEEHIE, George	200	Sergeant	Va. St. Line	3 yrs.	June 23, '84
3200	MARTIN, Thomas	444⅔	Lieutenant	Va. St. Line	7 yrs.	June 23, '84
3210	MATTHEWS, Thomas	6000	Lieut.-Col	Va. St. Line	3 yrs.	June 25, '84
3217	MARKS, John	100	Sailor	Va. St. Navy	3 yrs.	June 26, '84
3222	MOUNTJOY, William	4000	Captain			June 28, '84
3243	MOORE, Cleon (Res. of Gen. Assby., June 23, 1784)	4000	Captain			June 29, '84
3256	MORRISON, William (Robert Coleman, assee. of Hugh Morrison, heir at law)	200	Sergeant	Va. Cont. Line	3 yrs.	June 30, '84
3311	MILLER, Wellcome L.	100	Private	Va. Cont. Line	3 yrs.	July 2, 1784
3317	MILLIONS, Henry	100	Private	Va. Cont. Line	3 yrs.	July 6, 1784
3333	MAYFIELD, Micajah	100	Private	Va. St. Line	3 yrs.	July 19, '84
3356	MIDDLEBROOK, John	200	Private	Va. Cont. Line	war	July 23, '84

LAND BOUNTY WARRANTS.

Warrant.	Name.	Acres	Rank.	Department.	Term	Date.
3359	MILLER, Francis (Edward Valentine, assee.)	200	Private	Va. Cont. Line	war	July 24, '84
3386	MOORE, John (Peter Tardiveau, assee.)	400	Sergeant	Illinois Regiment	war	Aug. 6, 1784
3393	MILES, Michael (Daniel Brodhead, assee.)	400	Sergeant	Va. St. Line	war	Aug. 14, '84
3415	MULLIN, John (John Mullin, heir at law)	200	Sergeant	Va. St. Line	3 yrs.	Aug. 27, '84
3416	MULLIN, John (John Mullin, heir at law)	400	Sergeant	Va. St. Line	war	Aug. 27, '84
3431	MURPHEY, John	100	Private	Va. Cont. Line	3 yrs.	Aug. 31, '84
3453	MILTON, Charles	100	Private	Va. St. Line	3 yrs.	Oct. 2, 1784
3488	MARSHALL, Benjamin	200	Master at Arms	Va. St. Navy	3 yrs.	Oct. 28, '84
3573	MOTH, Thomas	100	Private	Va. St. Navy	3 yrs.	Dec. 15, '84
3577	MOUGHAN, Matthias	100	Private	Va. St. Line	3 yrs.	Dec. 15, '84
3580	MAINS, Thomas	2666⅔	Q'ter Master	Va. St. Navy	3 yrs.	Dec. 15, '84
3583	MANN, Clairborne (Olive Mann, legal rep.)	200	Private	Va. Cont. Line	war	Dec. 16, '84
3608	MOODY, William	100	Private	Va. St. Line	3 yrs.	Dec. 22, '84
3610	MOORE, John	100	Private	Va. St. Line	3 yrs.	Dec. 22, '84
3611	MAZARET, John	4000	Major	Va. St. Line	3 yrs.	Dec. 23, '84
3612	MAZARET, John	2333⅓	Major	Va. St. Line	3 yrs.	Dec. 23, '84
3614	MAY, Thomas	400	Corporal	Va. Cont. Line	war	Dec. 23, '84
3616	MARSHALL, Richard	200	Private	Va. Cont. Line	war	Dec. 23, '84
3618	MARTIN, Thomas	200	Private	Va. Cont. Line	war	Dec. 23, '84
3619	MORROUGH, George	100	Private	Va. Cont. Line	3 yrs.	Dec. 23, '84
3696	MADDER, Martin	200	Private	Va. Cont. Line	war	Jan. 20, '85
3700	MOFFETT, William	100	Private	Va. Cont. Line	3 yrs.	Jan. 20, '85
3719	MOORE, Richard	200	Corporal	Va. Cont. Line	3 yrs.	Jan. 24, '85
3696	MADDER, Martin	200	Private	Va. Cont. Line	war	Jan. 20, '85
3700	MOFFETT, William	100	Private	Va. Cont. Line	3 yrs.	Jan. 20, '85
3719	MOORE, Richard	200	Corporal	Va. Cont. Line	3 yrs.	Jan. 24, '85
3730	MACLIN, William	100	Private	State Line	war	Feb. 3, 1785
3737	MOODY, William	200	Private	Va. Cont. Line	war	Feb. 7, 1785
3750	MOORE, Nicholas	200	Private	Va. Cont. Line	war	Feb. 9, 1785
3773	MAUPIN, Gabriel	4000	Captain	Res. of Gen. Ass'by, June 16, 1784		
3806	MAYNOR, Henry	100	Private	Va. Cont. Line	3 yrs.	Mch. 10, '85
3814	MATTHIAS, Griffith	100	Private	Va. Cont. Line	3 yrs.	Apr. 14, '85
3830	MAJOR, John (William Bigger, assee. of Wm. Major, legal rep.)	100	Private	Va. St. Line	3 yrs.	Apr. 28, '85
3833	MAJOR, James	200	Private	Va. Cont. Line	war	Apr. 29, '85
3836	MICHAM, John	100	Private	Va. Cont. Line	3 yrs.	Apr. 29, '85
3842	MEAD, William (John Mead, heir at law)	2666⅔	Ensign	Va. Cont. Line		Apr. 29, '85
3850	MURLAT, Abraham	200	Private	Va. Cont. Line	war	May 6, 1785
3874	MORGAN, John (Charles Morgan, heir at law)	2666⅔	Ensign	Va. Cont. Line	3 yrs.	May 10, '85
3878	MANSFIELD, George	200	Private	Va. Cont. Line	war	May 20, '8F
3886	MIDDLETON, John (William Logan, assee.)	100	Private	Va. Cont. Line	war	June 1, 1785
3899	MINTER, Barker (William Reynolds, assee.)	200	Private	Va. Cont. Line	war	June 21, '85
3913	MALONE, John	100	Private	Va. Cont. Line	3 yrs.	June 21, '85
3920	MOOR, Alexander (William Askew, assee.)	200	Private	Va. Cont. Line	war	June 21, '85
3932	MALLOHORN, Thomas (William Reynolds, assee.)	100	Private	Va. Cont. Line	3 yrs.	Aug. 1, 1785
3958	MADDOX, William (William Reynolds, assee.)	100	Private	Va. Cont. Line	3 yrs.	Aug. 12, '85
4016	MOORE, William D	100	Private	Va. Cont. Line	3 yrs.	Dec. 2, 1785
4018	MOORE, James (Sarah Moore, rep.)	100	Private	Va. St. Line	3 yrs.	Dec. 3, 1785
4044	METCALF, Gordon	200	Q'ter Master	St. Navy	3 yrs.	Dec. 17, '85
4045	MADRID, Elisha	100	Private	St. Line	3 yrs.	Dec. 17, '85
4094	MAINE, Phillip	100	Private	Va. St. Line	3 yrs.	Jan. 23, '86
4119	MILLIGAN, John	200	Private	Va. Cont. Line	war	Mch. 7, 1786
4120	MILLIGAN, John	100	Private	Va. Cont. Line	3 yrs.	Mch. 7, 1786
4133	MOORE, Michael	200	Private	Va. Cont. Line	war	Mch. 18, '86
4166	MADDOX, Clairborne	200	Sergeant	Va. Cont. Line	3 yrs.	June 5, 1786
4174	MILLS, Moses	100	Private	Va. Cont. Line	3 yrs.	June 19, '86
4175	MARTIN, John	200	Private	Va. Cont. Line	3 yrs.	June 20, '86
4183	METCALF, Walter	100	Sailor	Va. St. Navy	3 yrs.	July 5, 1786
4187	MITCHELL, John	100	Private	Va. Cont. Line	3 yrs.	July 12, '86

LAND BOUNTY WARRANTS.   53

Warrant.	Name.	Acres	Rank.	Department.	Term	Date.
4205	Michael, Conrod	100	Private	Va. Cont. Line	3 yrs.	Aug. 31, '86
4209	Mercer, Isaac (Wm. Reynolds, assee. of Wm. Bigger, assee. of the rep. of)	1333⅓	Lieutenant	Va. St. Navy	3 yrs.	Sept. 27, '86
4210	Mercer, Isaac (Wm. Reynolds, assee. of Wm. Bigger, assee. of the rep. of)	1333⅓	Lieutenant	Va. St. Navy	3 yrs.	Sept. 27, '86
4220	Mahoney, Florence	100	Private	Va. St. Line	3 yrs.	Oct. 23, '86
4226	Muse, Jesse (Jeremiah Muse, heir at law)	2666⅔	Lieutenant	Va. St. Navy	3 yrs.	Nov. 6, 1786
4245	Massey, John (Hugh Donaghe, exor.)	100	Private	Va. Cont. Line	3 yrs.	Dec. 27, '86
4251	Mitchell, James	100	Private	Va. Cont. Line	3 yrs.	Jan. 12, '87
4270	Morgan, Jonas	200	Private	Va. Cont. Line	war	Apr. 7, 1787
4277	Miller, William	100	Private	Va. St. Line	3 yrs.	Apr. 7, 1787
4286	Miskel, John	200	Sergeant	Va. St. Line	3 yrs.	May 24, '87
4287	Miskel, Jonathan	200	Sergeant	Va. St. Line	3 yrs.	May 24, '87
4299	Moore, John	100	Private	Va. St. Line	3 yrs.	June 25, '87
4317	Macomber, Zenas	100	Private	Va. Cont. Line	3 yrs.	Oct. 23, '87
4352	Merrick, John (William Merrick, heir at law)	200	Private	Va. Cont. Line	war	Dec. 19, '87
4369	March, William (Wm. Reynolds, assee. of Richard March, Jr., rep.)	2666⅔	Midshipman	Va. St. Navy	3 yrs.	Jan. 23, '88
4374	Moss, Julius (William Reynolds, assee.)	100	Private	Va. St. Line	3 yrs.	Jan. 23, '88
4382	Mitchell, Thomas (Wm. Reynolds, assee.)	100	Sailor	Va. St. Navy	3 yrs.	Jan. 29, '88
4389	Maddox, John (William Reynolds, assee.)	100	Private	Va. Cont. Line	3 yrs.	Mch. 12, '88
4400	Monroe, John	100	Private	Va. St. Line	3 yrs.	May 9, 1788
4442	Myer, Christopher (Matthias Myer, heir at law)	2666⅔	Lieutenant	Va. Cont. Line	3 yrs.	Nov. 1, 1788
4446	Moore, Henly (Samuel Moore, heir at law)	200	Sergeant	Va. St. Line	3 yrs.	Dec. 26, '88
4464	Millisons, Wm. (Patrick Lockhart, assee.)	100	Private	Va. Cont. Line	3 yrs.	Sept. 18, '89
4518	Mills, Anthony	200	Sergeant	St. Line	3 yrs.	Feb. 24, '91
4601	Massenburg, Nicholas (John Massenburg, legal rep.)	2666⅔	Lieutenant	Cont. Line	war	Dec. 20, '92
4621	Morris, Samuel	100	Private	Cont. Line	3 yrs.	Sept. 13, '93
4622	Mason, William (the rep. or reps. of)	200	Private	St. Navy	war	Sept. 16, '93
4624	Merritt, Major (Francis Graves, assee.)	200	Private	Cont. Line	war	Sept. 19, '93

Mc

263	McDens, Daniel (Rev. Robert Andrews, assee.)	100	Private	St. Line	3 yrs.	Apr. 3, 1783
264	McClanachan, Elijah (Rev. Robert Andrews, assee.)	100	Private	St. Line	3 yrs.	Apr. 3, 1783
272	McHene, John (Dr. James McClung, assee.)	100	Private	St. Line	3 yrs.	Apr. 3, 1783
276	McDougal, John (Dr. James McClung, assee.)	100	Drummer	Va. St. Line	3 yrs.	Apr. 3, 1783
380	McCarty, Charles	200	Private	Va. St. Line	war	Apr. 22, '83
519	McNalley, James	200	Private	St. Line	war	May 1, 1783
604	McDonnan, James	100	Private	Va. Art. on Cont. Estab.	3 yrs.	May 20, '83
661	McIlehany, John	4000	Captain	Va. St. Line	3 yrs.	May 27, '83
665	McDonald, Terence	100	Private	Va. Cont. Art.	3 yrs.	May 28, '83
714	McMeckin, Joseph	200	Drum Major	Va. St. Art.	3 yrs.	June 2, 1783
719	McCall, Samuel	200	Sergeant	Va. Cont. Line	3 yrs.	June 3, 1783
828	McDowell, John	2666⅔	Lieutenant	Va. Cont. Line	3 yrs.	June 14, '83
862	McDowell, Matthew	100	Private	Va. Cont. Line	3 yrs.	June 18, '83
920	McNolly, Michael	100	Private	Va. Cont. Line	3 yrs.	June 20, '83
977	McKnight, William	100	Private	Cont. Line	3 yrs.	June 20, '83
1019	McKenny, John	100	Private	Va. Cont. Line	3 yrs.	June 23, '83
1026	McMeans, William	100	Private	Va. Cont. Line	3 yrs.	June 23, '83
1059	McIntosh, Alexander	200	Private	Va. Cont. Line	war	June 24, '83
1066	McKay, Eneas	200	Private	Va. Cont. Line	war	June 24, '83
1078	McCartney, Peter	200	Private	Va. Cont. Line	war	June 24, '83
1084	McClean, Laughlin	200	Private	Va. Cont. Line	war	June 24, '83
1085	McDonald, Edward	200	Private	Va. Cont. Line	war	June 24, '83

54   LAND BOUNTY WARRANTS.

Warrant.	Name	Acres	Rank	Department	Term	Date
1098	McElwin, Moses	200	Drummer	Va. Cont. Line	war	June 24, '83
1144	McCord, Samuel	200	Private	Va. Cont. Line	war	June 24, '83
1183	McLardy, Alexander	200	Corporal	Va. Cont. Line	3 yrs.	June 25, '83
1189	McCue, Henry	100	Private	Va. Cont. Line	3 yrs.	June 26, '83
1243	McMasters, Michael	100	Private	Va. Cont. Line	3 yrs.	June 27, '83
1283	McGuy, Bennett	200	Private	Va. Cont. Line	war	June 28, '83
1301	McCune, Patrick	100	Private	Va. St. Line	3 yrs.	June 30, '83
1334	McWilliams, Joshua	2666⅔	Midshipman	St. Navy	3 yrs.	July 5, 1783
1350	McClain, Thomas	100	Private	Cont. Line	3 yrs.	July 10, '83
1365	McIntosh, William	100	Private	St. Line	3 yrs.	July 12, '83
1412	McIntosh, William	233⅓	Private	Cont. Line	war	July 22, '83
1439	McKinley, John	233⅓	Private	St. Line	7 yrs.	July 28, '83
1490	McGuire, Andrew	233⅓	Private	Cont. Line	war	Aug. 4, 1783
1559	McSwain, Edward	200	Sergeant	St. Line	3 yrs.	Aug. 12, '83
1621	McCormack, Adam (original warrant gives name as David McCormack)	200	Private	Cont. Line	war	Aug. 22, '83
1646	McNamara, Timothy	200	Private	Va. Cont. Line	war	Aug. 23, '83
1804	McClanahan, Elijah	200	Private	Va. Cont. Line	war	Sept. 30, '83
1844	McQuillen, Robert	200	Private	Va. Cont. Line	war	Oct. 10, '83
1893	McMechen, William	6000	Surgeon	Va. Cont. Line	3 yrs.	Oct. 20, '83
1900	McClurg, James	6000	Director of Hospitals		3 yrs	Oct. 21, '83
1845	McCartney, Peter	200	Private	Va. Cont. Line	war	Oct. 31, '83
1884	McGann, James	200	Private		war	
1972	McMeehen, Robert	100	Private	Va. Cont. Line	3 yrs.	Nov. 26, '83
1996	McKenny, Daniel	100	Private	Va. Cont. Line	3 yrs.	Nov. 29, '83
2001	McMahon, Roger	100	Private	Va. Cont. Line	3 yrs.	Nov. 29, '83
2006	McIntire, William	200	Sergeant	Va. Cont. Line	3 yrs.	Dec. 2, 1783
2034	McTear, William	200	Sergeant	Va. Cont. Line	3 yrs.	Dec. 6, 1783
2035	McTear, Frizzel	200	Sergeant	Va. Cont. Line	3 yrs.	Dec. 6, 1783
2043	McDonald, Benjamin	200	Private	Va. Cont. Line	war	Dec. 9, 1783
2047	McConner, Christopher	400	Sergeant	Va. Cont. Line	war	Dec. 9, 1783
2108	McCrow, John (Francis McCrow, heir at law)	100	Private	Va. Cont. Line	3 yrs.	Dec. 12, '83
2185	McCant, James	200	Private	Va. Cont. Line	war	Dec. 22, '83
2300	McDowell, John	200	Private	Va. Cont. Line	war	Jan. 26, '84
2393	McNeal, David (Martin Hawkins, assee.)	100	Private	Va. Cont. Line	3 yrs.	Feb. 3, 1784
2499	McGuire, William	2666⅔	Lieutenant	Va. Cont. Line	3 yrs.	Feb. 3, 1784
2638	McAdam, Joseph (John McAdams, heir at law)	2666⅔	Surg.'s Mate	Va. Cont. Line	3 yrs.	Feb. 26, '84
2770	McConn, James (James Jenkins, assee.)	100	Private	Va. Cont. Line	3 yrs.	Mch. 18, '84
2859	McKnight, Benjamin	100	Private	Va. Cont. Line	3 yrs.	Apr. 2, 1784
2864	McCale, Michael	200	Private	Va. Cont. Line	3 yrs.	Apr. 2, 1784
2866	McComesky, Moss	100	Private	Va. Cont. Line	war	Apr. 2, 1784
2872	McDowell, John	233⅓	Private	Va. Cont. Line	3 yrs.	Apr. 5, 1784
2879	McGill, Daniel (Clay McGill, heir at law)	200	Private	Va. Cont. Line	war	Apr. 5, 1784
2882	McCune, Peter	200	Sergeant	Va. Cont. Line	3 yrs.	Apr. 5, 1784
2972	McClurg, Walter (Barbary Vance McClurg, devisee)	6000	Surgeon	Va. St. Navy	3 yrs.	Apr. 20, '84
2977	McCannon, Christopher	100	Private	Va. St. Line	3 yrs.	Apr. 20, '84
2993	McWilliams, John (Edward Valentine, assee.)	100	Private	Va. St. Line	3 yrs.	Apr. 21, '84
3000	McCarty, Richard (Daniel Clark, admr.)	4000	Captain	Va. St. Line	3 yrs.	Apr. 22, '84
3020	McCargo, Stephen (Benjamin McDonald, assee.)	200	Private	Va. Cont. Line	war	Apr. 26, '84
3098	McClure, William (James Fairs, assee.)	200	Private	Va. Cont. Line	war	May 24, '84
3124	McDonald, Reuben	100	Private	Va. St. Line	3 yrs.	June 5, 1784
3197	McNeal, Peter	100	Private	Vo. Cont. Line	3 yrs.	June 23, '84
3220	McKinsey, Alexander	400	Sergeant	Va. Cont. Line	war	June 26, '84
3286	McAdam, John	2666⅔	Lieutenant	Vo. Cont. Line	3 yrs.	July 1, 1784
3289	McClanahan, Alex (Res. Gen. Ass'by, June 23, 1784)	6666⅔	Colonel	Services		July 1, 1784
3302	McCorkle, Samuel (Catherine McCorkle, heir at law)	100	Private	Va. Cont. Line	3 yrs.	July 2, 1784
3303	McCorkle, Andrew (Catherine McCorkle, heir at law)	100	Private	Va. Cont. Line	3 yrs.	July 2, 1784
3348	McCoy, William	200	Private	Va. Cont. Line	war	July 23, '84
3369	McGannon, Darby (Peter Glasscock, assee.)	200	Sergeant	Va. Cont. Line	3 yrs.	July 31, '84

LAND BOUNTY WARRANTS. 55

Warrant.	Name.	Acres	Rank.	Department.	Term	Date.
3443	McCloud, Archibald	233½	Private	Va. Cont. Line	7 yrs.	Sept. 16, '84
3492	McKee, Richard	200	Private	Va. Cont. Line	war	Nov. 1, 1784
3512	McCartee, James	100	Private	Va. St. Line	3 yrs.	Nov. 8, 1784
3515	McIlhany, James	100	Private	Va. Cont. Line	3 yrs.	Nov. 9, 1784
3519	McKinley, Alexander	100	Private	Va. St. Line	3 yrs.	Nov. 11, '84
3581	McCawley, John	200	Private	Va. Cont. Line	war	Dec. 16, '84
3607	McKinney, Dennis	100	Private	Va. Cont. Line	3 yrs.	Dec. 22, '84
3693	McKinley, Charles	100	Private	Va. Cont. Line	3 yrs.	Jan. 20, '85
3697	McMullen, James	100	Private	Va. Cont. Line	3 yrs.	Jan. 20, '85
3705	McElroy, William	100	Private	Va. Cont. Line	3 yrs.	Jan. 20, '85
3718	McGraw, James	100	Private	Va. Cont. Line	3 yrs.	Jan. 24, '85
3728	McMahan, Andrew	400	Sergeant	Va. Cont. Line	war	Feb. 2, 1785
3791	McMahan, Andrew	100	Private	Va. St. Line	3 yrs.	Apr. 1, 1785
3816	McDonald, Angus (Mary McDonald, heir at law)	100	Private	Va. Cont. Line	3 yrs.	Apr. 21, '85
3844	McDonald, Benjamin (William Jackson, assee.)	100	Private	Va. Cont. Line	3 yrs.	May 2, 1785
3869	McKinney, James	100	Private	Va. Cont. Line	3 yrs.	May 10, '85
3871	McAdams, Alexander	100	Private	Va. Cont. Line	3 yrs.	May 10, '85
3906	McDorman, Daniel (William Reynolds, assee.)	200	Private	Va. Cont. Line	war	June 21, '85
3942	McFeely, John	100	Private	Va. Cont. Line	3 yrs.	Aug. 9, 1785
4056	McGinnes, Ambrose	100	Private	Va. Cont. Line	3 yrs.	Dec. 26, '85
4092	McDermot, Francis	200	Private	Va. St. Line	war	Jan. 23, '86
4097	McClain, Thomas (Samuel McClain, heir at law)	100	Private	Va. Cont. Line	3 yrs.	Jan. 25, '86
4110	McNutton, Daniel	100	Private	Va. Cont. Line	3 yrs.	Feb. 21, '86
4113	McCraw, Francis	200	Private	Va. Cont. Line	war	Mch. 4, 1786
4136	McDaniel, Andrew (Wm. Reynolds, assee. and rep.)	100	Private	Va. Cont. Line	3 yrs.	Mch. 24, '86
4186	McCarty, Timothy (Charles McCarty, rep.)	200	Drummer	Va. St. Line	war	July 11, '86
4196	McKennon, Martin (Courteny McKennon, rep.)	400	Sergeant	Va. Cont. Line	war	Aug. 14, '86
4227	McGovern, James (John McGovern, heir at law)	200	Private	Va. Cont. Line	war	Nov. 13, '86
4269	McGraw, James	100	Private	Va. Cont. Line	3 yrs.	Apr. 6, 1787
4303	McManay, John	100	Private	Va. Cont. Line	3 yrs.	Aug. 11, '87
4313	McCormick, James (Joseph Henderson and Elizabeth, his wife, late Elizabeth McCormick, rep. of Jas. McCormick)	100	Private	Va. Cont. Line	3 yrs.	Oct. 16, '87
4360	McCallister, John	200	Sergeant	Va. Cont. Line	3 yrs.	Jan. 7, 1788
4378	McCormack, Wm. (Wm. Reynolds, assee. of the rep.)	200	Private	Va. Cont. Line	war	Jan. 23, '88
4392	McGowan, William (William Russell, assee.)	200	Private	Va. Cont. Line	3 yrs.	Mch. 14, '88
4406	McDade, James (James Arnold, assee.)	100	Private	Va. Cont. Line	3 yrs.	June 12, '88
4418	McGraw, James (William Reynolds, assee. of the rep. of)	100	Private	Va. Cont. Line	3 yrs.	July 17, '88
4461	McLochlin, John	100	Private	Va. St. Line	3 yrs.	June 24, '89
4527	McDorman, David	200	Private	Va. Cont. Line	war	July 7, 1791
4572	McKannon, Christopher	400	Sergeant	Cont. Line	war	May 4, 1792
4591	McCannon, Christopher	100	Private	Va. St. Line	3 yrs.	Nov. 1, 1792

N

18	Nevill, Presley	7000	Lieut.-Col.	Va. Cont. Line	7 yrs.	Nov. 24, '82
315	Norvell, Lipscomb	2666⅔	Lieutenant	Va. Cont. Line	3 yrs.	Apr. 11, '83
337	Nickens, William	200	Drummer	St. Line	war	Apr. 15, '83
368	Nixon, Andrew	4000	Captain	Va. Cav	3 yrs.	Apr. 19, '83
375	Napier, James	400	Sergeant	St. Line	war	Apr. 19, '83
388	Nicholson, William	200	Private	St. Line	war	Apr. 23, '83
401	Newman, Thomas	400	Sergeant	Va. St. Line	war	Apr. 25, '83
433	New, Jesse	100	Private	Va. Cont. Line	3 yrs.	Apr. 26, '83
436	Nickers, John	200	Private	St. Line	war	Apr. 26, '83
584	Narvall, Aquilla	200	Sergeant	Cont. Line	3 yrs.	May 15, '83
739	Nawter, Benjamin	100	Private	Va. St. Line	3 yrs.	June 4, 1783
757	Newby, Thomas	100	Private	Va. St. Art.	3 yrs.	June 6, 1783
796	Nowell, Henry Holdcraft	200	Sergeant	Va. Cont. Line	3 yrs.	June 12, '83
850	Nance, Robert	4000	Captain	Va. Cont. Line	3 yrs.	June 18, '83
864	Norwood, Joseph	100	Private	Va. Cont. Line	3 yrs.	June 20, '83
937	Nevill, John	7777⅔	Colonel	Va. Cont. Line	7 yrs.	June 20, '83
938	Nance, Joseph	100	Private	Va. Cont. Line	3 yrs.	July 20, '83

LAND BOUNTY WARRANTS.

Warrant.	Name.	Acres	Rank.	Department.	Term	Date.
1461	Nincom, Solomon	200	Private	Cont. Line	war	Aug. 1, 1783
1477	Nickens, Richard	100	Seaman	St. Navy	3 yrs.	Aug. 2, 1783
1479	Newby, John	100	Private	St. Line	3 yrs.	Aug. 2, 1783
1519	Neil, Nicholas	466⅔	Sergeant	Cont. Line	7 yrs.	Aug. 7, 1783
1592	Nichols, John	100	Private	Cont. Line	3 yrs.	Aug. 20, '83
1708	Nuttal, Iverson	2666⅔	Midshipman.	Va. St. Navy	3 yrs.	Sept. 2, 1783
1716	Nicking, James	100	Sailor	Va. St. Navy	3 yrs.	Sept. 2, 1783
1735	Newell, John	200	Sergeant	Va Cont. Line	3 yrs.	Sept. 8, 1783
1790	Nelson, John	5333⅓	Major	Va. St. Cav	3 yrs.	Sept. 25, '83
1835	Noland, Pierce	2666⅔	Lieutenant	Cont. Line	3 yrs.	Oct. 7, 1783
⑨ 1856	Naughan, Richard	100	Private	Va. Cont. Line	3 yrs.	Nov. 5, 1783
⑥ 1924	Newman, Owen	466⅔	Sergeant	Va. Cont. Line	7 yrs.	Nov. 21, '83
1990	Norman, William	100	Seaman	Va. St. Navy	3 yrs.	Nov. 28, '83
2159	Nunnamaker, Lewis	100	Private	Va. St. Line	3 yrs.	Dec. 19, '83
2213	Nelson, William	6000	Lieut.-Col	Va. Cont. Line	3 yrs.	Dec. 27, '83
2236	Nelson, John	4000	Captain	Va. Cont. Line	3 yrs.	Jan. 12, '84
2350	Norl, Achilles (William Noel, rep.)	200	Sergeant	Va. Cont. Line	3 yrs.	Jan. 31, '84
2340	Noell, Richard	200	Corporal	Va. Cont. Line	3 yrs.	Jan. 31, '84
2398	Newman, Thomas (Thomas Aslin, assee.)	100	Private	Va. Cont. Line	3 yrs.	Feb. 3, 1784
2403	Nichols, John	200	Private	Va. Cont. Line	war	Feb. 4, 1784
2427	Nickens, Edward	100	Sailor	Va. St. Navy	3 yrs.	Feb. 9, 1784
2442	Needham, Isaac	200	Private	Va. Cont. Line	war	Feb. 9, 1784
2594	Napper, Moses (William Reynolds, assee.)	100	Private	Va. Cont. Line	3 yrs.	Feb. 23, '84
2605	Nunnaly, Obadiah	100	Private	Va. St. Line	3 yrs.	Feb. 24, '84
2635	Nunaly, Joseph (Obadiah Nunaly, heir at law)					
2636	Nunaly, John (Obadiah Nunally, heir at law)	100	Private	Va. Cont. Line	3 yrs.	Feb. 25, '84
2656	Nelms, Charles	400	Sergeant	Va. Cont. Line	war	Feb. 25, '84
2673	Neal, Charles	200	Sergeant	Va. Cont. Line	3 yrs.	Mch. 1, 1784
2747	Newman, Joseph	200	Sergeant	Va. Cont. Line	3 yrs.	Mch. 2, 1784
28⁄3	Nelson, Roger	200	Private	Va. Cont. Line	3 yrs.	Mch. 10, '84
28₄''	Nelson, Roger	1000	Lieutenant	Va. Cont. Line	3 yrs.	Mch. 29, '84
2911	Nichols, Charles (Daniel Perryman, assee.)	1666⅔	Lieutenant	Va. Cont. Line	3 yrs.	Mch. 29, '84
3008	Nance, Frederick	100	Private	Va. Cont. Line	3 yrs.	Apr. 9, 1784
3114	Nance, Zachariah (Thomas Warren, assee.)	200	Sergeant	Va. Cont. Line	3 yrs.	Apr. 23, '84
3121	Neal, Willia m	100	Private	Va. Cont. Line	3 yrs.	May 29, 1784
3273	Nightingale, Matthew	100	Private	Va. Cont. Line	3 yrs.	June 4, 1784
3275	Nutt, Thomas	200	Boatswain	Va. St. Navy	3 yrs.	July 1, 1784
3307	Newton, Thomas	100	Sailor	Va. St. Navy	3 yrs.	July 1, 1784
3308	Nicolls, Thomas	100	Private	Va. St. Line	3 yrs.	July 2, 1784
8586	Newby, Leroy (John Newby, heir at law)	100	Private	Va. St. Line	3 yrs.	July 2, 1784
3785	Nelson, George	200	Sergeant	Va. St. Line	3 yrs.	Dec. 17, '84
3793	Nunnamaker, John (Lewis Nunnamaker, heir at law)	200	Sergeant	Va. Cont. Line	3 yrs.	Mch. 25, '85
3904	Nowlin, Matthew (William Reynolds, assee.)	100	Private	Va. Cont. Line	3 yrs.	Apr. 1, 1785
3934	Nash, William (William Reynolds, assee. of Jno. Nash, Jr., who is heir at law)	200	Private	Va. Cont. Line	war	June 21, '85
4050	Newman, George (John Posey Newman, heir at law)	100	Private	Va. St. Line	3 yrs.	Aug. 1, 1785
4143	Nicholson, Jesse	100	Private	Cont. Line	3 yrs.	Dec. 21, '85
4148	Nunally, Daniel (Robt. Nunally, heir at law)	100	Private	Va. Cont. Line	3 yrs.	Mch. 22, '86
4150	Newland, John (Chas. Lewis, assee. of Jo. Woodward, assee. of)	100	Private	Va. St. Line	3 yrs.	Apr. 24, '86
⑨ 4310	Newcomb, Thomas (Wm. Reynolds, assee of Peter Newcomb, rep. of)	200	Corporal	Va. St. Line	3 yrs.	Apr. 29, '86
4468	Nickins, Nathaniel (William Biggs, assee.)	100	Private	Va. St. Line	3 yrs.	Oct. 6, 1787
4481	Newman, Joseph, Sr	100	Private	Va. Cont. Line	3 yrs.	Oct. 22, '89
4522	Norris, Bazaleel	200	Dragoon	Cont. Line	war	Nov. 25, '89
4551	Nash, Thomas (Harmon Nash, heir at law)	200	Private	Cont. Line	war	Apr. 23, '91
						Nov. 24, '91

LAND BOUNTY WARRANTS. 57

Warrant.	Name.	Acres	Rank.	Department.	Term	Date.
	O					
14	OLDHAM, Conway (Samuel Oldham, heir at law)	4000	Captain	Va. Cont. Line	3 yrs.	Nov. 11, '82
44	OVERTON, Thomas	2666⅔	Lieutenant	Va. Cont. Line	3 yrs.	Dec. 13, '82
153	OVERTON, John	4000	Captain	14th Cont. Va. Reg.	3 yrs.	Feb. 28, '83
250	ORR, Samuel	100	Private	2d Va. State Reg.	3 yrs.	Apr. 3, 1783
502	OLIVE, John	200	Private	St. Line	war	May 1, 1783
566	OWENS, Charles	200	Private	St. Line	war	May 9, 1783
693	OLIVER, William	4000	Capt.-Lieut.	Va. St. Art.	3 yrs.	May 30, '83
981	ORAM, Henry	100	Private	Cont. Line	3 yrs.	June 20, '83
1068	OSBURN, Samuel	200	Private	Va. Cont. Line	war	June 24, '83
1099	OVERLIN, William	200	Private	Va. Cont. Line	war	June 24, '83
1109	ORISH, James	200	Private	Va. Cont. Line	war	June 24, '83
1387	ONEAL, Ferdinand	4000	Captain	Cont. Cav	3 yrs.	July 17, '83
1403	OUST, George	400	Corporal	Cont. Line	war	July 21, '83
1544	OWL, Robert	200	Private	Cont. Line	war	Aug. 11, '83
1611	ONEAL, Farral	400	Sergeant	Cont. Line	war	Aug. 21, '83
1626	OGDEN, Matthew	200	Private	Cont. Line	war	Aug. 22, '83
1787	OSBURN, Elijah	200	Private	Va. Cont. Line	war	Sept. 24, '83
1799	ONEAL, William	100	Private	Va. Cont. Line	3 yrs.	Sept. 29, '83
②1908	OVERTON, Thomas	1333⅓	Captain	Va. Cont. Line	3 yrs.	Nov. 19, '83
2314	ONEAL, John	200	Private	Va. Cont. Line	war	Jan. 29, '84
2469	OAKLEY, George (George Taylor, assee.)	200	Sergeant	Va. St. Line	3 yrs.	Feb. 11, '84
2581	OLFER, Thomas (Lewis Ford, assee.)	200	Private	Va. Cont. Line	3 yrs.	Feb. 21, '84
2980	OWEN, Vincent	100	Private	Va. St. Line	3 yrs.	Apr. 20, '84
3013	OVERSTREET, Benone	200	Sergeant	Va. Cont. Line	3 yrs.	Apr. 24, '84
3026	OMENATE, John	100	Private	Va. Cont. Line	3 yrs.	Apr. 27, '84
3154	OWENS, Christopher	200	Sergeant	Va. Cont. Line	3 yrs.	June 12, '84
3216	OLIVER, William	100	Private	Va. St. Line	3 yrs.	June 26, '84
3371	O'CONNER, Timothy	100	Private	Va. Cont. Line	3 yrs.	Aug. 2, 1784
3643	OWENS, Ephraim	200	Corporal	Va. Cont. Line	3 yrs.	Dec. 30, '84
3811	OWENS, Evan (Mason Owens, legal rep.)	100	Private	Va. Cont. Line	3 yrs.	Apr. 4, '85
3837	ODELL, Reuben	100	Private	Va. Cont. Line	3 yrs.	Apr. 29, '85
3890	OVERSTREET, John (Robert Rankin, assee.)	100	Private	Va. Cont. Line	3 yrs.	June 15, '85
3952	OLIVER, Moses	200	Private	Va. Cont. Line	war	Aug. 12, '85
3956	OGAN, Thomas (William Reynolds, assee.)	200	Private	Va. Cont. Line	war	Aug. 12, '85
4038	OLEPHANT, Benjamin (Obediah Olephant, eldest brother and heir at law)	100	Private	Va. Cont. Line	3 yrs.	Dec. 15, '85
4153	OAKMAN, William	100	Private	Va. Cont. Line	3 yrs.	May 6, 1786
4208	OGILSBY, Robert	100	Private	Va. Cont. Line	3 yrs.	Aug. 31, '86
4219	OBRIEN, James	100	Private	Va. Cont. Line	3 yrs.	Oct. 16, '86
4291	OBANNION, Thomas (William Obannion, heir at law)	200	Private	Va. Cont. Line	war	June 9, 1787
4514	OGLE, Thomas	200	Sergeant	Va. Cont. Line	3 yrs.	Dec. 21, '90
	P					
4	PUCKETT, Womack	100	Private	Cont Line	3 yrs.	Aug. 27, '82
14	PUGH, Willis (Wm. Pugh, heir at law)	2666⅔	Ensign	15th Va. Reg.	3 yrs.	Nov. 9, 1782
15	PHILLIPS, Samuel (Salley Phillips, devisee)	2666⅔	Ensign	Va. Cont. Line	3 yrs.	Nov. 11, '82
55	PAYNE, Thomas	4000	Captain	9th Va. Cont. Reg.	3 yrs.	Dec. 17, '82
56	PEYTON, John	4000	Captain	Va. Cont. Line	3 yrs.	Dec. 17, '82
57	PORTERFIELD, Robert	4000	Captain		3 yrs.	Dec. 18, '82
58	PORTERFIELD, Charles (Robert Porterfield, heir at law)	6000	Lieut.-Col.		3 yrs.	Dec. 18, '82
113	PENDLETON, James	4666⅔	Captain	Art. in Va. Line	7 yrs.	Feb. 7, 1783
126	PAYOR, John	4000	Capt.-Lieut	Cont. Art	3 yrs.	Feb. 13, '83
197	POINTER, William	2666⅔	Lieutenant	Va. Cont. Line	3 yrs.	Mch. 25, '83
240	POSEY, Thomas	7000	Lieut.-Col.	Va. Line	7 yrs	Apr. 1, 1783
279	PELHAM, Charles (William Lewis, assee.)	6222	Major	Va. Cont. Line	7 yrs.	Apr. 3, 1783
283	PHILLIPS, Larkin	100	Private	Va. St. Line	3 yrs.	Apr. 3, 1783
293	PALMER, William	200	Corporal	Va. Cont. Line	3 yrs.	Apr. 5, 1783
332	PUNTER, Henry	200	Sergeant	Va. Art	3 yrs.	Apr. 14, '83
374	PORTER, Daniel	400	Sergeant	St. Line	war	Apr. 19, '83
384	PORTER, Calvert (Philip Daw, assee.)	200	Sergeant	Va. Cont. Line	3 yrs.	Apr. 23, '83

LAND BOUNTY WARRANTS.

Warrant.	Name.	Acres	Rank.	Department.	Term	Date.
386	Prithett, John	200	Sergeant	Va. Cont. Line	3 yrs.	Apr. 23, '83
398	Pemberton, Thomas	4000	Captain	Light Dragoons in Va. Cont. Line..	*	Apr. 25, '83
423	Palmer, David	400	Corporal	Va. St. Line	war	Apr. 26, '83
424	Phipps, George	200	Private	Va. St. Line	war	Apr. 26, '83
430	Perry, Hildry	400	Sergeant	Va. St. Line	war	Apr. 26, '83
442	Powell, John	200	Private	St. Line	war	Apr. 26, '83
448	Porter, William (Daniel Porter, rep.)	200	Private	St. Line	war	Apr. 28, '83
455	Phillips, Benjamin	200	Private	St. Line	war	Apr. 28, '83
479	Penny, John	100	Private	St. Line	3 yrs.	Apr. 30, '83
481	Pickett, Francis	400	Drummer	St. Line	war	Apr. 30, '83
491	Pickett, George	200	Drummer	St. Line	war	Apr. 30, '83
497	Pollard, Braxton	400	Corporal	St. Line	war	Apr. 30, '83
531	Parks, Henry	200	Private	St. Line	war	May 2, 1783
547	Pursley, William	200	Sergeant	St. Line	3 yrs.	May 5, 1783
574	Palmer, Thomas	100	Private	Va. Cont. Line	3 yrs.	May 14, '83
603	Peace, Samuel	200	Sergeant	Va. St. Line	3 yrs.	May 20, '83
608	Pair, George	200	Private	Va. Cont. Line	war	May 21, '83
664	Patterson, John	400	Sergeant	Va. St. Line	war	May 28, '83
670	Porter, William	2666⅔	Lieutenant	Va. Cont. Line	3 yrs.	May 29, '83
675	Pool, Robert	100	Private	Va. Cont. Cav.	3 yrs.	May 29, '83
679	Powell, Thomas (Seymour Powell, heir at law to)	2266⅔	Lieutenant	Va. St. Line	3 yrs.	May 29, '83
699	Payne, Tarlton	4666⅔	Captain	Va. Cont. Line	7 yrs.	May 31, '83
715	Perry, William	100	Drummer	Va. Cont. Line	3 yrs.	June 2, 1783
732	Parker, Thomas	4000	Captain	Va. Cont. Line	3 yrs.	June 4, 1783
735	Parker, Richard (Alexander Parker, heir at law)	6666⅔	Colonel	Va. Cont. Line	3 yrs.	June 4, 1783
768	Pate, Matthew	100	Private	St. Line	3 yrs.	June 7, 1783
779	Powell, Aaron	200	Sergeant	Va. St. Art	3 yrs.	June 10, '83
780	Parker, Robert	200	Corporal	Va. St. Line	3 yrs.	June 10, '83
792	Poulson, John	6222	Major	Va. Cont. Line	7 yrs.	June 12, '83
800	Parker, Wyatt	100	Private	St. Line	3 yrs.	June 13, '83
840	Perryman, Philip	100	Private	Va. St. Line	3 yrs.	June 16, '83
842	Purvear, Thomas	100	Private	Va. Cont. Line	3 yrs.	June 16, '83
858	Parker, Nicholas (Josiah Parker, heir at law to)	2666⅔	Lieutenant	Va. Cont. Line	3 yrs.	June 18, '83
903	Powell, Robert	4000	Captain	Va. Cont. Line	3 yrs.	June 20, '83
904	Pearson, Thomas	2666⅔	Lieutenant	Va. Cont. Line	3 yrs.	June 20, '83
984	Pollock, Thomas	100	Private	Cont. Line	3 yrs.	June 20, '83
989	Powle, William	100	Private	Cont. Line	3 yrs.	June 21, '83
1013	Parker, William Harwar	2666⅔	Lieutenant	Va. St. Navy	3 yrs.	June 28, '83
1018	Parsons, Thomas	100	Private	Va. Cont. Line	3 yrs.	June 23, '83
1032	Porter, Elisha	100	Private	Va. Cont. Line	3 yrs.	June 23, '83
1055	Phelps, George	200	Private	Va. Cont. Line	war	June 24, '83
1061	Paul, Edward	200	Private	Va. Cont. Line	war	June 24, '83
1107	Phillips, John	200	Private	Va. Cont. Line	war	June 24, '83
1118	Pailer, James	200	Private	Va. Cont. Line	war	June 24, '83
1196	Pulham, John	100	Private	Va. Cont. Line	3 yrs.	June 26, '83
1222	Poe, Thomas	100	Private	Va. St. Line	3 yrs.	June 26, '83
2145	Perkinton, William	200	Sergeant	Va. St. Art	3 yrs.	June 27, '83
1250	Pugh, Lewis	200	Private	Va. Cont Line	3 yrs.	June 27, '83
1296	Peyton, Valentine (Timothy Peyton, heir at law to)	4000	Captain	Va. Cont Line	3 yrs.	June 28, '83
1306	Perry, William	100	Private	Va. Cont Line	3 yrs.	June 30, '83
1321	Perkins, Joseph	200	Private	Va. Cont Line	war	June 30, '83
1346	Patman, William	200	Sergeant	St. Art	3 yrs.	July 10, '83
1353	Peters, Thomas	100	Private	St. Line	3 yrs.	July 11, '83
1369	Pickrel, Samuel	100	Drummer	St. Line	3 yrs.	July 12, '83
1370	Proctor, John	200	Sergeant	Cont. Line	3 yrs.	July 12, '83
1374	Poe, William	100	Private	St. Line	3 yrs.	July 15, '83
1391	Pendleton, Nathaniel	4666⅔	Captain	Cont. Line	7 yrs.	July 18, '83
1415	Powell, Peyton	1666⅔	Lieutenant	Cont. Line	3 yrs.	July 22, '83
1416	Powell, Peyton	1000	Lieutenant	Cont. Line	3 yrs.	July 22, '83
1455	Piper, William	200	Sergeant	St. Line	3 yrs.	July 31, '83
1462	Perry, Henry	100	Private	Cont. Line	3 yrs.	Aug. 1, 1783
1500	Pride, William (John Pride, heir at law)	2666⅔	Lieutenant	Cont. Line	3 yrs.	Aug. 5, 1783
1515	Patterson, Israel	200	Private	Cont. Line	war	Aug. 7, 1783
1548	Parker, Jeremiah	200	Sergeant	Cont. Line	3 yrs.	Aug. 11, '38
1554	Perryman, Benone	100	Fifer	Cont. Line	3 yrs.	Aug. 11, '83
1598	Purcell, John	200	Private	Cont. Line	war	Aug. 20, '83
1617	Perry, John	2666⅔	Cornet	Cont. Line	3 yrs.	Aug. 22, '83
1639	Plummer, Armstead	100	Private	Va. Cont. Line	3 yrs.	Aug. 23, '83
1642	Price, David	400	Sergeant	Va. Cont. Line	war	Aug. 23, '83

*From 17th December, 1776, to 15th January, 178—.

LAND BOUNTY WARRANTS. 59

Warrant.	Name.	Acres	Rank.	Department.	Term	Date.
1654	PAYNE, Joseph	1000	Lieutenant	Va. Cont. Line	3 yrs.	Aug. 23, '83
1655	PAYNE, Joseph	1000	Lieutenant	Va. Cont. Line	3 yrs.	Aug. 23, '83
1656	PAYNE, Joseph	666⅔	Lieutenant	Va. Cont. Line	3 yrs.	Aug. 23, '83
1658	PEARMAN, Harrison	200	Private	Va. Cont. Line	war	Aug. 23, '83
1687	POWELL, Charles	200	Sergeant	Va. Cont. Line	3 yrs.	Aug. 30, '83
1699	PLUMMER, William	200	Sergeant	Va. Cont. Line	3 yrs.	Aug. 30, '83
1726	PACKETT, Richard	100	Private	Va. St. Line	3 yrs.	Sept. 4, 1783
1710	PURYEAR, Jessee	100	Private	Va. Cont. Line	3 yrs.	Sept. 2, 1783
1742	PENN, John	100	Sailor	Va. St. Navy	3 yrs.	Sept. 11, '83
1747	POPE, Fortunatus	200	Sergeant	Va. St. Line	3 yrs.	Sept. 11, '83
1749	PUTTON, William	200	Sergeant	Va. St. Line	3 yrs.	Sept. 11, '83
1775	POWER, Robert	3110½	Cornet	Va. Cont. Line	7 yrs.	Sept. 19, '83
1784	PARKER, Warren	400	Sergeant	Va. Cont. Line	war	Sept. 24, '83
1789	PRITCHARD, James	200	Private	Va. Cont. Line	war	Sept. 24, '83
1810	PARKER, Joseph	200	Corporal	Va. Cont. Line	3 yrs.	Sept. 30, '83
1828	PEYTON, Francis	100	Private	Va. Cont. Line	3 yrs.	Oct. 7, 1783
1851	PLUNKET, Reuben	200	Corporal	Va. Cont. Line	3 yrs.	Oct. 13, '83
1858	PATILLO, James	200	Sergeant	Va. Cont. Line	3 yrs.	Oct. 14, '83
1868	PERRYMAN, Daniel	100	Private	Va. Cont. Line	3 yrs.	Oct. 15, '83
1895	PACE, William	200	Private	Va. Cont. Line	war	Oct. 20, '83
1896	PICKET, John	100	Private	Va. Cont. Line	3 yrs.	Oct. 20, '83
1927	POOL, Baxter	100	Private	Va. Cont. Line	3 yrs.	Oct. 28, '83
1934	POUND, William	200	Corporal	Va. St. Line	3 yrs.	Oct. 30, '83
ⓓ 1852	PARKER, Watts	200	Sergeant	Va. Cont. Line	3 yrs.	Nov. 4, 1783
ⓓ 1873	POPLAR, Hack	100	Seaman	Va. St. Navy	3 yrs.	Nov. 7, 1783
ⓓ 1874	PITMAN, Isaac	200	Sergeant	Va. Cont. Line	3 yrs.	Nov. 7, 1783
ⓓ 1878	POYTHRESS, William	4000	Capt.-Lieut	Art. in Va. Cont. Line	3 yrs.	Nov. 8, 1783
ⓓ 1892	PARKER, Alexander	5333⅓	Captain	Va. Cont. Line	8 yrs.	Nov. 12, '83
ⓓ 1920	PARKER, Josiah	6666⅔	Colonel	Va. Cont. Line	3 yrs.	Nov. 21, '83
1943	PASTEUR, Bluett	100	Seaman	Va. St. Navy	3 yrs.	Nov. 22, '83
1944	PASLEY, Joel	100	Private	Va. St. Line	3 yrs.	Nov. 22, '83
1956	PIGGOTT, Abraham	100	Private	Va. Cont. Line	3 yrs.	Nov. 26, '83
1973	PURVIS, William	100	Private	Va. Cont. Line	3 yrs.	Nov. 26, '83
1975	PARSONS, George	100	Private	Va. Cont. Line	3 yrs.	Nov. 29, '83
1995	PITMAN, George	200	Sergeant	Va. Cont. Line	3 yrs.	Dec. 10, '83
2078	PARISH, Peter	200	Sergeant	Va. Cont. Line	3 yrs.	Dec. 10, '83
2079	PAYNE, Jacob	200	Sergeant	Va. Cont. Line	3 yrs.	Dec. 10, '83
2088	PILE, Richard	100	Sergeant	Va. Cont. Line	3 yrs.	Dec. 12, '83
2104	POTTS, John	100	Private	Va. Cont. Line	3 yrs.	Dec. 19, '83
2151	PAYNE, John	200	Private	Va. Cont. Line	war	Dec. 20, '83
2169	POOL, Edward	200	Corporal	Va. St. Line	3 yrs.	Dec. 20, '83
2179	PIERCE, Thomas	100	Sailor	Va. St. Navy	3 yrs.	Dec. 20, '83
2182	PURCELL, Robert	100	Private	Va. St. Line	3 yrs.	Dec. 23, '83
2205	POWERS, William	100	Private	Va. Cont. Line	3 yrs.	Jan. 8, 1784
2225	PETRIE, Alexander	200	Sergeant	Va. Cont. Line	3 yrs.	Jan. 12, '84
2233	PEDIFORD, Edward	100	Private	Va. Cont. Line	3 yrs.	Jan. 16, '84
2251	PATTERSON, Tilman	400	Sergeant	Va. St. Line	war	Jan. 26, '84
2297	PEYTON, James	100	Private	Va. Cont. Line	3 yrs.	Jan. 30, '84
2321	PARSONS, William	4000	Captain	Va. Cont. Line	3 yrs.	Feb. 3, 1784
2383	PERKINS, Archelaus	2666⅔	Lieutenant	Va. Cont. Line	war	Feb. 7, 1784
2424	PETTUS, John (Stephen Pettus, legal rep.)	1000	Captain	Va. Cont. Line	3 yrs.	Feb. 7, 1784
2425	PETTUS, John (Stephen Pettus, legal rep.)	1000	Captain	Va. Cont. Line	3 yrs.	Feb. 7, 1784
2426	PETTUS, John (Stephen Pettus, legal rep.)	2000	Captain	Va. Cont. Line	3 yrs.	Feb. 9, 1784
2443	PIERCE, William	4666⅔	Captain	Va. Cont. Line	7 yrs.	Feb. 9, 1784
2508	PINCHBACK, Thomas	200	Sergeant	Va. Cont. Line	3 yrs.	Feb. 17, '84
2564	POWERS, William (William Reynolds, assee.)	200	Private	Va. Cont. Line	war	Feb. 20, '84
2567	PAYTON, William (William Reynolds, assee.)	100	Private	Va. Cont. Line	3 yrs.	Feb. 20, '84
2587	PARSONS, Williby (Francis Graves, assee.)	100	Private	Va. St. Line	3 yrs.	Feb. 32, '84
2595	PEARMAN, Thomas (John Depriest, assee.)	200	Private	Va. Cont. Line	war	Feb. 23, '84
2612	PULLIN, George (George Pickett, assee.)	100	Private	Va. Cont. Line	3 yrs.	Feb. 24, '84
2627	PATTON, Alexander (Daniel Flowerree, assee.)	100	Private	Va. Cont. Line	3 yrs.	Feb. 24, '84
2674	PAYNE, Josiah	2666⅔	Lieutenant	Va. Cont. Line	war	Mch. 3, 1784
2689	PERAULT, Michael	4000	Captain	Va. St. Line	3 yrs.	Mch. 3, 1784
2739	PATTERSON, Thomas (Charles Patterson, heir at law)	4000		Va. Cont. Line	war	Mch. 8, 1784
2796	PHILLIPS, John	100	Private	Va. Cont. Line	3 yrs.	Mch. 19, '84

LAND BOUNTY WARRANTS.

Warrant.	Name.	Acres	Rank.	Department.	Term	Date.
2820	PARISH, William (Joseph Hawkins, assee.)	200	Sergeant	Va. Cont. Line	3 yrs.	Mch. 26, '84
2891	PARTON, David	100	Private	Va. Cont. Line	3 yrs.	Apr. 5, 1784
2894	PORTER, William	2666⅔	Subaltern	Va. Cont. Line	3 yrs.	Apr. 6, 1784
2895	PORTER, Thomas	200	Sergeant	Va. Cont. Line	3 yrs.	Apr. 6, 1784
2939	POTTS, David	100	Private	Va. Cont. Line	3 yrs.	Apr. 17, '84
2942	POTTS, Jonathan	100	Private	Va. Cont. Line	3 yrs.	Apr. 17, '84
2944	PURSLEY, Lawrence	100	Private	Va. St. Line	3 yrs.	Apr. 17, '84
2962	POSEY, Zephaniah	100	Private	Va. Cont. Line	3 yrs.	Apr. 19, '84
2987	PRICE, Isaac (David Price, heir at law)	100	Private	Va. Cont. Line	3 yrs.	Apr. 21, '84
3029	PARKER, Thomas	4000	Captain	Va. Cont. Line	7 yrs.	Apr. 28, '84
3030	PARKER, Thomas	666⅔	Captain	Va. Cont. Line	7 yrs.	Apr. 28, '84
3040	PHILLIPS, Newton	100	Private	Va. Cont. Line	3 yrs.	May 4, 1784
3053	PLUNKETT, Thomas	200	Private	Va. Cont. Line	war	May 7, 1784
3057	PRITCHETT, Peter	200	Sergeant	Va. Cont. Line	3 yrs.	May 7, 1784
3143	PHILLIPS, John	200	Corporal	Va. Cont. Line	3 yrs.	June 10, '84
3147	POWELL, John (William Payne, assee.)	400	Sergeant	Va. Cont. Line	war	June 10, '84
3203	PRICE, Thomas	100	Private	Va. Cont. Line	3 yrs.	June 24, '84
3209	PAGE, Carter (Res. of Gen. Assby., May 26, 1784)	4000	Captain	Services		June 24, '84
3228	PEW, David (James Brown, heir at law)	200	Private	Va. Cont. Line	3 yrs.	June 28, '84
3234	PEYTON, Henry (Francis Peyton, heir at law)	5333⅓	Major	Va. Cont. Line	3 yrs.	June 29, '84
3235	PEYTON, Dade (Francis Peyton, heir at law)	2666⅔	Lieutenant	Va. Cont. Line	3 yrs.	June 29, '84
3241	PULLY, William	100	Private	Va. Cont. Line	3 yrs.	June 29, '84
3253	PETERSON, Conrad	100	Private	Va. Cont. Line	3 yrs.	June 30, '84
3268	PICKEN, Spencer M. (Sam'l Blackwell, assee.)	100	Sailor	Va. St. Navy	3 yrs.	July 1, 1784
3297	POLLARD, Absalom	200	Corporal	Va. St. Line	3 yrs.	July 1, 1784
3306	PRICE, George	100	Private	Va. St. Line	3 yrs.	July 2, 1784
3335	PIQUE, William	400	Sergeant	Va. St. Line	war	July 19, '84
3337	PILMAN, Buckner	200	Sergeant	Va. St. Line	3 yrs.	July 19, '84
3396	POWELL, Leven	2000	Lieutenant	Va. Cont. Line	3 yrs.	Aug. 17, '84
3397	POWELL, Leven	2000	Lieutenant	Va. Cont. Line	3 yrs.	Aug. 17, '84
3398	POWELL, Leven	2000	Lieutenant	Va. Cont. Line	3 yrs.	Aug. 17, '84
3401	PITTS, David (John Pitts, heir at law)	100	Private	Va. Cont. Line	3 yrs.	Aug. 18, '84
3402	PITTS, Bradley (John Pitts, heir at law)	100	Private	Va. Cont. Line	3 yrs.	Aug. 18, '84
3428	PARROT, James (William Reynolds, assee.)	100	Private	Va. St. Line	3 yrs.	Aug. 28, '84
3429	POWELL, Leven (Res. of Gen. Assby., June 18, 1784)	6000	Lieut.-Col.	Services		Aug. 30, '84
3437	PEYTON, George (Valentine Peyton, heir at law)	2666⅔	Ensign		3 yrs.	Sept. 11, '84
3438	PEYTON, Robert (Valentine Peyton, heir at law)	2666⅔	Lieutenant	Va. Cont. Line	3 yrs.	Sept. 11, '84
3440	PERKESON, James (William Reynolds, assee.)	200	Private	Va. Cont. Line	war	Sept. 15, '84
3462	PAMY, Moses	200	Sergeant	Va. Cont. Line	3 yrs.	Oct. 13, '84
3536	PETTIFORD, Elias (Samuel Parker, assee.)	100	Private	Va. St. Line	3 yrs.	Nov. 24, '84
3537	PETTIFORD, Drury	100	Private	Va. St. Line	3 yrs.	Nov. 24, '84
3552	POUGH, Michael	100	Private	Va. Cont. Line	3 yrs.	Dec. 6, 1784
3563	PURVIS, James (Res. of Gen. Assby., Dec. 2, 1784)	4000	Captain			Dec. 8, 1784
3594	PAYNE, Charles	100	Private	Va. Cont. Line	3 yrs.	Dec. 21, '84
3629	POWELL, Levin	200	Private	Va. Cont. Line	war	Dec. 29, '84
3646	PEYTON, Charles (Elijah Peyton, heir at law)	100	Private	Va. Cont. Line	3 yrs.	Dec. 31, '84
3660	PHILIPS, John (William Philips, heir at law)	100	Private	Va. Cont. Line	3 yrs.	Dec. 31, '84
3663	PRICE, Burdett	200	Private	Va. Cont. Line	war	Jan. 1, 1785
3664	PERRIN, John (William Mead, assee.)	100	Private	Va. Cont. Line	3 yrs.	Jan. 1, 1785
3678	POOL, Peter (Thomas Patterson, assee)	100	Private	Va. Cont. Line	3 yrs.	Jan. 8, 1785
3724	POPE, William	100	Private	Va. Cont. Line	3 yrs.	Jan. 31, '85
3752	PUCKETT, Josiah	200	Private	Va. Cont. Line	war	Feb. 11, '85
3760	PRITCHARD, Thomas	100	Private	Va. Cont. Line	3 yrs.	Feb. 25, '85

LAND BOUNTY WARRANTS.   61

Warrant.	Name.	Acres	Rank	Department	Term	Date
3801	Palmer, Charles (Lipscomb Norvell, assee. of Wm. Reynolds, who was assee. of)....	100	Private....	Va. St. Line.......	3 yrs.	Apr. 12, '85
3810	Payne, William (Res. of Gen. Assby. of Nov. 29, 1784)....	4000	Captain..	Services.........	3 yrs.	Apr. 18, '85
3815	Puller, John (Mary King, rep.)........................	100	Private....	Va. Cont. Line.....	3 yrs.	Apr. 21, '85
3819	Patton, William (William Phillips, assee.)	100	Private....	Va. Cont. Line.....	3 yrs.	Apr. 21, '85
3866	Pyatt, Benjamin	200	Sergeant...	Va. Cont. Line.....	3 yrs.	May 10, '85
3877	Powers, John	100	Private....	Va. St. Line........	3 yrs.	May 16, '85
3883	Putten, Henry	100	Private....	Va. Cont. Line.....	3 yrs.	May 25, '85
3892	Preston, Nathan (Robert Rankins, assee.)	100	Private....	Va. Cont. Line.....	3 yrs.	June 15, '85
3896	Pratt, John (William Reynolds, assee.)...................	100	Private....	Va. Cont. Line.....	3 yrs.	June 21, '85
3912	Pennry, Robert	100	Private....	Va. Cont. Line.....	3 yrs.	June 21, '85
3916	Pile, Richard	400	Private....	Va. Cont. Line.....	war	June 21, '85
3919	Pile, Benjamin (Daniel Buckley, assee.)	200	Private....	Va. Cont. Line.....	war	June 21, '85
3946	Peay, Thomas (William Reynolds, assee. of Geo. Peay, rep. of)	200	Corporal...	Va. Cont. Line.....	3 yrs.	Aug. 10, '85
3947	Peay, Elias (William Reynolds, assee. of Geo. Peay, rep. of).	200	Sergeant...	Va. Cont. Line.....	3 yrs.	Aug. 10, '85
3963	Pair, George (William Reynolds, assee.)	200	Private....	Va. Cont. Line.....	war	Aug. 13, '85
3970	Pruder, Henry (Samuel Couch, assee.)....................	200	Sergeant...	Va. Cont. Line.....	3 yrs.	Sept. 12, '85
3975	Powell, Richard (Thos. Brown, assee.).....................	100	Private....	Va. Cont. Line.....	3 yrs.	Sept. 16, '85
3982	Pritchard, James	200	Private....	Va. Cont. Line.....	war	Oct. 18, '85
3995	Paskill, George	200	Private....	Va. Cont. Line.....	war	Nov. 15, '85
3997	Pinkstone, Shadrack	100	Private....	Va. Cont. Line.....	3 yrs.	Nov. 19, '85
4032	Phillips, John	100	Private....	Va. Cont. Line.....	3 yrs.	Dec. 10, '85
4055	Penn, William (John and Gabriel Penn, exors.)..........	2666⅔	Lieutenant.	Va. Cont. Line.....	3 yrs.	Dec. 26, '85
4062	Powell, Benjamin	200	Private....	Va. Cont. Line.....	war	Dec. 31, '85
4109	Parish, Henry	200	Sergeant...	Va. Cont. Line.....	3 yrs.	Feb. 7, 1786
4162	Petty, William	100	Private....	Va. Cont. Line.....	3 yrs.	May 27, '86
4170	Parker, Thomas	100	Private....	Va. Cont. Line.....	3 yrs.	June 13, '86
②4204	Philips, Jacob	100	Private....	Va. Cont. Line.....	3 yrs.	Aug. 31, '86
4256	Poythress, Francis (Mary Randolph, rep.)	400	Sergeant...	Va. Cont. Line.....	war	Feb. 5, 1787
4298	Price, Ebenezer (William Reynolds, assee.)	2666⅔	Qtr. Master.	Va. St. Navy......	3 yrs.	June 21, '87
4314	Pottes, alias "Potts," Nathaniel	100	Private....	Va. Cont. Line.....	3 yrs.	Oct. 23, '87
4323	Piles, William	100	Private....	Va. Cont. Line.....	3 yrs.	Oct. 26, '87
4347	Pilkington, Drury	100	Private....	Va. Cont. Line.....	3 yrs.	Dec. 1, 1787
4368	Peters, James (William Reynolds, assee.)	100	Private....	Va. St. Line........	3 yrs.	Jan. 17, '88
4379	Prayle, John (William Bigger, assee.)....................	100	Sailor.....	Va. St. Navy......	3 yrs.	Jan. 23, '88
4411	Punch, Patrick	200	Private....	Va. Cont. Line.....	war	July 17, '88
4560	Parker, John (Jacob Parker, heir at law).................	200	Private....	Cont. Line	war	Dec. 15, '91
4592	Pettus, Samuel O...........	2666⅔	Lieutenant.	Cont. Line	war	Nov. 9, 1792
4600	Pemberton, Reuben (Francis Graves, assee.)	200	Private....	St. Line	war	Dec. 18, '92

Q

84	Quarles, James	4000	Captain...	St. Line	3 yrs.	Dec. 31, '82
150	Quarles, James	1333⅓	Major....	....	....	Feb. 26, '83
	(Note—Granted "in consideration of his services as a Major; 4,000 acres granted to said Quarles as a Captain, since promoted to the rank of Major; 1333⅓ completes his bounty as a Major.")					
378	Quarles, Nathaniel	200	Sergeant...	Va. Line	3 yrs.	Apr. 21, '83
③ 651	Quarles, Henry	4000	Captain..	Va. St. Line.....	3 yrs.	May 28, '83
799	Quarles, Thomas	2666⅔	Lieutenant.	St. Line	3 yrs.	June 13, '83
1294	Quarles, Abner	200	Private....	Va. Cont. Line.....	war	June 28, '83
1342	Quirk, Thomas	1000	Major....	St. Line	3 yrs.	July 9, 1783

LAND BOUNTY WARRANTS.

Warrant.	Name.	Acres	Rank.	Department.	Term	Date.
1343	QUIRK, Thomas	1000	Major	St. Line	3 yrs.	July 9, 1783
1344	QUIRK, Thomas	3333⅓	Major	St. Line	3 yrs.	July 9, 1783
1436	QUIN, Patrick	200	Private	Cont. Line	war	July 28, '83
2381	QUARLES, Robert	2666⅔	Lieutenant	Va. Cont. Line	war	Feb. 3, 1784
2569	QUARLES, William	2000	Lieutenant	Va. Cont. Line	war	Feb. 21, '84
2570	QUARLES, William	666⅔	Lieutenant	Va. Cont. Line	war	Feb. 21, '84
2651	QUINLEY, William (Samuel Trower, assee.)	200	Sergeant	Va. Cont. Line	3 yrs.	Feb. 28, '84
2666	QUARLES, John	4000	Capt.-Lieut.	Va. St. Line	3 yrs.	Mch. 2, 1784
2900	QUARLES, John (John Hooper, and Ann, his wife and heir at law to)	2666⅔	Lieutenant	Va. Cont. Line	3 yrs.	Apr. 6, 1784
3480	QUARLES, John (James Fear, assee.)	100	Private	Va. Cont. Line	3 yrs.	Oct. 25, '84
3902	QUARLES, Moses (William Reynolds, assee.)	200	Private	Va. Cont. Line	war	June 21, '85

R

33	REDDY, Dennis	200	Sergeant	Va. Cont. Line	3 yrs.	Dec. 30, '82
46	READ, Isaac (Clement Read, eldest son and heir at law)	6666⅔	Colonel	Army	3 yrs.	Dec. 14, '82
54	READE, Edmund	4000	Captain	Nielson's Corps of St. Cav.	3 yrs.	Dec. 16, '82
68	READ, Clement (John Read, eldest brother and heir at law)	2666⅔	Lieutenant	Maj. John Neilson's Corps of Cavalry		Dec. 23, '82
90	RICE, Nathaniel	2666⅔	Lieutenant	St. Art	3 yrs.	Jan. 3, 1783
92	ROANE, Christopher	4000	Captain	Art. in Dabney's Legion	3 yrs.	Jan. 3, 1783
98	RUCKER, Angus	4000	Captain	St. Infantry	3 yrs.	Jan. 21, '83
105	ROBERTS, John	6000	Surgeon	Va. Cont. Line	3 yrs.	Jan. 30, '83
128	RUDDER, Epaphroditus	2666⅔	Lieutenant	Va. Cav. Cont. Est.	3 yrs.	Feb. 13, '83
136	RUCKER, Elliott	2666⅔	Lieutenant	Va. St. Line	3 yrs.	Feb. 20, '83
148	ROGERS, John	3000	Captain	Va. St. Line	3 yrs.	Feb. 26, '83
149	ROGERS, John	1000	Captain	Va. St. Line	3 yrs.	Feb. 26, '83
154	ROY, Beverley	4000	Captain	Va. Line	3 yrs.	Mch. 3, 1783
165	RANKINS, Robert	2666⅔	Lieutenant	Va. Cont. Line	3 yrs.	Mch. 8, 1783
167	RANSDALL, Thomas	4000	Captain	Va. Line	3 yrs.	Mch. 9, 1783
249	RUSSELL, Charles	2666⅔	Lieutenant	St. Line	3 yrs.	Apr. 2, 1783
255	RIDDEN, Robert (Rev. Robert Andrews, assee.)	100	Private	St. Line	3 yrs.	Apr. 3, 1783
274	RICKETTS, William (Dr. James McClung, assee.)	100	Private	St. Line		
278	RUSSELL, John	2666⅔	Lieutenant	Va. St. Line	3 yrs.	Apr. 3, 1783
304	REARDEN, George	200	Sergeant	St. Line	3 yrs.	Apr. 3, 1783
331	RINGO, Burtus	200	Private	St. Cav	3 yrs.	Apr. 8, 1783
342	RUSSELL, Albert	2666⅔	Lieutenant	Va. Cont. Line	war	Apr. 14, '83
354	ROSE, George	200	Private	Va. St. Line	3 yrs.	Apr. 15, '83
371	REYNOR, John	200	Private	St. Line	war	Apr. 17, '83
376	REYNOLDS, Bernard	200	Private	Va. St. Line	war	Apr. 19, '83
397	RAGSDALE, Drury	4000	Captain	Cont. Line	*	Apr. 19, '83
414	ROBERTSON, William	2666⅔	Lieutenant	Va. Cont. Line	3 yrs.	Apr. 25, '83
435	ROWE, John	200	Private	St. Line	war	Apr. 26, '83
446	RANDOLPH, Adam	200	Private	Va. St. Line	war	Apr. 26, '83
458	ROBERTS, Anthony	200	Private	St. Line	war	Apr. 28, '83
460	RHODES, John (John Rhoads, legal rep.)	200	Private	Va. St. Line	war	Apr. 28, '83
466	RUSSELL, Thomas	200	Private	Va. Cav	war	Apr. 29, '83
489	REARDEN, George	400	Sergeant	St. Line	war	Apr. 30, '83
601	REID, Nathan or John	4000	Captain	Va. Cont. Line		May 20, '83
625	ROSS, John	200	Private	Va. Cont. Line		May 23, '83
636	ROBERTSON, George	100	Private	Va. Cont. Line	3 yrs.	May 24, '83
677	ROBERTS, Garrard	200	Sergeant	Va. St. Line	3 yrs.	May 29, '83
695	RICHESON, James	400	Sergeant	Va. St. Line	war	May 31, '83
709	ROBINSON, Cole	200	Sergeant	Va. Cont. Line	3 yrs.	May 31, '83
710	ROBINSON, William (Cole Robinson, heir and legal rep. of)	200	Private	Va. Cont. Line	3 yrs.	May 31, '83
733	RANGER, Joseph	100	Sailor	Va. St. Navy	3 yrs.	June 4, 1783
762	RUSSELL, William	100	Private	Va. St. Art	3 yrs.	June 6, 1783
782	RAVENSCRAFT, Thomas	4000	Captain	Va. Cont. Line	3 yrs.	June 10, '83
811	RANDOLPH, Robert	2666⅔	Gunner	Va. Cav	3 yrs.	June 13, '83
819	RYDMAN, John	200	Sergeant	St. Navy	3 yrs.	June 14, '83
823	RICHARDS, Thomas	100	Private	Va. Cont. Line	3 yrs.	June 14, '83
824	RYCROFT, Thomas	100	Private	Va. Cont. Line	3 yrs.	June 14, '83

*From 13th January, 1777, to date.

LAND BOUNTY WARRANTS.

Warrant.	Name.	Acres	Rank.	Department.	Term	Date.
847	Royal, Grief	100	Private	Va St. Art.	3 yrs.	June 17, '83
856	Rice, George	4000	Captain	Va Cont. Line	3 yrs.	June 17, '83
859	Rogers, William	4000	Lieutenant	Va. Cont. Line	3 yrs.	June 18, '83
873	Royall, Francis	100	Private	Va. Art	3 yrs.	June 19, '83
943	Ray, David	100	Private	Va. Cont. Line	3 yrs.	June 20, '83
978	Ragor, Bartholomew	100	Private	Cont. Line	3 yrs.	June 20, '83
979	Rumage, David	100	Private	Cont. Line	3 yrs.	June 20, '83
1009	Russell, James	200	Sergeant	Va. Art	3 yrs.	June 23, '83
1010	Routen, Richard	200	Corporal	Va. Cont. Line	3 yrs	June 23, '83
1054	Roach, Richard	200	Private	Va. Cont. Line	war	June 24, '83
1058	Reynolds, James	200	Private	Va. Cont. Line	war	June 24, '83
1073	Ravens, Michael	200	Private	Va. Cont. Line	war	June 24, '83
1101	Riley, John	200	Private	Va. Cont. Line	war	June 24, '83
1105	Rooke, John	200	Private	Cont. Line	war	June 24, '83
1108	Robertson, John	200	Private	Va. Cont. Line	war	June 24, '83
1114	Rucker, Jacob	200	Private	Va. Cont. Line	war	June 24, '83
1131	Robinson, Charles	200	Private	Va. Cont. Line	war	June 24, '83
1155	Richeson, John	200	Private	Va. Cont. Line	war	June 24, '83
1211	Robson, Green	100	Private	Va. St. Line	3 yrs.	June 26, '83
1260	Roach, William	466⅔		Va. Cont. Line	7 yrs.	June 27, '83
1291	Roberts, Ambrose	100	Private	Va. St. Line	3 yrs.	June 28, '83
1304	Rest, Tucker	200	Sergeant	Va. St. Line	3 yrs.	June 30, '83
1345	Ridley, John	200	Sergeant	St. Art	3 yrs.	July 10, '83
1419	Read, William	200	Corporal	Cont. Line	3 yrs.	July 22, '83
1431	Rust, Benjamin	2666⅔	Lieutenant	St. Navy	3 yrs.	July 27, '83
1452	Rhea, Matthew	2666⅔	Lieutenant	Cont. Line	3 yrs.	July 31, '83
1454	Rains, John	100	Private	Cont. Line	3 yrs	July 31, '83
1458	Rice, George	400	Corporal	Cont. Line	war	Aug. 1, 1783
1483	Rankins, William	100	Private	Cont. Line	3 yrs.	Aug. 2, 1783
1485	Rankins, Robert	200	Sergeant	Cont. Line	3 yrs.	Aug. 2, 1783
1497	Robertson, Hugh	200	Sergeant	Cont. Line	3 yrs.	Aug. 5, 1783
1501	Rice, William	200	Private	Cont. Line	war	Aug. 6, 1783
1507	Rodden, John	100	Private	St. Line	3 yrs.	Aug. 6, 1783
1511	Rich, William	466⅔	Corporal	Cont. Line	war	Aug. 7, 1783
1524	Rhoads, William	200	Sergeant	Cont. Line	3 yrs.	Aug. 8, 1783
1529	Richards, Thomas	200	Private	Cont. Line	war	Aug. 11, '83
1553	Ramble, Samuel	100	Private	Cont. Line	3 yrs.	Aug. 16, '83
1575	Rhoads, William	100	Private	St. Line	3 yrs.	Aug. 20, '83
1591	Roberts, John	200	Private	Cont. Line	war	Aug. 21, '83
1613	Roberts, Obedience	2666⅔	Lieutenant	Cont. Art	3 yrs.	Aug. 22, '83
1624	Richeson, Walker	200	Private	Cont. Line	war	Aug. 22, '83
1632	Ross, Valentine	100	Private	Va. Cont. Line	3 yrs.	Aug. 23, '83
1640	Ransone, Robert	200	Private	Va. Cont. Line	war	Sept. 2, '83
1707	Rutter, Adam	100	Private	Va. Cont. Line	3 yrs.	Sept. 13, '83
1761	Randolph, John	200	Private	Va. Cont. Line	war	Sept. 30, '83
1801	Robertson, David	666⅔	Captain	St. Line	7 yrs.	Sept. 30, '83
1808	Roane, Christopher	400	Sergeant	Va. St. Line	war	Oct. 2, 1783
1816	Rose, Archibald	2666⅔	Lieutenant	Va. Cont. Line	3 yrs.	Oct. 11, '83
1847	Robins, John	200	Sergeant	Va. St. Line	3 yrs.	Oct. 11, '83
1848	Royster, John	200	Private	Va. St. Line	war	Oct. 11, '83
1849	Robinson, Mordecai	200	Private	Va. St. Line	war	Oct. 14, '83
1862	Robinson, Green	200	Private	Va. St. Line	3 yrs.	Oct. 15, '83
1879	Robinett, Joseph	233⅓	Private	Va. Cont. Line	7 yrs.	Oct. 25, '83
1916	Russell, Nicholas	100	Private	Va. Cont. Line	3 yrs.	Oct. 31, '83
④1844	Rock, John	200	Private	Va. Cont. Line	war	Oct. 31, '83
④1850	Rose, Robert	7000	Surgeon	Va. Cont. Line	7 yrs.	Nov. 1, 1783
④1864	Rose, William	100	Private	Va. St. Line	3 yrs.	Nov. 6, 1783
④1865	Ross, Jesse	100	Private	Va. St. Line	3 yrs.	Nov. 6, 1783
④1886	Ramsey, Francis	200	Private	Va. Cont. Line	war	Nov. 12, '83
1947	Russell, John	100	Private	Va. Cont. Line	3 yrs.	Nov. 12, '83
1985	Russell, Charles (William Russell, heir at law)	200	Corporal	Va. Cont. Line	3 yrs.	Nov. 28, '83
2023	Russell, William	2666⅔	Colonel	Va. Cont. Line	3 yrs.	Dec. 6, 1783
2027	Richardson, Richard	200	Private	Va. Cont. Line	war	Dec. 6, 1783
2028	Robinson, William	400	Sergeant	Va. Cont. Line	3 yrs.	Dec. 6, 1783
2059	Robertson, Mordecai (Samuel Griffin, assee.)	100	Private	Va. Cont. Line	3 yrs.	Dec. 9, 1783
2103	Reatley, James	200	Private	Va. Cont. Line	war	Dec. 12, '83
2127	Ridley, Thomas	5333⅓	Major	Va. Cont. Line	3 yrs.	Dec. 15, '83
2158	Robinson, John	2666⅔	Lieutenant	Va. Cont. Line	3 yrs.	Dec. 19, '83
2176	Rudd, Benjamin	100	Sailor	Va. St. Navy	3 yrs.	Dec. 20, '83
2231	Robinson, James	200	Corporal	Va. Cont. Line	3 yrs.	Jan. 12, '84
2234	Richardson, Robert	100	Private	Va. Cont. Line	3 yrs.	Jan. 12, '84
2242	Roney, John	3110⅔	Lieutenant	Va. Cont. Line	7 yrs.	Jan. 12, '84

LAND BOUNTY WARRANTS.

Warrant.	Name.	Acres	Rank.	Department.	Term	Date.
2245	RICKMAN, William (Elizabeth Rickman, widow. Res. of Assby. of Dec. 3, 1783)	6666⅔	Colonel	Va. Cont. Line	3 yrs.	Jan. 13, '84
2266	ROBERTSON, George	100	Private	Va. Cont. Line	3 yrs.	Jan. 21, '84
2290	REYNOLDS, William	200	Sergeant	Va. St. Line	3 yrs.	Jan. 26, '84
2339	ROGERS, John	200	Private	Va. Cont. Line	war	Jan. 31, '84
2358	RYLAND, John	400	Corporal	Va. Cont. Line	war	Jan. 31, '84
2414	RICHESON, Robert (John Depriest, assee.)	100	Private	Va. St. Line	3 yrs.	Feb. 5, 1784
2448	RICHARDSON, William (William Price, assee.)	100	Private	Va. St. Line	3 yrs.	Feb. 10, '84
2463	RIDLEY, Alexander (Lewis Ford, assee. of)	100	Private	Va. Cont. Line	3 yrs.	Feb. 11, '84
2471	ROACH, John (Daniel Feagan, assee. of)	200	Corporal	Va. Cont. Line	3 yrs.	Feb. 11, '84
2472	RANKINS, Benjamin (Francis Peyton, assee. of)	100	Private	Va. Cont. Line	3 yrs.	Feb. 11, '84
2478	REAGEN, Daniel (Price Bailey, assee.)	200	Sergeant	Va. St. Line	3 yrs.	Feb. 11, '84
2490	REAVES, James	100	Sailor	Va. St. Navy	3 yrs.	Feb. 13, '84
2507	RICHESON, Holt	6000	Lieut.-Col.	Va. Cont. Line	3 yrs.	Feb. 17, '84
2520	ROE, William	100	Private	Va. Cont. Line	3 yrs.	Feb. 19, '84
2529	REASONS, William	100	Private	Va. Cont. Line	3 yrs.	Feb. 19, '84
2531	ROGERS, Bernard	200	Sergeant	Va. Cont. Line	3 yrs.	Feb. 19, '84
2572	RICHARDS, John	200	Steward	Va. St. Navy	3 yrs.	Feb. 21, '84
2597	ROUX, Anthony Lee	200	Private	Va. Cont. Line	war	Feb. 23, '84
2604	ROWMAN, John	100	Private	Va. Cont. Line	3 yrs.	Feb. 24, '84
2621	RICE, William (Daniel Flowerree, assee.)	100	Private	Va. St. Line	3 yrs.	Feb. 24, '84
2632	REDWOOD, John	100	Private	Va. Cont. Line	3 yrs.	Feb. 25, '84
2639	ROBERTS, William (Daniel Perryman, assee.)	100	Private	Va. Cont. Line	3 yrs.	Feb. 26, '84
2658	ROBERTSON, Joseph	200	Private	Va. Cont. Line	war	Mch. 1, 1784
2663	RAPHITE, Jean	100	Private	Va. Cont. Line	3 yrs.	Mch. 1, 1784
2701	ROSSER, John	100	Private	Va. Cont. Line	3 yrs.	Mch. 4, 1784
2720	ROCK, William	200	Private	Va. Cont. Line	war	Mch. 6, 1784
2732	ROWSEL, Thomas (George Rowsel, heir at law)	100	Private	Va. St. Line	3 yrs.	Mch. 6, '84
2762	ROW, James	200	Corporal	Va. St. Line	3 yrs.	Mch. 15, '84
2778	RICE, Bardill (James Jenkins, assee.)	100	Private	Va. Cont. Line	3 yrs.	Mch. 18, '84
2802	RICHEE, James (Edward Valentine, assee.)	100	Private	Va. St. Line	3 yrs.	Mch. 22, '84
2825	ROBERTSON, James	100	Private	Va. Cont. Line	3 yrs.	Mch. 26, '84
2857	RIDER, Adam	100	Private	Va. Cont. Line	3 yrs.	Apr. 1, 1784
2896	RILEY, Daniel (James Rayburn, assee.)	200	Private	Va. Cont. Line	war	Apr. 6, 1784
2899	READ, Alexander	466⅔	Sergeant	Va. Cont. Line	7 yrs.	Apr. 6, 1784
2927	ROBERTS, Thomas	200	Sergeant	Va. Cont. Line	3 yrs.	Apr. 13, '84
2945	ROSE, Isaac	200	Corporal	Va. Cont. Line	3 yrs.	Apr. 17, '84
2954	ROBINSON, Maximillion (Laban Skip, assee.)	100	Private	Va. Cont. Line	3 yrs.	Apr. 17, '84
2959	RINKIN, Edward	200	Sergeant	Va. Cont. Line	3 yrs.	Apr. 17, '84
2974	RYAN, George	100	Private	Va. Cont. Line	3 yrs.	Apr. 20, '84
2995	REELOR, Maximillion	100	Private	Va. Cont. Line	3 yrs.	Apr. 21, '84
3052	RHODES, Elijah	100	Private	Va. Cont. Line	3 yrs.	May 7, 1784
3100	ROBINS, William	100	Private	Va. St. Line	3 yrs.	May 26, '84
3140	REDDICK, Jason (Thomas Reddick, heir at law)	4000	Captain	Va. Cont. Line	3 yrs.	June 10, '84
3141	REDDICK, Willis	4000	Captain	Va. Cont. Line	3 yrs.	June 10, '84
3151	ROBERTS, John	100	Private	Va. St. Line	3 yrs.	June 11, '84
3188	ROBERTS, Daniel	100	Private	Va. Cont. Line	3 yrs.	June 23, '84
3261	REYNOLDS, Aaron	200	Corporal	Va. Cont. Line	3 yrs.	June 30, '84
3296	RAY, David (John Ray, heir at law)	100	Private	Va. Cont. Line	3 yrs.	July 1, 1784
3324	ROTH, Frederick	200	Private	Va. St. Line	war	July 15, '84
3338	RUPORT, George	200	Private	Va. St. Line	war	July 19, '84
3350	RITCHER, John	100	Private	Va. Cont. Line	3 yrs.	July 22, '84
3427	RUSSELL, Ephraim (William Reynolds, assee.)	200	Private	Va. Cont. Line	war	Aug. 28, '84
3457	RICHARDSON, Daniel	2666⅔	Lieutenant	Va. St. Navy	3 yrs.	Oct. 7, 1784
3467	ROCK, John (James Davis, assee.)	200	Private	Va. Cont. Line	war	Oct. 18, '84
3481	RUST, Vincent (Francis Graves, assee. of Mathew Rust, heir at law to)	200	Private	Va. Cont. Line	war	Oct. 25, '84

LAND BOUNTY WARRANTS.

War-rant.	Name.	Acres	Rank.	Department.	Term	Date.
3482	Rust, George (Francis Graves, assee. of Mathew Rust, heir at law)	200	Private	Va. Cont. Line	war	Oct. 25, '84
3490	Robins, John	266⅔	Midshipman	Va. St. Navy	3 yrs.	Oct. 29, '84
3499	Rinker, Jesse	100	Private	Va. Cont. Line	3 yrs.	Nov. 4, 1784
3630	Russell, Andrew (Pamila and Penelope Russell, heirs at law)	2666⅔	Major	Va. Cont. Line	3 yrs.	Dec. 29, '84
3631	Russel, Andrew (Pamila and Penelope Russell, heirs at law)	2666⅔	Major	Va. Cont. Line	3 yrs.	Dec. 29, '84
3632	Rains, Henry	100	Private	Va. Cont. Line	3 yrs.	Dec. 29, '84
3648	Rawlins, Moses	200	Private	Va. Cont. Line	war	Dec. 31, '84
3659	Ray, Thomas	100	Private	Va. Cont. Line	3 yrs.	Dec. 31, '84
3667	Rutherford, Julius	100	Private	Va. Cont. Line	3 yrs.	Jan. 3, 1785
3694	Rankins, James	100	Private	Va. Cont. Line	3 yrs.	Jan. 20, '85
3698	Ritchie, Abraham	100	Private	Va. Cont. Line	3 yrs.	Jan. 20, '85
3699	Roberts, William	100	Private	Va. Cont. Line	3 yrs.	Jan. 20, '85
3702	Richard, Thomas	100	Private	Va. Cont. Line	3 yrs.	Jan. 20, '85
3706	Ritchie, William	100	Private	Va. Cont. Line	3 yrs.	Jan. 20, '85
3738	Roberts, John	400	Sergeant	Va. Cont. Line	war	Feb. 7, 1785
3746	Rains, Robert	200	Private	Va. Cont. Line	war	Feb. 7, 1785
3753	Roots, John (George Washington, assee. of)	3000	(See Foot Note.)			Feb. 14, '85
3756	Robertson, John	100	Private	Va. Cont. Line	3 yrs.	Feb. 18, '85
3779	Richardson, Mourning	100	Private	Va. Cont. Line	3 yrs.	Mch. 15, '85
3858	Resner, John (Jacob Campbell, assee.)	200	Private	Va. Cont. Line	war	May 6, 1785
3861	Ross, Elijah	100	Private	Va. St. Line	3 yrs.	May 7, 1785
3888	Randolph, Henry	200	Corporal	Va. Cont. Line	3 yrs.	June 9, 1785
3908	Roberts, Elisha (William Reynolds, assee. of Mary McDonald, heir at law)	200	Private	Va. Cont. Line	war	June 21, '85
3911	Russell, Thomas	100	Private	Va. Cont. Line	3 yrs.	June 21, '85
3954	Russell, Vincent (William Reynolds, assee.)	100	Private	Va. Cont. Line	3 yrs.	Aug. 12, '85
3985	Rowe, William	100	Private	Va. Cont. Line	3 yrs.	Oct. 21, '85
3993	Rose, Alexander	2000	Captain	Va. Cont. Line	3 yrs.	Nov. 11, '85
3994	Rose, Alexander	2000	Captain	Va. Cont. Line	3 yrs.	Nov. 11, '85
4005	Rosson, William (Thos. Rosson, heir at law)	100	Private	Va. Cont. Line	3 yrs.	Nov. 23, '85
4028	Roberts, George	200	Sergeant	Va. Cont. Line	3 yrs.	Dec. 9, 1785
4046	Robertson, Benjamin	200	Sergeant	Cont. Line	3 yrs.	Dec. 19, '85
4063	Riggs, Jacob	200	Private	Va. Cont. Line	war	Dec. 31, '85
4096	Ralph, Ephraim	2666⅔	Lieutenant	Va. Cont. Line	3 yrs.	Jan. 25, '86
4101	Ross, James	100	Private	Va. St. Line	3 yrs.	Jan. 30, '86
4111	Russell, William	100	Private	Va. Cont. Line	3 yrs.	Feb. 22, '86
4114	Rogers, Bowling (William Croghan, assee. of James Fair, assee. of)	200	Private	Va. Cont. Line	war	Mch. 4, 1786
4123	Richards, Boswell (George Richards, heir at law)	100	Private	Va. Cont. Line	3 yrs.	Mch. 10, '86
4137	Robinson, Andrew (William Reynolds, assee.)	100	Private	Va. St. Line	3 yrs.	Mch. 24, '86
4154	Ramsey, James	100	Private	Va. Cont. Line	3 yrs.	May 6, 1786
4177	Richards, Clement	100	Private	Va. Cont. Line	3 yrs.	June 20, '86
4180	Roe, William (William Reynolds, assee.)	2666⅔	Surgeon	Va. St. Navy	3 yrs.	June 22, '86
4198	Roberts, William (Margaret Roberts, wife)	100	Sailor	Va. St. Navy	3 yrs.	Aug. 26, '86
4214	Rollins, Dan'l (Sam'l Lamm, assee. of Wm. Reynolds, assee. of)	100	Private	Va. St. Line	3 yrs.	Oct. 4, 1786
4221	Ranger, Joseph	100	Sailor	Va. St. Navy	3 yrs.	Oct. 4, 1786
4236	Redman, Solomon (Jeremiah Bolling, heir at law)	100	Private	Va. Cont. Line	3 yrs.	Dec. 13, '86
4264	Reynolds, Wm	2666⅔	Lieutenant	Va. Cont. Line	3 yrs.	Mch. 25, '86
4288	Reason, Reuben (William Reason, heir at law)	100	Private	Va. Cont. Line	3 yrs.	May 25, '86
4380	Rice, Isaac (Wm. Reynolds, assee. of the rep.)	100	Private	Va. St. Line	3 yrs.	Jan. 29, '88
4404	Ravenscraft, Francis	100	Private	Va. Cont. Line	3 yrs.	June 11, '88
4425	Riggin, William (James Guthrie, rep)	100	Private	Va. St. Line	3 yrs.	July 17, '88

Note—("For a military warrant of 3,000 acres of land granted to John Roots by Lord Dunmore the 7th day of December, 1773, and assd. by the said Roots to George Washington, Esq., the 14th of February, 1774; exchanged by resolution of Assembly, passed the 30th of December, 1784.")

LAND BOUNTY WARRANTS.

Warrant.	Name.	Acres	Rank.	Department.	Term	Date.
4439	RADFORD, William (Wm. Reynolds, assee. of Francis Pierce, assee. of Jno. Radford, rep. of)	400	Sergeant	Va. Cont. Line	war	Oct. 25, '88
4513	ROBINSON, Cole	2666⅔	Ensign	Va. St. Line	3 yrs.	Dec. 9, 1790
4516	RYALLS, James	200	Private	Va. Cont. Line	war	Feb. 1, 1791
4556	RAMSEY, James (Peter Tardiveau, assee.)	200	Private	St. Line	war	Dec. 3, 1791

S

26	STITH, John	4000	Captain	Va. Cont. Line	3 yrs.	Nov. 30, '82
39	STEWART, William	100	Private	St. Art	3 yrs.	Dec. 11, '82
45	SLAYDEN, Daniel	100	Private	4th Reg. Lt. Drags.	3 yrs.	Dec. 13, '82
51	SCOTT, Joseph, Sr.	4666⅔	Captain	Va. Cont. Reg.	7 yrs.	Dec. 14, '82
63	SANSUM, Philip	4000	Captain	1st Va. Cont. Reg.	3 yrs.	Dec. 20, '82
69	SLAUGHTER, Phil	4000	Captain	Va. Cont. Line	3 yrs.	Dec. 23, '82
70	SMITH, Francis	2666⅔	Lieutenant	Army	3 yrs.	Dec. 24, '82
86	SWOPE, John	1000	Surgeon	St. Navy	3 yrs.	Jan. 2, 1783
87	SWOPE, John	5000	Surgeon	St. Navy	3 yrs.	Jan. 2, 1783
95	SPILLER, William	4000	Captain	Art. in St. Line	3 yrs.	Jan. 21, '83
104	STEUBEN, Maj.-Gen	15000	Maj.-Gen.	Per Act of Gen. Assby.	M'lty Serv.	Jan. 30, '83
111	SHELTON, Clough	4000	Captain	Cont. Va. Line	3 yrs.	Feb. 3, 1783
118	SAVAGE, Nathaniel	2666⅔	Lieutenant	Cav. of St. Line	3 yrs.	Feb. 8, 1783
124	SMITH, Gregory	6666⅔	Colonel	St. Line	3 yrs.	Feb. 13, '83
127	SMITH, Jonathan	2666⅔	Lieutenant	Va. Line	3 yrs.	Feb. 13, '83
137	STARK, Richard	2666⅔	Lieutenant	Va. Line	3 yrs.	Feb. 20, '83
146	SMITH, Wm. S.	2666⅔	Lieutenant	6th Va. Cont. Reg.	3 yrs.	Feb. 24, '83
175	SAUNDERS, Caley (John Saunders, heir at law and legal rep.)	4666⅔	Captain	St. Navy		Mch. 12, '83
185	SMITH, Aaron	200	Private	Va. Cont. Line	war	Mch. 19, '83
200	SMITH, Ballard	2666⅔	Lieutenant	Va. Line	3 yrs.	Mch. 26, '83
212	SLAUGHTER, William	2666⅔	Lieutenant	Va. St. Line	3 yrs.	Mch. 31, '83
222	SPRINGER, Uriah	2000	Captain	Va. Cont. Line	3 yrs.	Apr. 1, 1783
223	SPRINGER, Uriah	2000	Captain	Va. Cont. Line	3 yrs.	Apr. 1, 1783
228	SPRINGER, Jacob	1300	Captain	Va. Cont. Line	3 yrs.	Apr. 1, 1783
229	SPRINGER, Jacob	1366⅔	Lieutenant	Va. Cont. Line	3 yrs.	Apr. 1, 1783
246	SLAUGHTER, Lawrence (Thomas Slaughter, heir at law)	2666⅔	Lieutenant	St. Line	3 yrs.	Apr. 1, 1783
252	STEWART, Solomon (Rev. Robert Andrews, assee.)	100	Private	St. Line	3 yrs.	Apr. 3, 1783
290	SHEPHERD, Abraham	4000	Captain	Va. Cont. Line	3 yrs.	Apr. 5, 1783
341	SWEARINGEN, Joseph	4000	Captain	Va. Cont. Line	3 yrs.	Apr. 15, '83
347	STEPHENSON, David	6222	Major	Va. Cont. Line	7 yrs.	Apr. 16, '83
351	SIMMS, Charles	6000	Lieut.-Col.	Va. Line	3 yrs.	Apr. 17, '83
403	SIMMS, Edward	200	Sergeant	Va. St. Line	3 yrs.	Apr. 25, '83
413	SMITH, William	200	Private	Va. St. Line	war	Apr. 25, '83
419	STAVES, William	200	Private	Va. St. Line	war	Apr. 26, '83
422	SUMMERS, James	200	Private	Va. St. Line	war	Apr. 26, '83
500	SANDERFORD, Samuel	200	Private	St. Line	war	May 1, 1783
509	SHELTON, Thomas	200	Private	St. Line	war	May 1, 1783
511	SCOTT, James	200	Private	St. Line	war	May 1, 1783
522	SHEFFIELD, Peter (James Fear, assee.)	200	Private	St. Line	war	May 1, 1783
523	SANFORD, John	200	Private	St. Line	war	May 1, 1783
535	SPRATLEY, Richard	200	Corporal	Va. Cont. Line	3 yrs.	May 2, 1783
543	SMITH, Underwood	100	Private	St. Line		May 3, 1783
567	SCOTT, William	400	Sergeant	Va. St. Line	war	May 9, 1783
569	SIMMONS, George	100	Sergeant	Va. St. Line	3 yrs.	May 12, '83
572	SINGLETON, Joshua	2666⅔	Lieutenant	St. Navy		May 12, '83
573	SMAW, John	200	Sergeant	Va. Cont. Line	3 yrs.	May 13, '83
597	SPOTTSWOOD, John	4000	Captain	Va. Cont. Line	3 yrs.	May 20, '83
602	STEEL, John	2666⅔	Lieutenant	Va. Cont. Line	3 yrs.	May 20, '83
605	SAUNDERS, William	4000	Captain	Va. St. Navy	3 yrs.	May 20, '83
616	STUBBS, Francis	100	Private	Va. St. Line	3 yrs.	May 21, '83
619	SMITH, Larkin	4000	Captain	Va. Cont. Line	3 yrs.	May 22, '83
623	SHEARMAN, Robert	200	Fife Major	Va. Cont. Line	3 yrs.	May 23, '83
644	SLAUGHTER, John	100	Private	Va. Cont. Line	3 yrs.	May 26, '83
685	SMITH, Obadiah	2666⅔	Lieutenant	Va. Cont. Line	3 yrs.	May 30, '83
704	SYKES, George	100	Private	Va. St. Line	3 yrs.	May 31, '83
736	SKINNER, Alexander	6000	Reg. Surg'n.	Va. Cont. Line	3 yrs.	June 4, 1783
752	SMART, Richard	2666⅔	M'ter's Mate	Va. St. Navy	3 yrs.	June 5, 1783
767	SMITH, Michael	200	Sergeant	Va. Cont. Line	3 yrs.	June 7, 1783
793	STOKELEY, Charles	2666⅔	Lieutenant	Va. Cont. Line	3 yrs.	June 12, '83

LAND BOUNTY WARRANTS. 67

Warrant.	Name	Acres	Rank	Department	Term	Date
815	Scott, Charles	11 666⅔	Brig. Gen...	Va. Cont. Line.....	3 yrs.	June 14, '83
826	Steed, John	4000	Captain ...	Va. Cont. Line.....	3 yrs.	June 14, '83
865	Shurles, Benjamin	100	Private	Va. Cont. Art.....	3 yrs.	June 18, '83
878	Spence, Henry	100	Private	Va. Cont. Art.....	3 yrs.	June 19, '83
899	Sublett, Benjamin	200	Sergeant ...	Va. Cont. Line.....	3 yrs.	June 20, '83
907	Stokes, Robert	200	Private	Va. Cont. Line.....	war	June 20, '83
908	Sparks, Samuel	200	Private	Va. Cont. Line.....	war	June 20, '83
914	Stotherd, Thomas	100	Private	Va. Cont. Line.....	3 yrs.	June 20, '83
930	Smith, George	100	Private	Va. Cont. Line.....	3 yrs.	June 20, '83
933	Stump, Michael	100	Private	Va. Cont. Line.....	3 yrs.	June 20, '83
950	Sollers, William	100	Private	Va. Cont. Line.....	3 yrs.	June 20, '83
954	Smith, John	100	Private	Va. Cont. Line.....	3 yrs.	June 20, '83
992	Smith, Francis	100	Fifer	Va. St. Line......	3 yrs.	June 21, '83
996	Stribling, Segismond	4666⅔	Captain ...	Va. Cont. Line.....	7 yrs.	June 21, '83
998	Solloman, George	100	Private	Va. Cont. Line.....	3 yrs.	June 21, '83
1002	Simmons, Bryan	100	Private	Va. Cont. Line.....	3 yrs.	June 21, '83
1022	Smock, Jacob	200	Sergeant ...	Va. Cont. Line.....	3 yrs.	June 23, '83
1023	Shores, Thomas	100	Private	Va. Cont. Line.....	3 yrs.	June 23, '83
1025	Shannon, Patrick	200	Sergeant ...	Va. Cont. Line.....	3 yrs.	June 23, '83
1041	Smith, John	200	Drummer ..	Va. Cont. Line.....	war	June 24, '83
1057	Smith, William	200	Private	Va. Cont. Line.....	war	June 24, '83
1062	Smith, Samuel	200	Private	Va. Cont. Line.....	war	June 24, '83
1074	Sharrow, Richard	200	Private	Va. Cont. Line.....	war	June 24, '83
1075	Smith, Michael	200	Private	Va. Cont. Line.....	war	June 24, '83
1086	Smith, James	200	Private	Va. Cont. Line.....	war	June 24, '83
1115	Shea, John	200	Private	Va. Cont. Line.....	war	June 24, '83
1136	Stackpole, James	200	Private	Va. Cont. Line.....	war	June 24, '83
1141	Stephard, Edward	200	Private	Va. Cont. Line.....	war	June 24, '83
1142	Skinner, Henry	200	Private	Va. Cont. Line.....	war	June 24, '83
1159	Snead, Smith	6222	Major	Va. Cont. Line.....	7 yrs.	June 24, '83
1171	Stubblefield, George (Benjamin Stubblefield, heir at law)	2666⅔	Ensign	Va. Cont. Line.....	3 yrs.	June 25, '83
1176	Spruce, John	100	Private	Va. Cont. Line.....	3 yrs.	June 25, '83
1203	Stubblefield, Beverly	4000	Captain ...	Va. Cont. Line.....	3 yrs.	June 26, '83
1206	Straughan, John	100	Private ...	Va. Cont. Line.....	3 yrs.	June 26, '83
1235	Simmons, Joshua	400	Fife Major.	Va. Cont. Line.....	war	June 27, '83
1240	Shields, James	100	Private ...	Va. Cont. Line.....	3 yrs.	June 27, '83
1247	Simms, Isaac	200	Private	Va. Cont. Line.....	war	June 27, '83
1253	Simmons, James	200	Private	Va. Cont. Line.....	war	June 27, '83
1265	Sell, George	200	Private	Va. Cont. Line.....	war	June 27, '83
1266	Smithy, Benjamin	100	Private	Va. Cont. Line.....	3 yrs.	June 27, '83
1280	Simmons, Williamson	233⅓	Private	Va. Cont. Line.....	7 yrs.	June 28, '83
1281	Sample, James	100		Va. Cont. Line.....	war	June 28, '83
1293	Southworth, Thomas	200	Private ...	Va. St. Line......	war	June 28, '83
1315	Scott, William	233⅓	Drummer ..	Va. Cont. Line.....	7 yrs.	July 1, 1783
1319	Skinner, Richard	100	Private ...	Va. Cont. Line.....	3 yrs.	July 2, 1783
1323	Son, Anthony	400	Sergeant ...	Va. Cav	war	July 3, 1783
1333	Splann, Thomas	100	Private ...	St. Line	3 yrs.	July 5, 1783
1363	Snead, Holman	100	Private ...	Va. Art	3 yrs.	July 12, '83
1364	Sullivan, John	200	Corporal ..	St. Line	war	July 12, '83
1396	Stokes, John	4666⅔	Captain ...	Cont. Line	7 yrs.	July 19, '83
1401	Steneham, Henry	400	Corporal ...	Cont. Line	war	July 21, '83
1405	Stephens, Thomas	466⅔	Corporal ...	Cont. Line	7 yrs.	July 21, '83
1421	Smith, Elijah	100	Private ...	Cont. Line	3 yrs.	July 22, '83
1430	Smith, William	200	Sergeant ...	Cont. Line	3 yrs.	July 27, 83
1453	Smith, Jacob	100	Private ...	Cont. Line	3 yrs	July 31, '83
1459	Stur, Thomas	100	Sailor	St. Navy	3 yrs.	Aug. 1, 1783
1489	Smith, John	200	Private ...	Cont. Line	war	Aug. 4, 1783
1508	Slate, James	400	Corporal ...	Cont. Line	war	Aug. 6, 1783
1510	Stewart, Patrick	100	Private ...	Cont. Line	3 yrs.	Aug. 6, 1783
1513	Satterwhite, John	400	Sergeant ..	Cont. Line	war	Aug. 6, 1783
1516	Shay, Dennis	200	Private ...	Cont. Line	war	Aug. 7, 1783
1527	Span, Richard	100	Private ...	Cont. Line	3 yrs.	Aug. 8, 1783
1528	Span, James	100	Private ...	Cont. Line	3 yrs.	Aug. 8, 1783
1562	Salmon, George	400	Sergeant ...	Cont. Line	war	Aug. 12, '83
1566	Stern, Charles	200	Sergeant ...	Cont. Line	3 yrs.	Aug. 13, '83
1569	Stokely, Charles	444	Lieutenant .	Cont. Line	7 yrs.	Aug. 14, '83
1579	Summerson, Gavin	2666⅔	Midshipman.	St. Navy	3 yrs.	Aug. 18, '83
1593	Swart, James	200	Private ...	Cont. Line	war	Aug. 20, '83
1628	Smithers, Stephen	466⅔	Sergeant ...	Cont. Line	7 yrs.	Aug. 22, '83
1635	Scott, John	200	Private ...	Va. Cont. Line.....	3 yrs.	Aug. 23, '83
1648	Smith, James	200	Private ...	Va. Cont. Line.....	war	Aug. 23, '83
1672	Steel, William	1000	Lieutenant .	Va. St. Navy.....	3 yrs.	Aug. 26, '83
1673	Steel, William	1666⅔	Lieutenant .	Va. St. Navy.....	3 yrs.	Aug. 26, '83
1689	Simpson, John	100	Private ...	Va. Cont. Line.....	3 yrs	Aug. 30, '83
1714	Stacey, John	100	Private ...	Va. St. Line......	3 yrs.	Sept. 2, 1783

LAND BOUNTY WARRANTS.

Warrant.	Name.	Acres	Rank.	Department.	Term	Date.
1715	ST. LEGER, William	100	Private	Va. St. Line	3 yrs.	Sept. 2, 1783
1717	SANDERS, Presley	200	Sergeant	Va. Cont. Line	3 yrs.	Sept. 2, 1783
1718	SANDERS, Joseph	2666⅔	Lieutenant	Va. St. Navy	3 yrs.	Sept. 2, 1783
1722	SHEARMAN, Martin	2666⅔	Midshipman	Va. St. Navy	3 yrs.	Sept. 2, 1783
1729	SMITH, John	100	Private	Va. Cont. Line	3 yrs.	Sept. 2, 1783
1736	SHELTON, David	100	Private	Va. Cont. Line	3 yrs.	Sept. 8, 1783
1770	SMITH, William	200	Drummer	Va. Cont. Line	3 yrs.	Sept. 10, '83
1778	SCOTT, Robert	200	Corporal	Va. Cont. Line	war	Sept. 17, '83
1782	SOMERS, William	200	Corporal	Va. Cont. Line	3 yrs.	Sept. 20, '83
1791	STEVENS, William	2666⅔	Lieutenant	Va. Cont. Line	3 yrs.	Sept. 23, '83
1793	SMITH, Stephen	100	Private	Va. St. Line	3 yrs.	Sept. 25, '83
1798	SCOTT, Walter	2666⅔	Lieutenant	Va. St. Line	3 yrs.	Sept. 25, '83
1813	SAUNDERS, Richard	2666⅔	Midshipman	Va. St. Navy	3 yrs.	Sept. 29, '83
1839	STEVENS, John (Joseph Stevens, heir at law)	200	Sergeant	Va. Cont. Line	3 yrs.	Oct. 1, 1783
1843	SMITH, William	2666⅔	Lieutenant	Va. Cont. Line	3 yrs.	Oct. 9, 1783
1852	STITH, John	4000	Captain	Va. Cont. Line	3 yrs.	Oct. 10, '83
1854	STEWART, Benjamin	233⅓	Private	Va. Cont. Line	7 yrs.	Oct. 13, '83
1865	SINGLETON, Joshua	200	Sergeant	Va. St. Line	3 yrs.	Oct. 14, '83
1884	SCOTT, John	4000	Captain	Va. St. Line	3 yrs.	Oct. 16, '83
1887	SCOTT, Joseph, Jr.	4000	Captain	Va. Cont. Line	3 yrs.	Oct. 17, '83
1901	STARKS, Wm., alias "Harrison"	100	Drummer	Va. Cont. Line	3 yrs.	Oct. 21, '83
1907	SUMMERSON, George	200	Private	Va. Cont. Line	war	Oct. 23, '83
1923	STRAUGHAN, Presley (Presley Straughan, heir at law)	100	Private	Va. Cont. Line	3 yrs.	Oct. 27, '83
②1879	SPENCER, Abraham	200	Private	Va. St. Navy	war	Nov. 8, 1783
②1896	SHELDON, Thomas, alias "Chilton"	533½	Fife Major	Va. Cont. Line	8 yrs.	Nov. 12, '83
③1902	SLAVEN, Cornelius (Cornelius Slaven, Jr., heir at law)	100	Private	St. Line	3 yrs.	Nov. 17, '83
②1917	STEVENS, Edward	5000	Brig. Gen.	Va. Cont. Line	3 yrs.	Nov. 21, '83
②1918	STEVENS, Edward	3000	Brig. Gen.	Va. Cont. Line	3 yrs.	Nov. 21, '83
③1919	STEVENS, Edward	2000	Brig. Gen.	Va. Cont. Line	3 yrs.	Nov. 21, '83
1941	SANDEFER, Samuel	100	Private	Va. Cont. Line	3 yrs.	Nov. 22, '83
1945	SCOTT, James	100	Private	Va. Cont. Line	3 yrs.	Nov. 22, '83
1980	SCARS, Thomas	100	Private	Va. Cont. Line	3 yrs.	Nov. 24, '83
1999	SMITH, Thomas	100	Private	Va. Cont. Line	3 yrs.	Nov. 29, '83
2012	SCOTT, Major-General Charles	1666⅔	Brigadier	Va. Cont. Line	8th yr	Dec. 5, 1783
2015	STANLEY, William	100	Private	Va. Cont. Line	3 yrs.	Dec. 5, 1783
2016	STONE, William	100	Private	Va. St. Line	3 yrs.	Dec. 5, 1783
2036	STACEY, Simon	100	Private	Va. Cont. Line	3 yrs.	Dec. 6, 1783
2066	SORRELL, James (Samuel Griffin, assee.)	100	Private	Va. St. Line	3 yrs.	Dec. 9, 1783
2076	SAMMONS, John	100	Private	Va. St. Line	3 yrs.	Dec. 10, '83
2085	SMALL, Henry	100	Private	Va. Cont. Line	3 yrs.	Dec. 10, '83
2087	SCOTT, William	100	Private	Va. Cont. Line	3 yrs.	Dec. 10, '83
2112	SLATE, John	200	Corporal	Va. Cont. Line	3 yrs.	Dec. 13, '83
2120	SINGLETON, Anthony	4000	Captain	Va. Cont. Line	3 yrs.	Dec. 13, '83
2123	STOKES, Christopher (Bowler Clark, assee.)	200	Sergeant	Va. Cont. Line	3 yrs.	Dec. 13, '83
2132	SANLEE, William	100	Private	Va. St. Line	3 yrs.	Dec. 15, '83
2188	SIMPSON, Spencer	100	Private	Va. Cont. Line	3 yrs.	Dec. 22, '83
2206	SOLES, William	100	Private	Va. Cont. Line	3 yrs.	Dec. 23, '83
2207	SHACKLEFORD, Mag	100	Private	Va. Cont. Line	3 yrs.	Dec. 23, '83
2208	SHACKLEFORD, Henry	100	Private	Va. Cont. Line	3 yrs.	Dec. 23, '83
2228	SLAUGHTER, Nathaniel (John Slaughter, heir at law)	100	Private	Va. Cont. Line	3 yrs.	Dec. 23, '83
2254	SEAY, Reuben (Samuel Dyer, assee.)	100	Private	Va. St. Line	3 yrs.	Jan. 12, '84
2270	SOUTHALL, Stephen	2666⅔	Lieutenant	Va. Cont. Line	war	Jan. 21, '84
2277	SALUSBURY, Newman	200	Private	Va. Cont. Line	war	Jan. 22, '84
2291	SELDON, Samuel	2666⅔	Lieutenant	Va. Cont. Line	war	Jan. 23, '84
2306	STAPE, Thomas	200	Private	Va. Cont. Line	3 yrs.	Jan. 26, '84
2330	SHEPHERD, David (John Depriest, assee.)	100	Private	Va. Cont. Line	war	Jan. 28, '84
2334	SPENCER, Beverley	100	Private	Va. Cont. Line	3 yrs.	Jan. 31, '84
2338	STEWART, Philip	100	Private	Va. Cont. Line	3 yrs.	Jan. 31, '84
2344	SHIRES, Nicholas (William Reynolds, assee.)	2666⅔	Lieutenant	Va. Cont. Line	war	Jan. 31, '84
2363	SCOTT, Drury	200	Private	Va. Cont. Line	war	Jan. 31, '84
2409	SHEPHERD, James	200	Private	Va. Cont. Line	war	Feb. 2, 1784
2413	STEPHENS, Richard	200	Sergeant	Va. St. Line	3 yrs.	Feb. 5, 1784
2418	SEARS, Thomas	100	Private	Va. Cont. Line	3 yrs.	Feb. 5, 1784
2423	SAVOY, John	2666⅔	Lieutenant	Va. Cont. Line	war	Feb. 6, 1784
		200	Private	Va. St. Line	war	Feb. 6, 1784

LAND BOUNTY WARRANTS. 69

Warrant.	Name.	Acres	Rank.	Department.	Term	Date.
2433	Starke, William (Lewis Starke, assee. of Burwell Starke, who was legal rep.)	2666⅔	Lieutenant	Va. Cont. Line	3 yrs.	Feb. 9, 1784
2444	Scott, Charles	2666⅔	Cornet	Va. Cont. Line	war	Feb. 10, '84
2446	Shelton, Clough	666⅔	Captain	Va. Cont. Line	7th yr	Feb. 10, '84
2451	Spencer, William	2666⅔	Lieutenant	Va. St. Line	war	Feb. 11, '84
2498	Slaughter, John	2666⅔	Subaltern	Va. Cont. Line	3 yrs.	Feb. 14, '84
2506	Self, Larkin	200	Private	Va. Cont. Line	war	Feb. 17, '84
2510	Sneed, John (Ambrose Lipscomb, assee. of)	100	Private	Va. Cont. Line	3 yrs.	Feb. 18, '84
2524	Sutton, Benjamin	200	Corporal	Va. Cont. Line	3 yrs.	Feb. 19, '84
2526	Sutton, Rowland	100	Private	Va. Cont. Line	3 yrs.	Feb. 19, '84
2534	Strother, William	400	Sergeant	Va. Cont. Line	war	Feb. 19, '84
2544	Smithy, Robert	100	Private	Va. Cont. Line	3 yrs.	Feb. 19, '84
2548	Scott, John	100	Private	Va. Cont. Line	3 yrs.	Feb. 20, '84
2549	Scott, Joseph	100	Private	Va. Cont. Line	3 yrs.	Feb. 20, '84
2600	Spearman, James	200	Sergeant	Va. St. Line	3 yrs.	Feb. 23, '84
2609	Scott, John	2666⅔	Subaltern	Va. Cont. Line	war	Feb. 24, '84
2617	Strange, William (Daniel Flowerree, assee.)	100	Private	Va. St. Line	3 yrs.	Feb. 24, '84
2623	Smith, Andrew (Daniel Flowerree, assee.)	100	Private	Va. St. Line	3 yrs.	Feb. 24, '84
2628	Savage, Joseph	2666⅔	Surg's Mate	Va. Cont. Line	3 yrs.	Feb. 25, '84
2643	Stokes, Silvanus	100	Private	Va. Cont. Line	3 yrs.	Feb. 26, '84
2659	Swillivant, James	100	Private	Va. Cont. Line	3 yrs.	Mch. 1, 1784
2676	Stevens, James	100	Private	Va. St. Line	3 yrs.	Mch. 3, 1784
2692	Sixton, William (Benoni Perryman, assee.)	100	Private	Va. Cont. Line	3 yrs.	Mch. 3, 1784
2707	Stacey, Stephen	100	Private	Va. Cont. Line	3 yrs.	Mch. 4, 1784
2722	Sebry, William	200	Private	Va. Cont. Line	war	Mch. 6, 1784
2734	Smothers, William	200	Private	Va. Cont. Line	war	Mch. 6, 1784
2746	Suddoth, William	100	Private	Va. Cont. Line	3 yrs.	Mch. 10, '84
2750	Stevens, John (Joshua Stevens, heir at law)	100	Private	Va. Cont. Line	3 yrs.	Mch. 10, '84
2771	Smith, John (James Jenkins, assee.)	100	Private	Va. Cont. Line	3 yrs.	Mch. 18, '84
2773	Saymore, William (James Jenkins, assee.)	100	Private	Va. Cont. Line	3 yrs.	Mch. 18, '84
2776	Seay, James (James Jenkins, assee.)	100	Private	Va. Cont. Line	3 yrs.	Mch. 18, '84
2786	Smith, Isaac	100	Private	Va. Cont. Line	3 yrs.	Mch. 18, '84
2791	Smith, Isaac	200	Sergeant	Va. Cont. Line	3 yrs.	Mch. 19, '84
2805	Stevens, John (Edward Valentine, assee.)	100	Private	Va. St. Line	war	Mch. 22, '84
2810	Stubbs, Allen	200	Private	Va. Cont. Line	war	Mch. 23, '84
2813	Spencer, John (William Reynolds, assee.)	2666⅔	Lieutenant	Va. St. Line	3 yrs.	Mch. 24, '83
2828	Sims, Thomas (George Sims, legal rep.)	200	Sergeant	Va. Cont. Line	3 yrs.	Mch. 26, '84
2835	Sebastian, Benjamin (Lawrence Muse, assee.)	233⅓	Private	Va. Cont. Line	3 yrs.	Mch. 27, '84
2838	Sneed, Thomas	100	Private	Va. Cont. Line	3 yrs.	Mch. 27, '84
2850	Stockdell, John	100	Private	Va. Cont. Line	3 yrs.	Mch. 30, '8
2858	Settle, Strother	2666⅔	Lieutenant	Va. Cont. Line	war	Apr. 2, 1784
2865	Shanks, James	100	Private	Va. Cont. Line	3 yrs.	Apr. 2, '84
2870	Stoll, William	2666⅔	Lieutenant	Va. St. Navy	3 yrs.	Apr. 3, 1784
2889	Simpson, Jeremiah	200	Sergeant	Va. Cont. Line	3 yrs.	Apr. 5, 1784
2915	Settle, Benjamin	200	Corporal	Va. St. Line	3 yrs.	Apr. 12, '84
2919	Smith, John	100	Private	Va. Cont. Line	3 yrs.	Apr. 12, '84
2928	Sledd, Seaton (William Reynolds, assee.)	100	Private	Va. Cont. Line	3 yrs.	Apr. 13, '84
2930	Shackleford, William (Wm. Reynolds, assee. of John Shackleford, the rep. of William Shackleford)	2666⅔	Lieutenant	Va. Cont. Line	3 yrs.	Apr. 13, '84
2932	Smith, Granville	2666⅔	Ensign	Va. St. Line	3 yrs.	Apr. 15, '84
2956	Street, John	100	Private	Crockett's St. Bat'l.	3 yrs.	Apr. 17, '84
2960	Smith, Nathan	2666⅔	Surg's Mate	Va. Cont. Line	war	Apr. 19, '84
2979	Sallards, Eliphalet	100	Private	Va. St. Line	3 yrs.	Apr. 20, '84
2988	Stephenson, Hugh (Richard Stephenson, heir at law)	6666⅔	Colonel	Va. Cont. Line	3 yrs.	Apr. 21, '84
3006	Scott, Littleberry	200	Private	Va. Cont. Line	war	Apr. 23, '84
3039	Swan, John	4666⅔	Captain	Va. Cont. Line	7 yrs.	May 3, 1784
3041	Shields, John (John Shields, heir at law)	4000	Captain	Va. St. Line	3 yrs.	May 4, 1784

LAND BOUNTY WARRANTS.

Warrant.	Name.	Acres	Rank.	Department.	Term	Date.
3044	Stringfellow, David (Henry Stringfellow, heir at law)....	400	Sergeant	Va. Cont. Line.....	war	May 4, 1784
3045	Southerland, William	233½	Private	Va. Cont. Line.....	7 yrs.	May 4, 1784
3046	Shirley, James	100	Private	Va. Cont. Line.....	3 yrs.	May 5, 1784
3064	Smith, Francis	100	Private	Va. Cont. Line.....	3 yrs.	May 10, '84
3073	Suddoth, John (William Reynolds, assee.)	100	Private	Va. Cont. Line.....	3 yrs.	May 11, '84
3075	Slaughter, William	666⅔	Lieutenant .	Va. St. Line.......	7th yr.	May 12, '84
3085	Sydnor, Fortunatus	200	Private	Va. Cont. Line.....	war	May 21, '84
3095	Sorrell, Richard (James Sorrell, heir at law)..........	100	Private	Va. Cont. Line.....	3 yrs.	May 24, '84
3101	Scott, Matthew (William Scott, assee.).................	200	Sergeant	Va. Cont. Line.....	3 yrs.	May 26, '84
3131	Slaughter, Francis L........	200	Private	Va. Cont. Line.....	war	June 5, 1784
3146	Smith, Joseph	100	Private	Va. Cont. Line.....	3 yrs.	June 10, '84
3150	Sanders, John	200	Private	Va. Cont. Line.....	war	June 11, '84
3155	Salurons, Henry	100	Private	Va. Cont. Line.....	3 yrs.	June 12, '84
3176	Skinner, Alexander	1000	Regtl. Surg.	Va. Cont. Line.....	7th yr	May 12, '84
3182	Smith, William	100	Private	Va. Cont. Line.....	3 yrs.	June 22, '84
3186	Standley, Moses	100	Private	Va. St. Line.......	3 yrs.	June 22, '84
3187	Scott, John	2666⅔	Subaltern . .	Va. Cont. Line.....	3 yrs.	June 23, '84
3218	Scott, John	100	Sailor	Va. St. Navy......	3 yrs.	June 26, '84
3259	Sullivan, Craven	100	Private	Va. St. Line.......	3 yrs.	June 30, '84
3291	Stanback, Littleberry	100	Sailor	Va. St. Navy......	3 yrs.	July 1, 1784
3304	Smith, John	100	Private	Va. Cont. Line.....	3 yrs.	July 2, 1874
3323	Stoakes, Zachariah (James Taylor, assee.)	100	Private	Va. St. Line.......	3 yrs.	July 14, '84
3328	Smith, William	200	Private	Va. St. Line.......	war	July 19, '84
3347	Sanderson, Samuel	100	Private	Va. Cont. Line.....	3 yrs.	July 22, '84
3349	Stephens, Edward	200	Sergeant	Va. Cont. Line.....	3 yrs.	July 22, '84
3355	Sullivan, Frederick (Thomas Clay, assee.)	100	Private	Va. St. Line.......	3 yrs.	July 23, '84
3366	Stewart, Edward	100	Private	Va. St. Line.......	3 yrs.	July 29, '84
3379	Sheffield, Thomas	100	Private	Va. St. Line.......	3 yrs.	Aug. 5, 1784
3385	Stevens, Peter (Matthew Pate, assee. of Robt. Taylor, who was assee. of)...............	200	Sergeant	Va. Cont. Line.....	3 yrs.	Aug. 10, '84
3389	Sturdivan, John	200	Private	Va. Cont. Line.....	war	Aug. 11, '84
3407	Stubbs, Allen (Samuel Brooking, assee.).................	100	Private	Va. Cont. Line.....	3 yrs.	Aug. 23, '84
3410	Shepherd, David	100	Private	Va. Cont. Line.....	3 yrs.	Aug. 25, '84
3414	Scarbrough, John	2666⅔	Lieutenant .	Va. Cont. Line.....	3 yrs.	Aug. 26, '84
3435	Spinner, Richard	100	Private	Va. St. Line.......	3 yrs.	Sept. 10, '84
3436	Snugss, George	100	Private	Va. Cont. Line.....	3 yrs.	Sept. 10, '84
3478	Stribling, William	400	Sergeant	Va. Cont. Line.....	war	Oct. 22, '84
3495	Suddoth, William	200	Corporal . .	Va. Cont. Line.....	3 yrs.	Nov. 3, '784
3504	Stackhouse, John	100	Private	Va. Cont. Line.....	3 yrs.	Nov. 4, 1784
3507	Smith, William (Samuel Demovell, assee. of)............	100	Boatswain .	Va. St. Navy......	3 yrs.	Nov. 8, 1784
3517	Smith, Minor	100	Private	Va. Cont. Line.....	3 yrs.	Nov. 11, '84
3525	Shackleford, Alexander	100	Private	Va. St. Line.......	3 yrs.	Nov. 20, '84
3535	Scott, George	100	Private	Va. Cont. Line.....	3 yrs.	Nov. 24, '84
3538	Slaughter, George	2500	Major	Per Res. of Gen. Assby. of 6th Nov., 1784		Nov. 24, '84
3539	Slaughter, George	1000	Major	Per Res. of Gen. Assby. of 6th Nov., 1784		Nov. 24, '84
3540	Slaughter, George	1833½	Major	Per Res. of Gen. Assby. of 6th Nov., 1784		Nov. 24, '84
3541	Slaughter, Augustine	3000	Surgeon . .	Per Res. of Gen. Assby. of 6th Nov., 1784		Nov. 24, '84
3542	Slaughter, Augustine	3000	Surgeon . .	Per Res. of Gen. Assby., 6th Nov., 1784		Nov. 24, '84
3547	Stokes, John (Benjamin Stokes, heir at law)...............	100	Private	Va. St. Line.......	3 yrs.	Nov. 30, '84
3551	Sanduskie, Jonathan (Samuel Sanduskie, heir at law)......	100	Private	Va. Cont. Line.....	3 yrs.	Dec. 6, 1784
3525	Shackleford, Alexander	100	Private	Va. Cont. Line.....	3 yrs.	Dec. 6, 1784
3561	Sinah, John	100	Private	Va. Cont. Line.....	3 yrs.	Dec. 8, 1784
3585	Sommers, Simon	4000	Adjutant . .	Va. Cont. Line.....	3 yrs.	Dec. 17, '84
3601	Shoup, William (John Bartlett, assee.)...................	400	Sergeant	Va. Cont. Line.....	war	Dec. 21, '84
3605	Samuel, Gray	200	Sergeant	Va. St. Line.......	3 yrs.	Dec. 22, '84

LAND BOUNTY WARRANTS.

Warrant.	Name.	Acres	Rank.	Department.	Term	Date.
3613	STRINGFELLOW, Henry	200	Private	Va. Cont. Line	war	Dec. 23, '84
3620	STEPHENS, John	100	Private	Va. Cont. Line	3 yrs.	Dec. 23, '84
3623	SAYERS, Robert (Res., Gen. Assby., Dec. 18, 1784)	1000	Captain	Va. Cont. Line		Dec. 27, '84
3624	SAYERS, Robert (Res., Gen. Assby., Dec. 18, 1784)	1000	Captain	Va. Cont. Line		Dec. 27, '84
3625	SAYERS, Robert (Res., Gen. Assby., Dec. 18, 1784)	1000	Captain	Va. Cont. Line		Dec. 27, '84
3626	SAYERS, Robert (Res., Gen. Assby., Dec. 18, 1784)	1000	Captain	Va. Cont. Line		Dec. 27, '84
3628	STEVENS, Warrington	100	Private	Va. St. Line	3 yrs.	Dec. 29, '84
3634	SMITH, Weedon	100	Private	Va. Cont. Line	3 yrs.	Dec. 29, '84
3649	STORY, John (Francis Story, heir at law)	100	Private	Va. Cont. Line	3 yrs.	Dec. 31, '84
3650	SULSER, Matthew	100	Private	Va. Cont. Line	3 yrs.	Dec. 31, '84
3658	STAPLES, Joseph	100	Private	Va. Cont. Line	3 yrs.	Dec. 31, '84
3666	SAXTON, John	100	Private	Va. Cont. Line	3 yrs.	Jan. 3, 1785
3668	SMITH, Richard (Zachariah Johnston, assee.)	200	Private	Va. Cont. Line	war	Jan. 4, 1785
3673	SIMPKINS, James	100	Private	Va. Cont. Line	3 yrs.	Jan. 5, 1785
3674	SIMPKINS, Garrott	100	Private	Va. Cont. Line	3 yrs.	Jan. 5, 1785
3682	SANDFORD, Thomas (William Reynolds, assee.)	100	Private	Va. Cont. Line	war	Jan. 11, '85
3707	SHEENER, Matthias	200	Sergeant	Va. Cont. Line	3 yrs.	Jan. 20, '85
3745	SELLARS, Michael	200	Private	Va. Cont. Line	war	Feb. 7, 1785
3751	SPITZFATHOM, John	200	Sergeant	Va. Cont. Line	3 yrs.	Feb. 9, 1785
3765	SPILLER, Benjamin (Res. of Assby.)	4000	Captain	Va. Cont. Line	3 yrs.	Feb. 28, '85
3778	STEWART, Marks	100	Private	Va. St. Line	3 yrs.	Mch. 12, '85
3787	SMITH, James (John Smith, legal rep.)	100	Private	Va. Cont. Line	3 yrs.	Mch. 25, '85
3807	SLEDD, Seaton (completes his allowance, having assd. 100 acres—No. 2928—to Wm. Reynolds)	300	Sergeant	Va. Cont. Line	war	Apr. 14, '85
3813	SPALDING, Charles (William Spalding, heir at law)	100	Private	Va. St. Line	3 yrs.	Apr. 21, '85
3817	SPENCER, Moses	100	Private	Va. Cont. Line	3 yrs.	Apr. 21, '85
3831	SMITH, William	200	Sergeant	Va. Cont. Line	3 yrs.	Apr. 28, '85
3834	STRATTON, Seth	200	Private	Va. Cont. Line	war	Apr. 29, '85
3851	SUSONG, Andrew	100	Private	Va. Cont. Line	3 yrs.	May 6, 1785
3856	SMITH, John	200	Sergeant	Va. Cont. Line	3 yrs.	May 6, 1785
3864	SHAVER, George	100	Private	Va. Cont. Line	3 yrs.	May 10, '85
3865	SHAVER, John	100	Private	Va. Cont. Line	3 yrs.	May 10, '85
3867	SHAW, William	100	Private	Va. Cont. Line	3 yrs.	May 10, '85
3898	SIMKINS, Reuben (William Reynolds, assee.)	200	Private	Va. Cont. Line	war	June 21, '85
3935	STRONG, William	200	Corporal	Va. St. Line	3 yrs.	Aug. 1, 1785
3936	SHANER, George	100	Private	Va. Cont. Line	3 yrs.	Aug. 2, 1785
3938	SPANG, David	100	Private	Va. Cont. Line	3 yrs.	Aug. 2, 1785
3959	SULLINS, William (William Reynolds, assee. of Edward Valentine, assee. of John Sullins, heir at law to William Sullins)	200	Private	Va. Cont. Line	war	Aug. 12, '85
3976	SIMPSON, Daniel (Thos. Brown, assee.)	200	Corporal	Va. St. Line	3 yrs.	Sept. 16, '85
3980	SHELDON, Peter F.	200	Fifer	Va. Cont. Line	war	Oct. 15, '85
3996	SMITHER, Benjamin	200	Private	Va. Cont. Line	war	Nov. 15, '85
4000	STEWART, John (Wm. Pettyjohn, assee. of Joshua Humphreys, who was assee. of)	100	Private	Va. St. Line	3 yrs.	Nov. 15, '85
4013	SEBURN, Jacob	200	Private	Va. Cont. Line	war	Dec. 2, 1785
4041	SHACKLETT, Edward	100	Private	Va. Cont. Line	3 yrs.	Dec. 15, '85
4051	SEWELL, Thomas	200	Sergeant	Va. Cont. Line	3 yrs.	Dec. 21, '85
4054	SMITHER, Benjamin	100	Private	Va. Cont. Line	3 yrs.	Dec. 22, '85
4066	SEARS, Joseph	200	Private	Va. Cont. Line	war	Jan. 6, 1786
4067	SMITH, James	200	Corporal	Va. Cont. Line	3 yrs.	Jan. 6, 1786
4093	SHIBLER, Frederick	100	Private	Va. Cont. Line	3 yrs.	Jan. 23, '86
4103	SALIMES, Henry (Francis Graves, assee.)	200	Private	Va. Cont. Line	war	Feb. 1, 1786
4117	SMITH, Thomas	400	Drum Major	Va. Cont. Line	war	Mch. 7, 1786
4130	SHAW, Matthew	200	Private	Va. Cont. Line	war	Mch. 18, '86
4132	SICKNER, John Simon	200	Private	Va. Cont. Line	war	Mch. 18, '86
4140	STEVENSON, William (Francis Stevenson, heir at law)	2666⅔	Lieutenant	Va. Cont. Line	3 yrs.	May 22, '86

LAND BOUNTY WARRANTS.

Warrant.	Name.	Acres	Rank.	Department.	Term	Date.
4158	Spencer, William	100	Private	Va. Cont. Line	3 yrs.	Apr. 5, 1786
4161	Stonnett, alias "Stoner," Richard (Jesse Ewell, assee.)	200	Private	Va. Cont. Line	war	May 27, '86
4163	Stewart, Robert (Patrick Stewart, assee.)	100	Private	Va. Cont. Line	3 yrs.	May 29, '86
4178	Saunders, William	666⅔	Captain	Va. St. Navy	3 yrs.	June 21, '86
4181	Savage, George (John Savage, heir at law)	100	Private	Va. Cont. Line	3 yrs.	June 29, '86
4201	Spencer, Benjamin (Susanna Spencer, rep.)	200	Private	Va. St. Line	war	Aug. 28, '86
4202	Selman, Joseph	100	Private	Va. St. Line	3 yrs.	Aug. 29, '86
4203	Smith, Major (Francis Smith, heir at law)	100	Private	Va. Cont. Line	3 yrs.	Aug. 30, '86
4207	Smith, William	100	Private	Va. Cont. Line	3 yrs.	Aug. 31, '86
4215	Satterwhite, Wm. (Sam'l Lamm, assee. of Wm. Reynolds, assee. of)	200	Sergeant	Va. St. Line	3 yrs.	Oct. 4, 1786
4217	Smith, Charles	100	Private	Va. Cont. Line	3 yrs.	Oct. 13, '86
4218	Smith, Richard (Stephen Smith, heir at law)	100	Private	Va. Cont. Line	3 yrs.	Oct. 13, '86
4253	Singleton, Frederick (Joshua Singleton, heir at law)	200	Private	Va. St. Line	war	Jan. 27, '87
4272	Smith, John	100	Private	Va. Cont. Line	3 yrs.	Apr. 7, 1787
4275	Stillwell, Joseph	100	Private	Va. Cont. Line	3 yrs.	Apr. 7, 1787
4295	Smith, Stephen (Daniel Smith, heir at law)	200	Private	Va. Cont. Line	war	June 14, '87
4324	Sutton, Martin	100	Private	Va. Cont. Line	3 yrs.	Nov. 1, 1787
4325	Simmons, James (Annie, Elizabeth, Catherine, Mary and Eppa Simmons, co-heiresses to)	100	Private	Va. Cont. Line	3 yrs.	Nov. 3, 1787
4339	Smith, William (Samuel Smith, oldest brother)	2666⅔	Lieutenant	Va. Cont. Line	3 yrs.	Nov. 23, '87
4354	Sprig, Nathan	100	Private	Va. St. Navy	3 yrs.	Dec. 20, '87
4359	Simpkins, William	100	Private	Va. Cont. Line	3 yrs.	Jan. 4, 1788
4372	Spencer, William (Wm. Reynolds, assee. of Rich. Bennett, assee. of the rep. of Wm. Spencer)	200	Private	Va. Cont. Line	war	Jan. 23, '88
4387	Slaughter, John	100	Private	Va. Cont. Line	3 yrs.	Feb. 11, '88
4440	Smith, Isaac (Mathew Walton, assee. of Edmund Thomas, assee. of Johnston Smith, heir at law to)	100	Private	Va. Cont. Line	3 yrs.	Oct. 27, '88
4449	Spur, John (Wm. Reynolds, assee of Richard Burnett, assee of the rep.)	200	Sergeant	Va. Cont. Line	3 yrs.	Feb. 26, '89
4454	Spencer, John (Wm. Reynolds, assee. of William DuVall, assee.)	100	Private	Va. Cont. Line	3 yrs.	Apr. 6, 1789
4459	Sharp, Josiah (Robert Sharp, heir at law)	100	Private	Va. Cont. Line	3 yrs.	May 25, '89
4478	Swearinger, Joseph	666⅔	Captain	Va. Cont. Line	7 yrs.	Nov. 19, '89
4479	Stevens, Joseph (Geo. Rice, assee. of Ansel George, assee. of)	200	Sergeant	Va. Cont. Line	3 yrs.	Nov. 21, '89
4480	Scott, Isaac (Reuben Slaughter, assee. of Wm. Price, assee. of Patience Scott, rep. of Isaac Scott)	100	Private	Va. St. Line	3 yrs.	Nov. 21, '89
4487	Sharpless, John (Courtney Sharpless, widow)	6000	Surgeon	Va. St. Navy	3 yrs.	Jan. 2, 1790
4500	Seavres, John (Thos. Seayres, heir at law to)	6000	Lieut.-Col.	Va. Cont. Line	3 yrs.	Sept. 4, 1790
4510	Scantlin, William (John Hume, assee.)	200	Sergeant	Va. St. Line	3 yrs.	Dec. 7, 1790
4515	Stephens, John (Rich. Smith, assee. of Ansel George, assee. of Jos. Stephens, heir at law to)	200	Private	Va. Cont. Line	war	Feb. 1, 1791
4525	Smith, James	400	Sergeant	Cont. Line	war	May 31, '91
4548	Stewart, Henry (John Stewart, heir at law)	200	Private	Cont. Line	war	Nov. 15, '91
4558	Sampson, George (Wm. Bigger, assee. of Reuben Sampson, heir at law to)	100	Private	Cont. Line	3 yrs.	Dec. 8, 1791

LAND BOUNTY WARRANTS.

Warrant.	Name	Acres	Rank	Department	Term	Date
4564	SCULLEY, James	200	Private	Cont. Line	war	Jan. 21, '92
4567	SMITH, James (Robert Means and James Vaughan, Jr., assees. of)	100	Private	Cont. Line	3 yrs.	Jan. 31, '92
4584	STERN, David	400	Sergeant	Cont. Line	war	July 11, '92
4585	SINGLETON, Anthony	666⅔	Captain	Cont. Line	7 yrs.	Sept. 15, '92
4604	SCOTT, Stephen (William Bigger, assee. of Wm. Patman, assee. of the rep. of)	200	Private	Cont. Line	war	Jan. 25, '93
4607	SANDERS, Thomas (the rep. or the reps. of)	200	Private	Cont. Line	war	Mch. 23, '93
4608	SANDERS, David (the rep. or the reps. of)	200	Private	Cont. Line	war	Mch. 23, '93
4616	SWEENY, Thomas (the rep. or reps. of)	200	Private	Cont. Line	war	June 20, '93
4623	STUART, James (Robert Means, assee. of Francis Graves, assee. of)	200	Private	Cont. Line	war	Sept. 18, '93
4625	SHAVER, Frederick	200	Private	Cont. Line	war	Sept. 13, '93

T

Warrant.	Name	Acres	Rank	Department	Term	Date
36	THOMPSON, William	4000	Captain	St. Reg. Art.	3 yrs.	Dec. 10, '82
59	TUNSTALL, Edward	200	Sergeant	St. Art	3 yrs.	Dec. 19, '82
100	TOWERS, John	100	Private	St. Line	3 yrs.	Jan. 23, '83
132	TAYLOR, William	5333⅓	Major	Va. Line	3 yrs.	Feb. 19, '83
133	TAYLOR, Richard	5333⅓	Captain	Navy of the Comth.	3 yrs.	Feb. 19, '83
203	TERRY, Stephen	200	Corporal	St. Line	3 yrs.	Mch. 26, '83
205	THWEATT, Thomas	4000	Captain	Va. Line	3 yrs.	Mch. 27, '83
213	TUPMAN, John	2666⅔	Master	St. Navy	3 yrs.	Apr. 1, 1783
234	TANNEHILL, Josiah	1333⅓	Lieutenant	Va. Cont. Line	3 yrs.	Apr. 1, 1783
235	TANNEHILL, Josiah	1333⅓	Lieutenant	Va. Cont. Line	3 yrs.	Apr. 1, 1783
245	TRIPLETT, George	2666⅔	Lieutenant	Va. Line	3 yrs.	Apr. 1, 1783
254	TOWNSHEND, George (Rev. Robert Andrews, assee.)	100	Private	St. Line	3 yrs.	Apr. 3, 1783
266	THOMPSON, Littleberry (Doctor James McClung, assee.)	100	Private	St. Line	3 yrs.	Apr. 3, 1783
312	TYREE, William	100	Private	Va. Cont. Cav.	3 yrs.	Apr. 11, '83
313	TABB, Augustine	4000	Captain	Va. St. Line	3 yrs.	Apr. 11, '83
333	TAYLOR, Bartholomew	200	Private	St. Cav	war	Apr. 14, '83
334	TAYLOR, Samuel	100	Private	Va. Cont. Line	3 yrs.	Apr. 14, '83
336	TAYLOR, Major	200	Private	St. Cav	war	Apr. 14, '83
364	TYSER, Cornelius	100	Private	St. Line	3 yrs.	Apr. 18, '83
369	TUTT, Charles (James Tutt, heir at law)	2666⅔	Lieutenant	Va. Cont. Line		Apr. 19, '83
404	TOMPKINS, Robert (William Tompkins, heir at law)	2666⅔	Lieutenant	Cont. Line	3 yrs.	Apr. 25, '83
405	TOMPKINS, Henry (William Tompkins, heir at law)	2666⅔	Ensign	Va. Cont. Line	3 yrs.	Apr. 25, '83
438	TATE, Adam	200	Fifer	St. Line	war	Apr. 26, '83
467	TRIPLETT, Daniel	200	Sergeant	St. Line	3 yrs.	Apr. 29, '83
526	THOMAS, William	400	Corporal	St. Line	war	May 2, 1783
540	THOMAS, Amos	200	Private	St. Line	war	May 3, 1783
541	THOMAS, William	200	Private	St. Line	war	May 3, 1783
559	TALLIAFERRO, Benjamin	4666⅔	Captain	Va. Cont. Line	7 yrs.	May 8, 1783
592	TRECKLE, John	100	Private	Va. Cont. Line	3 yrs.	May 17, '83
615	TUCKER, William	100	Private	Va. St. Line	3 yrs.	May 21, '83
648	TOWERS, John	200	Private	Va. St. Line	war	May 28, '83
649	TRENT, Lawrence	4000	Captain	Va. Cont. Cav.	3 yrs.	May 28, '83
662	THOMPSON, Daniel	100	Private	Va. St. Line	3 yrs.	May 28, '83
666	TREACLE, John	100	Private	Va. St. Line	3 yrs.	May 29, '83
667	TREACLE, Dawson	100	Private	Va. St. Line	3 yrs.	May 29, '83
668	TAYLOR, Humphrey	100	Private	Va. St. Line	3 yrs.	May 29, '83
676	TREACLE, William	100	Private	Va. St. Line	3 yrs.	May 29, '83
737	TRIPLETT, William	200	Sergeant	Va. St. Line	3 yrs.	June 4, 1783
846	THORNTON, Presley	4000	Captain	Va. Cav. on Cont. Establishment	3 yrs.	June 17, '83
854	TALIAFERRO, Nicholas	2666⅔	Lieutenant	Va. Cont. Line	3 yrs.	June 17, '83
855	TOWLES, Oliver	6000	Lieut.-Col.	Va. Cont. Line	3 yrs.	June 17, '83
921	TAPP, Venct	100	Private	Va. Cont. Line	3 yrs.	June 20, '83
925	TOLIN, Elias	200	Sergeant	Va. Cont. Line	3 yrs.	June 20, '83
939	THOMPSON, James	100	Private	Cont. Line	3 yrs.	June 20, '83
964	TOMLIN, John	100	Private	Cont. Line	3 yrs.	June 20, '83
1012	TAYLOR, Benjamin	2666⅔	Midshipman	Va. St. Navy	3 yrs.	June 23, '83
1037	TANNEHILL, Thomas	400	Sergeant	Va. Cont. Line	war	June 24, '83

LAND BOUNTY WARRANTS.

Warrant.	Name.	Acres	Rank.	Department.	Term	Date.
1122	THORNTON, Pat	200	Private	Va. Cont. Line	war	June 24, '83
1180	TOLER, William	100	Corporal	Va. St. Art	3 yrs.	June 25, '83
1205	TIMBERLAKE, Joseph	233⅓	Private	Va. St. Line	7 yrs.	June 26, '83
1237	THOMPSON, Thomas	100	Private	Va. Cont. Line	3 yrs.	June 27, '83
1238	TURK, James (Thomas Turk, heir at law)	100	Private	Va. Cont. Line	3 yrs.	June 27, '83
1242	TURK, Robert (Thomas Turk, heir at law)	100	Private	Va. St. Line	3 yrs.	June 27, '83
1256	THOMAS, Daniel	200	Private	Va. Cont. Line	war	June 27, '83
1276	TAYLOR, Isaac	466⅔	Sergeant	Va. Cont. Line	war	June 28, '83
1284	THOMPSON, Robert	200	Private	Va. Cont. Line	war	June 28, '83
1321	THORNBURN, John	200	Private	St. Line	war	July 2, 1783
1322	TAPP, Vincent	200	Sergeant	Va. Cont. Line	3 yrs.	July 3, 1783
1330	TIBBS, Thomas (John Tibbs, heir)					
1389	TOWNSEND, William	400	Captain	Va. Cont. Line	3 yrs.	July 5, 1783
1394	TERRELL, William	200	Private	Cont. Line	war	July 17, '83
1422	THOMPSON, Clanders	400	Corporal	Cont. Line	war	July 19, '83
1443	TURNER, William	400	Corporal	Cont. Line	war	July 23, '83
1448	TILLERY, John	100	Private	Cont. Line	3 yrs.	July 30, '83
1496	TAYLOR, Ferguson	200	Private	Cont. Line	war	July 31, '83
1499	TAYLOR, James	100	Fifer	Cont. Line	3 yrs.	Aug. 5, 1783
1552	TUCKER, James	200	Sergeant	Cont. Line	3 yrs.	Aug. 5, 1783
1602	TAYLOR, Archibald	200	Sergeant	Cont. Line	3 yrs.	Aug. 11, '83
1630	TAPLEY, Thomas	200	Private	Cont. Line	war	Aug. 20, '83
1634	TINSLEY, Jonathan	200	Private	Cont. Line	war	Aug. 22, '83
1637	THAYER, William	466⅔	Private	Cont. Line	war	Aug. 22, '83
1734	TAYLOR, Richard	6000	Serg.-Maj.	Va. Cont. Line	7 yrs.	Aug. 23, '83
1763	TURNER, Francis	100	Lieut.-Col.	Va. Cont. Line	3 yrs.	Sept. 8, 1783
1859	TAYLOR, William	100	Private	Va. Cont. Line	3 yrs.	Sept. 13, '83
②1859	TEAR, Hammer	100	Private	Va. St. Line	3 yrs.	Sept. 14, '83
ⓢ1870	TUGLER, William	200	Private	Va. Cont. Line	3 yrs.	Nov. 6, 1783
1876	TURNSTALL, Thomas, Jr.	200	Private	Va. Cont. Line	war	Nov. 7, 1783
1932	TELKINS, John	100	Sergeant	Va. Cont. Line	3 yrs.	Oct. 15, '83
②1936	TAYLOR, Reuben	4000	Private	Va. Cont. Line	3 yrs.	Oct. 29, '83
ᒡ1937	TAYLOR, Francis	5333⅓	Captain	Va. Cont. Line	3 yrs.	Nov. 22, '83
1963	TALIAFERRO, William (William Taliaferro, heir at law)	6000	Major	Va. Cont. Line	3 yrs.	Nov. 22, '83
1974	TERRELL, Edmund	200	Lieut.-Col	Va. Cont. Line	3 yrs.	Nov. 25, '83
1986	TOWNS, John	2666⅔	Sergeant	Va. Cont. Line	3 yrs.	Nov. 26, '83
2017	TINSLEY, Samuel	2666⅔	Lieutenant	Va. Cont. Line	3 yrs.	Nov. 28, '83
2019	TURVEY, William	200	Cornet	Va. St. Line	3 yrs.	Dec. 5, 1783
2026	THORNTON, William	200	Private	Va. Cont. Line	war	Dec. 5, 1783
2050	TRIPLETT, Nathaniel	400	Private	Va. Cont. Line	war	Dec. 6, 1783
2056	TAYLOR, Charles (Samuel Griffin, assee.)		Sergeant	Va. Cont. Line	war	Dec. 9, 1783
2058	THOMAS, William (Samuel Griffin, assee.)	100	Private	Va. St. Line	3 yrs.	Dec. 9, 1873
2094	THOMPSON, Patrick	200	Private	Va. St. Line	3 yrs.	Dec. 9, 1783
2128	TUNE, William	200	Sergeant	Va. Cont. Line	3 yrs.	Dec. 10, '83
2147	TUGGLES, Joshua	100	Sergeant	Va. Cont. Line	3 yrs.	Dec. 15, '83
2189	TASKER, James	100	Private	Va. Cont. Line	3 yrs.	Dec. 18, '83
2280	THARP, Elkanah	466⅔	Private	Va. Cont. Line	3 yrs.	Dec. 22, '83
2341	TAYLOR, James	100	Sergeant	Va. Cont. Line	7 yrs.	Jan. 24, '84
2353	TREACLE, William (Martin Hawkins, assee.)		Private	Va. St. Line	3 yrs.	Jan. 31, '84
2370	TRENT, Thomas	100	Private	Va. St. Line	3 yrs.	Jan. 31, '84
2377	TREZVANT, Doctor John	200	Sergeant	Va. Cont. Line	3 yrs.	Feb. 3, 1784
2396	TONY, Vincent (Thomas Olson, assee.)	6000	Surgeon	Va. Cont. Line	war	Feb. 3, 1784
2399	TUGGLE, Henry (Thomas Aslin, assee.)	100	Private	Va. Cont. Line	3 yrs.	Feb. 3, 1784
2407	TURNER, John	100	Private	Va. Cont. Line	3 yrs.	Feb. 3, 1784
2417	TEMPLE, Benjamin	2666⅔	Lieutenant	Va. St. Line	war	Feb. 5, 1784
2422	TAYLOR, James	1000	Lieutenant	Va. Cont. Line	3 yrs.	Feb. 6, 1784
2439	THOMPSON, Royal (William Furbush, assee.)	200	Sergeant	Va. St. Line	3 yrs.	Feb. 6, 1784
2481	THOMPSON, George (Lucy Thompson, legal heir and rep.)	100	Private	Va. Cont. Line	3 yrs.	Feb. 9, 1784
2484	TOMLIN, William	2666⅔	Lieutenant	Va. St. Line	3 yrs.	Feb. 12, '84
2497	TOMPKINS, Christopher (Bennett Thompson, legal rep.)	200	Sergeant	Va. Cont. Line	3 yrs.	Feb. 13, '84
2515	TRABUE, John	2666⅔	Subaltern	Va. Cont. Line	3 yrs.	Feb. 14, '84
2539	THOMAS, Massey	2666⅔	Lieutenant	Va. Cont. Line	war	Feb. 18, '84
		100	Private	Va. Cont. Line	3 yrs.	Feb. 19, '84

LAND BOUNTY WARRANTS. 75

Warrant.	Name.	Acres	Rank.	Department.	Term	Date.
2580	Todd, Robert	4000	Captain ...	Va. St. Line	3 yrs.	Feb. 21, '84
2601	Terry, Nathaniel	4666⅔	Captain ...	Va. Cont. Line	7 yrs.	Feb. 23, 84
2611	Thompson, John (Richard Claiborne, assee.)	200	Sergeant ...	Va. Cont. Line	3 yrs.	Feb. 24, '84
2648	Tatum, Zachariah	2666⅔	Subaltern ..	Va. Cont. Line	3 yrs.	Feb. 28, '84
2653	Travis, Edward	5333⅓	Captain	Va. St. Navy	3 yrs.	Feb. 28, '84
2667	Tompkins, Daniel (James Tompkins, legal rep.)	1000	Lieutenant .	Va. Cont. Line	3 yrs.	Mch. 2, 1784
2668	Tompkins, Daniel (James Tompkins, legal rep.)	1666⅔	Lieutenant .	Va. Cont. Line	3 yrs.	Mch. 2, 1784
2686	Taylor, Isaac	4000	Captain ...	Va. St. Line	3 yrs.	Mch. 3, 1784
2713	Tukeway, Joseph	100	Private ...	Va. Cont. Line	3 yrs.	Mch. 5, 1784
2729	Trabue, William	200	Sergeant ...	Va. Cont. Line	3 yrs.	Mch. 6, 1784
2753	Thomas, Lewis	4000	Captain ...	Va. Cont. Line	6 yrs.	Mch. 11, '84
2765	Thomas, Jacob (Edward Valentine, assee.)	100	Private	Va. Cont. Line	3 yrs.	Mch. 16, '84
2774	Tunstill, Henry (James Jenkins, assee.)	200	Sergeant ...	Va. Cont. Line	3 yrs.	Mch. 18, '84
2783	Tyler, William	200	Private ...	Va. Cont. Line	war	Mch. 18, '84
2788	Thompson, Henry (William Thompson, legal rep.)	100	Private	Va. Cont. Line	3 yrs.	Mch. 18, '84
2795	Tallom, Peter	100	Private	Va. Cont. Line	3 yrs.	Mch. 19, '84
2816	Thompson, John	100	Private	Va. St. Line	3 yrs.	Mch. 24, '84
2875	Trotter, John	200	Private	Va. Cont. Line	war	Apr. 5, 1784
2877	Taylor, James (Jean Taylor, heir at law)	200	Private	Va. Cont. Line	war	Apr. 5, 1784
2892	Thomas, Henry	100	Private	Va. Cont. Line	3 yrs.	Apr. 5, 1784
2903	Tanner, William	100	Private	Va. Cont. Line	3 yrs.	Apr. 6, 1784
2940	Thomas, William	100	Private	Va. Cont. Line	3 yrs.	Apr. 17, '84
2958	Turpin, Obediah	200	Sergeant ...	Va. St. Line	3 yrs.	Apr. 17, '84
2981	Tucker, Michael (Lewis Ford, assee. of Wm. Tucker, heir at law to)	200	Sergeant ...	Va. Cont. Line	3 yrs.	Apr. 21, '84
3004	Thompson, Smith	100	Private	Va. Cont. Line	3 yrs.	Apr. 22, '84
3018	Tripps, Adam	200	Sergeant ...	Va. Cont. Line	3 yrs.	Apr. 26, '84
3134	Triller, William	200	Corporal ...	Va. Cont. Line	3 yrs.	June 8, 1784
3177	Thomas, Joseph	100	Private	Va. Cont. Line	3 yrs.	June 21, '84
3206	Throckmorton, Albion, Jr.	1000	Subaltern. .	Va. Cont. Line	war	June 24, '84
3207	Throckmorton, Albion, Jr.	1666⅔	Subaltern. .	Va. Cont. Line	war	June 24, '84
3238	Tomlinson, Littleberry (Alex Tomlinson, heir at law)	100	Private	Va. Cont. Line	3 yrs.	June 29, '84
3239	Tomlinson, Herbert (Hamlin Tomlinson, heir at law)	100	Private	Va. Cont. Line	3 yrs.	June 29, '84
3240	Tomlinson, Joseph (Alex Tomlinson, heir at law)	100	Private	Va. Cont. Line	3 yrs.	June 29, '84
3254	Thornhill, Thomas	200	Private	Va. Cont. Line	war	June 30, '84
3257	Turnham, Thomas	100	Private	Va. Cont. Line	3 yrs.	June 30, '84
3298	Temple, John	100	Private	Va. Cont. Line	3 yrs.	July 1, 1784
3301	Tyler, John (Nathaniel Tyler, heir at law)	2666⅔	Lieutenant .	Va. Cont. Line	3 yrs.	July 1, 1784
3318	Tapscott, John (Francis Graves, assee. of Jo. Sanders, who was assee. of)	100	Sailor	Va. St. Navy	3 yrs.	July 6, 1784
3319	Tapscott, Ezekial (Francis Graves, assee. of Jo. Sanders, who was assee. of)	100	Sailor	Va. St. Navy	3 yrs.	July 6, 1784
3332	Thompson, William	200	Corporal ...	Va. St. Line	3 yrs.	July 19, '84
3342	Theel, Levi	100	Private	Va. St. Line	3 yrs.	July 19, '84
3364	Taylor, Robert (James Fear, assee.)	200	Sergeant ...	Va. Cont. Line	3 yrs.	July 29, '84
3422	Tennell, George	200	Private	Va. Cont. Line	war	Aug. 28, '84
3446	Taylor, Thornton	2666⅔	Lieutenant	Services	3 yrs.	Sept. 20, '84
3448	Timmons, John	200	Sergeant ...	Va. Cont. Line	3 yrs.	Sept. 23, '84
3450	Turner, Richard	200	Private	Va. Cont. Line	war	Sept. 25, '84
3463	Thomas, Elisha	100	Private	Va. Cont. Line	3 yrs.	Oct. 15, '84
3464	Thomas, Joseph	100	Private	Va. Cont. Line	3 yrs.	Oct. 15, '84
3509	Thorn, Richard	200	Private	Va. Cont. Line	war	Nov. 8, 1784
3565	Trice, Dabney (William Reynolds, assee. of Jno. Heath, who is heir at law)	100	Private	Va. St. Line	3 yrs.	Dec. 9, 1784
3566	Trice, William (William Reynolds, assee. of Jno. Heath, who is heir at law to)	100	Private	Va. St. Line	3 yrs.	Dec. 9, 1784
3579	Townsend, Ewel	200	Corporal ...	Va. Cont. Line	3 yrs.	Dec. 15, '84
3584	Terrant, Manlove	400	Sergeant ...	Va. Cont. Line	war	Dec. 16, '84

LAND BOUNTY WARRANTS.

Warrant.	Name.	Acres	Rank.	Department.	Term	Date.
3636	TAYLOR, William (Alne Taylor, heir at law)	200	Sergeant	Va. St. Line	3 yrs.	Dec. 31, '84
3654	TYREE, John (William Tyree, heir at law)	100	Private	Va. Cont. Line	3 yrs.	Dec. 31, '84
3688	TATE, Robert (William Reynolds, assee.)	100	Private	Va. Cont. Line	3 yrs.	Jan. 11, '85
3796	TOWNSEND, John	200	Private	Va. Cont. Line	war	Apr. 6, 1785
3797	TALLEY, John, Sr.	200	Private	Va. Cont. Line	war	Apr. 6, 1785
3798	TALLEY, John, Jr.	200	Private	Va. Cont. Line	war	Apr. 6, 1785
3824	TEMPLE, Alexander (William Reynolds, assee.)	100	Sailor	St. Navy	3 yrs.	Apr. 23, '85
3854	TAYLOR, Robert	100	Private	Va. Cont. Line	3 yrs.	May 6, 1785
3863	TILBURY, George	200	Private	Va. Cont. Line	war	May 7, 1785
3884	TYLER, Benjamin	200	Private	Va. Cont. Line	war	May 26, '85
3914	TOAT (Toole), Joseph	200	Private	Va. Cont. Line	war	June 21, '85
3931	THOMPSON, George (William Reynolds, assee.)	100	Private	Va. Cont. Line	3 yrs.	Aug. 1, 1785
3939	TATE, James	100	Private	Va. Cont. Line	3 yrs.	Aug. 2, 1785
3961	TERRY, James (William Reynolds, assee. of Stept. Terry, assee. of Thos. Terry, heir at law)	100	Private	Va. St. Line	3 yrs.	Aug. 12, '85
3974	TOWLER, John (Samuel Couch, assee.)	100	Private	Va. Cont. Line	3 yrs.	Sept. 13, '85
3991	TONEY, Reuben	100	Private	Va. Cont. Line	3 yrs.	Nov. 9, 1785
3992	TONEY, Archibald	100	Private	Va. Cont. Line	3 yrs.	Nov. 9, 1785
4011	THURSTIEN, William (Henry Banks, assee.)	100	Private	Va. Cont. Line	3 yrs.	Dec. 2, 1785
4047	TAYLOR, John (William Taylor, heir at law)	100	Private	Va. Cont. Line	3 yrs.	Dec. 20, '85
4052	TAYLOR, James	100	Drum Major	Va. Cont. Line	3 yrs.	Dec. 21, '85
4071	THOMAS, John	4000	Captain	Va. St. Navy	3 yrs.	Jan. 13, '86
4074	TAYLOR, William	200	Private	Va. Cont. Line	3 yrs.	Jan. 13, '86
4099	TRIPLETT, William	2666⅔	Lieutenant	Va. Cont. Line	3 yrs.	Jan. 28, '86
4102	TURNER, John (Charles Turner, heir at law)	200	Sergeant	Va. St. Line	3 yrs.	Jan. 31, '86
4131	TIMES, Peter	200	Private	Va. Cont. Line	war	Mch. 18, '86
4149	TRAVIS, Miles	100	Private	Va. Cont. Line	3 yrs.	Apr. 26, '86
4169	THOMPSON, John	400	Corporal	Va. Cont. Line	war	June 12, '86
4195	THRALL, John	2666⅔	Lieutenant	Va. St. Navy	3 yrs.	Aug. 9, 1786
4334	TURLINGTON, Jacob	100	Private	Va. Cont. Line	3 yrs.	Nov. 13, '87
4383	TATE, Robert (William Reynolds, assee.)	100	Sailor	Va. St. Navy	3 yrs.	Jan. 29, '88
4415	TALLEY, Thomas (Richard Burnett, assee. of the rep.)	100	Private	Va. Cont. Line	3 yrs.	July 17, '88
4417	TURNER, G. (William Reynolds, assee. of the rep.)	100	Private	Va. Cont. Line	3 yrs.	July 17, '88
4421	TURNER, William (William Reynolds, assee of Richard Burnett, assee of the rep. of)	100	Private	Va. Cont. Line	3 yrs.	July 17, '88
4429	TUCKER, Reuben (Turner Morris, assee. of John Bailey, assee. of Ed. Davis, assee. of R. Burnett, assee. of the rep.)	100	Private	Va. Cont. Line	3 yrs.	Aug. 4, 1788
4447	TANNER, John	100	Private	Va. St. Line	3 yrs.	Jan. 9, 1789
4458	TIPTON, Abraham (Samuel Tipton, heir at law)	4000	Captain	Va. St. Line	3 yrs.	May 18, '89
4483	TURNER, Isham	100	Private	Va. Cont. Line	3 yrs.	Dec. 4, 1789
4484	TURNER, Thomas	100	Private	Va. Cont. Line	3 yrs.	Dec. 4, 1789
4528	TRIPLETT, Roger	1000	Lieutenant	St. Line	3 yrs.	July 21, '91
4529	TRIPLETT, Roger	1000	Lieutenant	St. Line	3 yrs.	July 21, '91
4530	TRIPLETT, Roger	666⅔	Lieutenant	St. Line	3 yrs.	July 21, '91
4544	TOMPKINS, Christopher (the rep. of)	2666⅔	Lieutenant	St. Navy	3 yrs.	Nov. 14, '91
4545	TOMPKINS, Robert (the rep. of)	4000	Captain	St. Navy	3 yrs.	Nov. 14, '91
4555	TURNER, George (Wm. Bigger, assee.)	100	Private	Cont. Line	3 yrs.	Nov. 29, '91
4574	TAPSCOTT, John (the rep. of)	200	Sergeant	Cont. Line	3 yrs.	May 5, 1792
4578	TEAGLE, Severn	4000	Captain	Cont. Line	3 yrs.	June 4, 1792
4626	TAYLOR, James	200	Private	Cont. Line	war	Oct. 26, '93

LAND BOUNTY WARRANTS. 77

Warrant.	Name.	Acres	Rank.	Department.	Term	Date.
	U					
340	Upshaw, Thomas	4000	Captain	St. Line	3 yrs.	Apr. 15, '83
590	Underwood, Gideon	200	Sergeant	Va. St. Line	3 yrs.	May 17, '83
1367	Usher, William	100	Private	St. Line	3 yrs.	July 12, '83
①1913	Utterback, Benjamin	100	Private	Va. Cont. Line	3 yrs.	Nov. 20, '83
3276	Upshaw, James (Res., Gen. Assby., June 16, 1784)	4000	Captain			July 1, 1784
	V					
21	Voglusan, Armand	4000	Captain	St. Cav	3 yrs.	Nov. 25, '82
97	Vawter, William	2666⅔	Lieutenant	St. Line	3 yrs.	Jan. 21, '83
139	Vandewall, Markes	2666⅔	Lieutenant	Cont. Va. Line	3 yrs.	Feb. 21, '83
161	Vowles, Charles	2666⅔	Lieutenant	St. Line	3 yrs.	Mch. 7, 1783
162	Vowles, Henry	4000	Capt.-Lieut	Art. in St. Line	3 yrs.	Mch. 7, 1783
163	Vowles, Walter (Henry Vowles, heir at law)	4666⅔	Captain	St. Line		Mch. 7, 1783
179	Valentine, Jacob	4000	Captain	Va. St. Line	3 yrs.	Mch. 14, '83
744	Vanmeter, Joseph	2666⅔	Ensign	Va. Cont. Line	3 yrs.	June 5, 1783
790	Vaiden, John	200	Corporal	Va. St. Line	3 yrs.	June 20, '83
850	Vance, Robert	4000	Captain	Va. Cont. Line	3 yrs.	June 17, '83
917	Veal, Solomon	200	Sergeant	Va. Cont. Line	3 yrs.	June 12, '83
938	Vance, Joseph	100	Private	Va. Cont. Line	3 yrs	June 20, '83
1067	Vann, Henry	200	Private	Va. Cont. Line	war	June 24, '83
1104	Violet, John	200	Private	Va. Cont. Line	war	June 24, '83
①1856	Vaughan, Richard	100	Private	Va. Cont. Line	3 yrs.	Nov. 5, 1783
2301	Vaughan, Thomas	100	Private	Va. St. Line	3 yrs.	Jan. 27, '84
2390	Vassar, Isham (Martin Hawkins, assee.)	200	Corporal	Va. Cont. Line	3 yrs.	Feb. 3, 1784
2556	Vaughan, Clairborn	2666⅔	Surg.'s Mate	Va. Cont. Line	3 yrs.	Feb. 20, '84
2568	Vaughan, John	2666⅔	Lieutenant	Va. St. Line	3 yrs.	Feb. 21, '84
2603	Vasser, Daniel	200	Sergeant	Va. Cont. Line	3 yrs.	Feb. 24, '84
2634	Viras, Joel (Daniel Viras, heir at law)	100	Private	Va. Cont. Line	3 yrs.	Feb. 25, '84
2761	Valentine, Edward	4000	Captain	Va. St. Line	3 yrs.	Mch. 15, '84
2780	Veroney, Joseph	200	Private	Va. Cont. Line	war	Mch. 18, '84
2916	Vernon, Thomas	100	Private	Va. Cont. Line	3 yrs.	Apr. 12, '84
3193	Vickers, William (Daniel Thompson, assee. of Francis Graves, assee. of)	200	Private	Va. St. Line	war	June 23, '84
3161	Vickers, William (Daniel Thompson, assee. of Francis Graves, assee. of)	100	Private	Va. St. Line	3 yrs.	July 27, '84
3362	Vest, George	100	Private	Va. Cont. Line	3 yrs.	July 27, '84
3506	Vadon, Bradock	200	Private	Va. Cont. Line	war	Nov. 5, 1784
3554	Vause, William	4000	Captain	Va. Cont. Line	3 yrs.	Dec. 6, 1784
3600	Valentine, Isham	100	Private	Va. Cont. Line	3 yrs.	Dec. 21, '84
3792	Vawter, Beverley (John Vawter, heir at law)	100	Private	Va. Cont. Line	3 yrs.	Apr. 1, 1785
3855	Vaughan, Patrick	100	Private	Va. Cont. Line	3 yrs.	May 6, 1785
4124	Vaughan, Sherwood	200	Sergeant	Va. Cont. Line	3 yrs.	Mch. 10, '86
4228	Vaughan, James	200	Sergeant	Va. St. Line	3 yrs.	Nov. 15, '86
4466	Vincent, John	200	Corporal	Va. Cont. Line	3 yrs.	Oct. 5, 1789
4541	Vaughan, John	200	Sergeant	St. Line	3 yrs.	Nov. 10, '91
4590	Valentine, Joseph	100	Private	Cont. Line	3 yrs.	Oct. 30, '92
	W					
2	Wilson, Willis	2666⅔	Lieutenant	11th Va. Cont. Reg.	3 yrs.	Aug. 15, '82
42	Wright, Patrick	4000	Captain	St. Art	3 yrs.	Dec. 12, '82
91	Weedon, George	10000	Brig. Gen.	Cont. Line	3 yrs.	Jan. 3, 1783
99	White, William	2666⅔	Lieutenant	St. Inf	3 yrs.	Jan. 21, '83
102	Wallace, Gustavus B.	7000	Lieut.-Col.	Va. Cont. Line	7 yrs.	Jan. 30, '83
116	Webb, John	6000	Lieut.-Col.	7th Va. Reg.	3 yrs.	Feb. 8, 1783
117	Wily, George, Jr	200	Serg.-Maj.	1st Va. Reg.	3 yrs.	Feb. 8, 1783
120	Wyatt, Carey	4000	Capt.-Lieut	St. Art	3 yrs.	Feb. 8, 1783
131	Whiting, Francis	2666⅔	Lieutenant	Cav. of Va. Line	3 yrs.	Feb. 19, '83
134	Whitlow, Francis	100	Private	St. Line	3 yrs.	Feb. 19, '83
135	Washington, George	2666⅔	Lieutenant	Va. Line	3 yrs.	Feb. 20, '83
155	Williams, John	4000	Captain	Art. in St. Line	3 yrs.	Mch. 3, 1783
174	White, William	4000	Captain	Va. Cont. Line	3 yrs.	Mch. 15, '83
180	Woodson, Robert	4000	Captain	Va. Cont. Line	7 yrs.	Mch. 15, '83
181	Woodson, Robert	666⅔	Captain	Va. Cont. Line	7 yrs.	Mch. 15, '83
183	Worsham, Richard	1000	Lieutenant	Va. Cont. Line	3 yrs.	Mch. 18, '83

LAND BOUNTY WARRANTS.

Warrant.	Name.	Acres	Rank.	Department.	Term	Date.
184	WORSHAM, Richard	1666⅔	Lieutenant	Va. Cont. Line	3 yrs.	Mch. 18, '83
238	WINLOCK, Joseph	1333⅓	Lieutenant	Va. Cont. Line	3 yrs.	Apr. 1, 1783
239	WINLOCK, Joseph	1333⅓	Lieutenant	Va. Cont. Line	3 yrs.	Apr. 1, 1783
251	WOODWARD, Charles (Rev. Robert Andrews, assee.)	100	Private	St. Line	3 yrs.	Apr. 3, 1783
259	WILLIAMS, Zebediah (Rev. Robert Andrews, assee.)	100	Private	St. Line	3 yrs.	Apr. 3, 1783
260	WILLIAMS, Thomas (Rev. Robert Andrews, assee.)	100	Private	St. Line	3 yrs.	Apr. 3, 1783
262	WILLIAMS, William (Rev. Robert Andrews, assee.)	100	Private	St. Line	3 yrs.	Apr. 3, 1783
269	WADE, David (Dr. James McClung, assee.)	100	Private	St. Line	3 yrs.	Apr. 3, 1783
282	WALDEN, Zachariah	100	Private	Va. St. Line	3 yrs.	Apr. 3, 1783
297	WOOD, James	1000	Colonel	Va. Cont. Line	3 yrs.	Apr. 7, 1783
298	WOOD, James	1000	Colonel	Va. Cont. Line	3 yrs.	Apr. 7, 1783
299	WOOD, James	4666⅔	Colonel	Va. Cont. Line	3 yrs.	Apr. 7, 1783
303	WHITE, Robert	4000	Lieutenant	Va. Cont. Line	3 yrs.	Apr. 8, 1783
311	WESTCOTT, Wright	4000	Captain	St. Navy	3 yrs.	Apr. 11, '83
326	WOOD, Edward	200	Private	Va. St. Line	war	Apr. 12, '83
343	WILLIAMS, John	200	Private	St. Line	war	Apr. 15, '83
360	WOODCOCK, John	100	Private	Va. Cont. Line	3 yrs.	Apr. 18, '83
366	WILLIAMS, Philemon	200	Private	St. Line	war	Apr. 19, '83
385	WALKER, William	100	Serg. (Sldr.)	Va. Cont. Line	3 yrs.	Apr. 23, '83
392	WEAVER, John	200	Private	Va. St. Line	war	Apr. 24, '83
393	WILLIS, John	200	Private	Va. St. Line	war	Apr. 24, '83
399	WEBB, Richard	200	Private	Va. St. Line	war	Apr. 25, '83
425	WINSLOW, Benjamin (Thomas Winslow, heir at law)	2666⅔	Ensign	Va. Cont. Line	3 yrs.	Apr. 26, '83
431	WOOD, Robert	200	Private	St. Line	war	Apr. 26, '83
440	WHELLER, John	200	Private	St. Line	war	Apr. 26, '83
441	WHALE, John	200	Private	St. Line	war	Apr. 26, '83
443	WEALCH, Nathaniel	4000	Captain	Va. St. Line	3 yrs.	Apr. 26, '83
445	WILLIAMS, Christopher	200	Private	Va. St. Line	war	Apr. 26, '83
447	WALLER, William	200	Private	St. Line	war	Apr. 28, '83
449	WATSON, William	400	Corporal	Va. St. Line	war	Apr. 28, '83
462	WILDAY, George	400	Corporal	Va. St. Line	war	Apr. 29, '83
470	WOODSON, Frederick	4000	Captain	St. Line	3 yrs.	Apr. 29, '83
473	WILLIAMSON, Lawrence Lot.	100	Private	St. Line	3 yrs.	Apr. 29, '83
492	WOOD, Philip	200	Private	St. Line	war	Apr. 30, '83
496	WHITAKER, James	200	Private	Va. St. Line	war	Apr. 30, '83
512	WHITMORE, William	400	Private	St. Line	war	May 1, 1783
517	WALKINS, William	200	Private	St. Line	war	May 1, 1783
577	WELCH, Lang	200	Private	Va. St. Line	war	May 14, '83
598	WILLIAMS, James	5666⅔	Captain	Va. Cont. Line	7 yrs.	May 20, '83
607	WYATT, Benjamin	200	Private	Va. Cont. Line	war	May 21, '83
610	WINSTON, John	4000	Captain	Va. Cont. Line	3 yrs.	May 21, '83
620	WARMAN, Thomas	2000	Captain	Va. Cont. Line	3 yrs.	May 22, '83
621	WARMAN, Thomas	1000	Captain	Va. Cont. Line	3 yrs.	May 22, '83
622	WARMAN, Thomas	1000	Captain	Va. Cont. Line	3 yrs.	May 22, '83
639	WHEELY, John	100	Private	Va. St. Line	3 yrs.	May 26, '83
642	WINTER, George	100	Private	Va. Cont. Line	3 yrs.	May 26, '83
651	WHITE, John (the rep. of)	2666⅔	Lieutenant	Va. Cav. on Cont. Estab.		May 27, '83
684	WYATT, John	100	Private	Va. Cont. Line	3 yrs.	May 30, '83
702	WALLACE, William B.	2666⅔	Lieutenant	Va. Cont. Line	3 yrs.	May 31, '83
725	WHITE, James	200	Private	Va. St. Cav.	war	June 3, 1783
726	WHITE, James	100	Private	Va. Cont. Line	war	June 3, 1783
743	WILLIAMS, Edward	2666⅔	Ensign	Va. Cont. Line	3 yrs.	June 5, 1783
753	WILLIS, John	6222	Major	Va. Cont. Line	7 yrs.	June 6, 1783
756	WYATT, William	100	Private	Va. Cont. Line	3 yrs.	June 6, 1783
758	WORTH, William	100	Sailor	Va. St. Navy	3 yrs.	June 6, 1783
770	WALLACE, John	100	Private	Va. Cont. Line	3 yrs.	June 7, 1783
776	WRIGHT, Robert	100	Private	Va. Cont. Line	3 yrs.	June 10, '83
795	WADE, Moses	100	Private	Va. Cont. Line	3 yrs.	June 12, '83
798	WEEDON, George	1666⅔	Brig. Gen.	Military Service	7 yrs.	June 13, '83
814	WALKER, Jacob (David Walker, heir and legal rep.)	1000	Captain	Va. Art	3 yrs.	June 14, '83
829	WARNECK, Frederick	5000 in part	Lieut.-Col.	Va. St. Line	3 yrs.	June 14, '83
830	WARNECK, Frederick	200 in part	Lieut.-Col.	Va. St. Line	3 yrs.	June 14, '83
831	WARNECK, Frederick	200 in part	Lieut.-Col.	Va. St. Line	3 yrs.	June 14, '83

LAND BOUNTY WARRANTS. 79

Warrant.	Name.	Acres	Rank.	Department.	Term	Date.
832	Warneck, Frederick	in part 200	Lieut.-Col.	Va. Line	3 yrs.	June 14, '83
833	Warneck, Frederick	in part 200	Lieut.-Col.	Va. Line	3 yrs.	June 14, '83
834	Warneck, Frederick	in part 200	Lieut.-Col.	Va. Line	3 yrs.	June 14, '83
839	Warick, William	200	Sergeant	Va. St. Art.	3 yrs.	June 16, '83
860	Williams, David	2666⅔	Lieutenant	Va. Cont. Line	3 yrs.	June 18, '83
882	Williams, George	200	Private	Va. Cont. Line	war	June 20, '83
887	Williams, John	400	Sergeant	Va. Cont. Line	war	June 20, '83
888	Williams, John	200	Private	Va. Cont. Line	war	June 20, '83
891	Warner, John	200	Musician	Va. Cont. Line	war	June 20, '83
892	Warner, John	100	Musician	Va. Cont. Line	war	June 20, '83
952	Wafield, George	100	Private	Va. Cont. Line	3 yrs.	June 20, '83
983	Waller, William	100	Private	Cont. Line	3 yrs.	June 20, '83
1003	Waggoner, Andrew	6222	Private	Va. Cont. Line	3 yrs.	June 21, '83
1004	Wallace, James	6000	Surgeon	Va. Cont. Line	3 yrs.	June 23, '83
1016	Wright, Thomas	100	Private	Va. Cont. Line	3 yrs.	June 23, '83
1033	Willis, Henry	4000	Captain	Va. Cont. Line	3 yrs.	June 23, '83
1035	Wood, Thomas	400	Serg.-Maj.	Va. Cont. Line	war	June 24, '83
1036	Williams, John	400	Serg.-Maj.	Va. Cont. Line	war	June 24, '83
1097	Ware, Moses	400	Serg.-Maj.	Va. Cont. Line	war	June 24, '83
1120	Woods, William	200	Private	Va. Cont. Line	war	June 24, '83
1123	Walker, Edward	200	Private	Va. Cont. Line	war	June 24, '83
1125	Woodman, John	200	Private	Va. Cont. Line	war	June 24, '83
1138	Winters, Stephen	200	Private	Va. Cont. Line	war	June 24, '83
1149	Welch, Jonathan	200	Private	Va. Cont. Line	war	June 24, '83
1150	Wood, Joseph	200	Private	Va. Cont. Line	war	June 24, '83
1241	Wilson, James	100	Private	Va. Cont. Line	3 yrs.	June 27, '83
1258	White, Richard	200	Private	Va. Cont. Line	war	June 27, '83
1261	Wilson, Stacey	400	Sergeant	Va. Cont. Line	war	June 27, '83
1268	Walden, John	200	Corporal	Va. St. Line	3 yrs.	June 28, '83
1271	Walden, George	200	Sergeant	Va. St. Line	3 yrs.	June 28, '83
1282	Williams, William	200	Private	Va. Cont. Line	war	June 28, '83
1300	Weeden, Augustine	200	Sergeant	Va. Cont. Line	3 yrs.	June 30, '83
1331	Warters, Richard	4000	Capt.-Lieut	Cont. Art	3 yrs.	July 5, 1783
1336	Wright, Richard	100	Private	St. Line	3 yrs.	July 7, 1783
1357	Ware, William	100	Private	Cont. Line	3 yrs.	July 12, '83
1375	White, Tarpley	4000	Captain	Cont. Line	3 yrs.	July 15, '83
1376	White, John	2666⅔	Lieutenant	Cont. Line	3 yrs.	July 15, '83
1449	Wedgbar, William	200	Private	Cont. Line	war	July 31, '83
1456	Willis, William	200	Private	Cont. Line	war	July 31, '83
1457	Wilkins, Thomas	200	Drummer	Cont. Line	war	Aug. 1, 1783
1463	Warren, John	200	Private	Cont. Line	war	Aug. 1, 1783
1512	Webb, James	100	Sailor	St. Navy	3 yrs.	Aug. 6, 1783
1526	Welch, Robert	200	Private	Cont. Line	war	Aug. 8, 1783
1531	Wallace, James	100	Private	St. Line	3 yrs.	Aug. 8, 1783
1567	Waller, John	200	Sergeant	Cont. Line	3 yrs.	Aug. 13, '83
1572	White, William (John White, heir at law)	4000	Captain	Cont. Line	3 yrs.	Aug. 15, '83
1581	Williams, Henry	100	Private	Cont. Line	3 yrs.	Aug. 18, '83
1606	Woodford, William (John Woodford, heir at law)	10000	Brig. Gen.	Cont. Line	3 yrs.	Aug. 20, '83
1625	Wood, James	200	Private	Cont. Line	war	Aug. 22, '83
1633	Wood, Nicholas	200	Private	Cont. Line	war	Aug. 22, '83
1638	Wood, William	400	Corporal	Va. Cont. Line	war	Aug. 23, '83
1677	Winston, William	2666⅔	Lieutenant	Va. Cont. Line	3 yrs.	Aug. 27, '83
1679	Woolfork, Francis	200	Sergeant	Va. Cont. Line	3 yrs.	Aug. 27, '83
1684	Winfrey, John	100	Private	Va. Cont. Line	3 yrs.	Aug. 29, '83
1692	Ward, George	100	Private	Va. Cont. Line	3 yrs.	Aug. 30, '83
1721	Winder, Jesse	200	Sergeant	Va. Cont. Line	3 yrs.	Sept. 2, 1783
1743	Webb, Thomas	100	Private	Va. St. Line	3 yrs.	Sept. 11, '83
1751	Woodson, Hughes	4000	Captain	Va. Cont. Line	3 yrs.	Sept. 11, '83
1795	Wood, Jesse	100	Private	Va. Cont. Line	3 yrs.	Sept. 26, '83
1803	White, Edward	100	Private	Va. Cont. Line	3 yrs.	Sept. 30, '83
1845	Walker, John	200	Private	Va. Cont. Line	ʃ ar	Oct. 10, '83
1875	Walker, Henry	100	Private	Va. Cont. Line	3 yrs.	Oct. 15, '83
1878	Walker, John	100	Private	Va. Cont. Line	3 yrs.	Oct. 15, '83
1890	Walker, David	2666⅔	Lieutenant	Va. Cont. Line	3 yrs.	Oct. 18, '83
1928	Woodson, Tarlton	5333⅓	Major	Va. Cont. Line	3 yrs.	Oct. 28, '83
1936	Watts, John	4666⅔	Captain	Va. Cont. Line	7 yrs	Oct. 31, '83
1938	Walker, Jeremiah	100	Private	Va. Cont. Line	3 yrs	Oct. 31, '83
①1848	Waters, James	400	Sergeant	Va. Cont. Line	war	Nov. 1, 1783
①1899	Waters, Thomas	200	Private	Va. Cont. Line	war	Nov. 15, '83
①1933	Wren, Alexander	100	Private	Va. St. Line	3 yrs.	Nov. 22, '83

LAND BOUNTY WARRANTS.

Warrant.	Name.	Acres	Rank.	Department.	Term	Date.
1954	WHITFIELD, Haynes	100	Sailor	Va. St. Navy	3 yrs.	Nov. 22, '83
1961	WHITCLORS, Levi	200	Private	Va. Cont. Line	war	Nov. 24, '83
1997	WELLS, James	100	Private	Va. Cont. Line	3 yrs	Nov. 29, '83
2008	WATTS, Gideon	200	Private	Va. Cont. Line	war	Dec. 3, 1783
2040	WYNE, Benjamin	200	Private	Va. Cont. Line	war	Dec. 9, 1783
2075	WILKS, Burwell	200	Sergeant	Va. Cont. Line	3 yrs.	Dec. 10, '83
2090	WRIGHT, John	100	Private	Va. Cont. Line	3 yrs.	Dec. 10, '83
2109	WOOD, John	200	Sergeant	Va. Cont. Line	3 yrs.	Dec. 12, '83
2121	WHITAKER, William	2666⅔	Lieutenant	Va. Cont. Line	3 yrs.	Dec. 13, '83
2134	WATERFIELD, Peter	100	Private	Va. Cont. Line	3 yrs.	Dec. 15, '83
2140	WILSON, John	100	Private	Va. Cont. Line	3 yrs.	Dec. 16, '83
2165	WATTERSON, Robert	200	Corporal	Va. Cont. Line	3 yrs.	Dec. 20, '83
2170	WATERS, James	100	Sailor	Va. St. Navy	3 yrs.	Dec. 20, '83
2204	WILLIAMS, Rice	100	Private		3 yrs.	Dec. 23, '83
2222	WATERS, Richard	666⅔	Capt.-Lieut.	Va. Cont. Art.	7th yr	Jan. 7, 1784
2246	WEBB, Isaac	2000	Lieutenant	Va. Cont. Line	3 yrs.	Jan. 13, '84
2248	WHITE, John	444	Lieutenant	Va. Cont. Line	7th yr	Jan. 15, '84
2250	WOMACK, Ephraim	200	Corporal	Va. Cont. Line	3 yrs.	Jan. 16, '84
2263	WASHINGTON, William	7000	Lieut.-Col.	Va. Cont. Line	7 yrs.	Jan. 21, '84
2287	WILSON, Isaac	200	Sergeant	Va. St. Line	3 yrs.	Jan. 26, '84
2316	WOOLFORK, William	200	Sergeant	Va. Cont. Line	3 yrs.	Jan. 29, '84
2320	WHITE, Thomas	2666⅔	Lieutenant	Va. St. Line	3 yrs.	Jan. 30, '84
2345	WHITEHEND, John (William Reynolds, assee.)	100	Sailor	Va. St. Navy	3 yrs.	Jan. 31, '84
2349	WHITING, Henry	4000	Captain	Va. Cont. Line	3 yrs.	Jan. 31, '84
2361	WOOTEN, Thomas	200	Private	Va. Cont. Line	war	Feb. 2, 1784
2364	WELCH, Patrick	200	Sergeant	Va. Cont. Line	3 yrs.	Feb. 2, 1784
2376	WALKER, Levin	2666⅔	Lieutenant	Va. St. Line	3 yrs.	Feb. 3, 1784
2387	WOODSON, Absalom (Martin Hawkins, assee.)	100	Private	Va. Cont. Line	3 yrs.	Feb. 3, 1784
2401	WILLOUGHBY, William (Martin Hawkins, assee.)	100	Private	Va. Cont. Line	3 yrs.	Feb. 3, 1784
2404	WEAVER, John	100	Private	Va. Cont. Line	war	Feb. 4, 1784
2405	WILLIAMS, John	200	Private	Va. Cont. Line	war	Feb. 4, 1784
2429	WILDER, James	100	Sailor	St. Navy	3 yrs.	Feb. 9, 1784
2434	WOLLARD, John (Thomas Warren, assee.)	100	Private	Va. St. Line	3 yrs.	Feb. 9, 1784
2454	WRIGHT, Paul (Lewis Ford, assee.)	100	Private	Va. Cont. Line	3 yrs.	Feb. 11, '84
2455	WOOSLEY, Moses (Lewis Ford, assee.)	100			3 yrs.	Feb. 11, '84
2470	WHITE, Thomas (Daniel Feagan, assee. of)	100	Private	Va. Cont. Line	3 yrs.	Feb. 13, '84
2486	WISE, Samuel	100	Private	Va. Cont. Line	3 yrs.	Feb. 13, '84
2489	WILDER, George	100	Sailor	Va. St. Navy	3 yrs.	Feb. 13, '84
2491	WEST, William	100	Sailor	Va. St. Navy	3 yrs.	Feb. 13, '84
2501	WASH, Thomas	200	Sergeant	Va. Cont. Line	3 yrs.	Feb. 16, '84
2502	WASH, Benjamin	100	Private	Va. Cont. Line	3 yrs.	Feb. 16, '84
2504	WHITE, William	666⅔	Captain	Va. Cont. Line	7th yr	Feb. 17, '84
2523	WOLF, George	100	Private	Va. Cont. Line	3 yrs.	Feb. 19, '84
2528	WILHEBY, Jesse	100	Private	Va. Cont. Line	3 yrs.	Feb. 19, '84
2579	WALLER, William (James Bedford, assee.)	200	Private	Va. Cont. Line	war	Feb. 21, '84
2640	WILKERSON, David (Jno. W. Price, assee.)	200	Private	Va. Cont. Line	war	Feb. 26, '84
2647	WORSHAM, John (William Worsham, heir at law)	2666⅔	Lieutenant	Va. Cont. Line	3 yrs.	Feb. 27, '84
2650	WHITLOW, Michael (Samuel Trower, assee.)	200	Private	Va. Cont. Line	war	Feb. 28, '84
2657	WELCH, Isaac	100	Private	Va. Cont. Line	3 yrs.	Mch. 1, 1784
2662	WEBBER, Philip	200	Sergeant	Va. Cont. Line	3 yrs.	Mch. 1, 1784
2664	WILKERSON, Drury (George Marple, assee.)	100	Private	Va. Cont. Line	3 yrs.	Mch. 1, 1784
2670	WOOSLEY, Thomas (Francis Graves, assee.)	200	Private	Va. Cont. Line	war	Mch. 2, 1874
2671	WOOSLEY, Aaron (Francis Graves, assee.)	200	Private	Va. Cont. Line	war	Mch. 2, 1874
2672	WADE, Aca (William Reynolds, assee.)	200	Private	Va. Cont. Line	war	Mch. 2, 1874
2682	WILLIAMS, Jarrett	2666⅔	Lieutenant	Va. St. Line	3 yrs.	Mch. 3, 1784
2695	WALKER, Jeremiah (Martin Hawkins, assee.)	200	Private	Va. Cont. Line	war	Mch. 3, 1784
2704	WILLIAMS, Charles (Francis Graves, assee.)	100	Private	Va. St. Line	3 yrs.	Mch. 4, 1784
2709	WILKERSON, Thomas	200	Private	Va. Cont. Line	3 yrs.	Mch. 5, 1784

LAND BOUNTY WARRANTS. 81

War-rant.	Name.	Acres	Rank.	Department.	Term	Date.
2710	WILKERSON, Barnabas	200	Sergeant	Va. Cont. Line	3 yrs.	Mch. 5, 1784
2725	WOOD, John	100	Private	Va. St. Art	3 yrs	Mch. 6, 1784
2726	WOSTER, William	400	Private	Va. Cont. Line	war	Mch. 6, 1784
2728	WYATT, George	200	Sergeant	Va. St. Art	3 yrs.	Mch. 6, 1784
2740	WRIGHT, James	4666⅔	Captain	Va. Cont. Line	7 yrs.	Mch. 9, 1784
2748	WALTON, Tilman	200	Sergeant	Va. Cont. Line	3 yrs.	Mch. 10, '84
2757	WATKINS, John	200	Sergeant	Va. Cont. Line	3 yrs.	Mch. 12, '84
2758	WELCH, Sylvester	100	Private	Va. Cont. Line	3 yrs.	Mch. 12, '84
2759	WELCH, Benjamin	100	Private	Va. Cont. Line	3 yrs.	Mch. 12, '84
2775	WILMINGTON, John (James Jenkins, assee.)	200	Private	Va. Cont. Line	3 yrs.	Mch. 18, '84
2781	WATTS, Martin	200	Private	Va. Cont. Line	war	Mch. 18, '84
2787	WELCH, Dominick	200	Private	Va. St. Line	war	Mch. 18, '84
2808	WIMBISH, John	200	Sergeant	Va. Cont. Line	3 yrs.	Mch. 23, '84
2814	WESTMORELAND, Jesse	100	Private	Va. St. Line	3 yrs.	Mch. 24, '84
2815	WESTMORELAND, Joseph	100	Private	Va. St. Line	3 yrs.	Mch. 24, '84
2830	WILSON, James	200	Sergeant	Va. Cont. Line	3 yrs.	Mch. 26, '84
2841	WHITE, George (William King, assee.)	100	Private	Va. Cont. Line	3 yrs.	Mch. 29, '84
2849	WALKER, Levin	2666⅔	Lieutenant	Va. St. Line	3 yrs.	Mch. 30, '84
2869	WILSON, Willis	5333⅓	Captain	Va. St. Navy	3 yrs.	Apr. 3, 1784
2873	WEIGHT, James	100	Private	Va. Cont. Line	3 yrs.	Apr. 5, 1784
2886	WALKERHOLT, Jacob	100	Private	Va. Cont. Line	3 yrs.	Apr. 5, 1784
2890	WHITE, William	100	Private	Va. Cont. Line	3 yrs.	Apr. 5, 1784
2913	WHITE, William (Gideon Johnston, assee.)	100	Private	Va. Cont. Line	3 yrs.	Apr. 10, '84
2917	WILSON, Peter	100	Private	Va. St. Line	3 yrs.	Apr. 12, '84
2923	WALDEN, Elijah (Nicholas Payne, assee.)	100	Private	Va. Cont. Line	3 yrs.	Apr. 12, '84
2936	WRIGHT, Moses	100	Private	Va. Cont. Line	3 yrs.	Apr. 16, '84
2943	WOFLER, John	100	Private	Va. Cont. Line	3 yrs.	Apr. 17, '84
2950	WINGATE, Martin (Richard Claiborne and John Hopkins, assees.)	100	Private	Va. Cont. Line	3 yrs.	Apr. 17, '84
2963	WHERLEY, Matthew	100	Private	Va. Cont. Line	3 yrs.	Apr. 19, '84
2994	WILLIAMS, Alexander	100	Private	Va. Cont. Line	3 yrs.	Apr. 21, '84
3022	WHITE, James (Edward Valentine, assee.)	100	Private	Va. Cont. Line	3 yrs.	Apr. 26, '84
3024	WHITFIELD, Edward (John Whitfield, heir at law)	100	Private	Va. St. Line	3 yrs.	Apr. 27, '84
3058	WHITE, John	100	Sailor	Va. St. Navy	3 yrs.	May 7, 1784
3067	WYATT, Pitman (Edward Valentine, assee.)	100	Private	Va. St. Line	3 yrs.	May 10, '84
3071	WALLACE, Edward (William Reynolds, assee.)	100	Private	Va. St. Line	war	May 11, '84
3081	WHISTLOR, Sawney	200	Private	Va. Cont. Line	war	May 17, '84
3108	WHITE, Robert	100	Private	Va. Cont. Line	3 yrs.	May 28, '84
3116	WAYLAND, Joshua	100	Private	Va. Cont. Line	3 yrs.	June 3, 1784
3130	WETHERALL, John	100	Private	Va. Cont. Line	3 yrs.	June 5, 1784
3145	WEST, Thomas	100	Private	Va. St. Line	3 yrs.	June 10, '84
3159	WALLER, Daniel	100	Private	Va. St. Line	3 yrs.	June 15, '84
3163	WEST, Randolph	100	Private	Va. Cont. Line	3 yrs.	June 16, '84
3194	WALLACE, James (Sam'l Wallace, heir at law)	2666⅔	Ensign	Va. Cont. Line	3 yrs.	June 23, '84
3195	WALLACE, Adam (Sam'l Wallace, heir at law)	4000	Captain	Va. Cont. Line	3 yrs.	June 23, '84
3196	WALLACE, Andrew (Sam'l Wallace, heir at law)	4000	Captain	Va. Cont. Line	3 yrs.	June 23, '84
3232	WHITE, James	100	Private	Va. St. Line	3 yrs.	June 29, '84
3236	WILLIAMS, Daniel (Henry Eaton, assee.)	100	Private	Va. Cont. Line	3 yrs.	June 29, '84
3242	WEST, Charles (Res. of Gen. Assby., June 23, 1784)	5333⅓	Major			June 29, '84
3258	WARD, John	100	Private	Va. Cont. Line	3 yrs.	June 30, '84
3267	WALKER, James	100	Sailor	Va. St. Navy	3 yrs.	July 1, 1784
3281	WADDY, Shapleigh	2666⅔	Midshipman	Va. St. Navy	3 yrs.	July 1, 1784
3283	WILLIAMS, Moses (Samuel Blackwell, assee.)	100	Sailor	Va. St. Navy	3 yrs.	July 1, 1784
3300	WILSON, John M.	100	Private	Va. Cont. Line	3 yrs.	July 1, 1784
3309	WATKINS, Robert	200	Sergeant	Va. Cont. Line	3 yrs.	July 2, 1784
3312	WIDDOWS, Robert	100	Private	Va. St. Line	3 yrs.	July 2, 1784
3313	WARD, Lawrence	100	Private	Va. Cont. Line	3 yrs.	July 3, 1784
3314	WIGLEY, Job	100	Private	Va. St. Line	3 yrs.	July 3, 1784
3315	WALLS, George	7110⅔	Major	Va. St. Line	8 yrs.	July 3, 1784
3339	WATKINS, Samuel	200	Private	Va. St. Line	war	July 19, '84

82   LAND BOUNTY WARRANTS.

Warrant.	Name.	Acres	Rank	Department	Term	Date
3345	Whitten, Daniel (Dan'l Brodhead, assee. of Jno. Joynes, devisee of)	200	Private	Va. St. Line	war	July 19, '84
3353	Weldy, William	200	Private	Va. Cont. Line	war	July 22, '84
3354	Whitson, Anthony	100	Private	Va. Cont. Line	3 yrs.	July 22, '84
3358	Wren, Travis	100	Private	Va. Cont. Line	3 yrs.	July 24, '84
3360	White, Abraham	100	Private	Va. St. Line	3 yrs.	July 26, '84
3406	Warner, John (Samuel Brooking, assee.)	200	Sergeant	Va. Cont. Line	3 yrs.	Aug. 23, '84
3454	Waggoner, William	200	Sergeant	Va. Cont. Line	3 yrs.	Oct. 2, 1784
3470	Williams, John (Nathaniel Williams, heir at law)	200	Private	Va. Cont. Line	war	
3533	Worsham, William (Peter Talbot, heir at law)	2666⅔	Lieutenant	Va. Cont. Line	3 yrs.	Nov. 23, '84
3548	Wilkerson, Benjamin (Richard Baylor, assee.)	100	Private	Va. St. Line	3 yrs.	Nov. 30, '84
3569	Whaling, John	200	Private	Va. St. Line	3 yrs.	Dec. 13, '84
3592	Whitmore, William	100	Private	Va. Cont. Line	3 yrs.	Dec. 21, '84
3647	Watts, Reuben (Aaron Watts, heir at law)	100	Private	Va. Cont. Line	3 yrs.	Dec. 31, '84
3656	Wheeler, John	100	Private	Va. Cont. Line	3 yrs.	Dec. 31, '84
3657	Wheeler, James	100	Private	Va. Cont. Line	3 yrs.	Dec. 31, '84
3661	Whirley, Peter	100	Private	Va. Cont. Line	3 yrs.	Dec. 31, '84
3672	Williams, Thomas	100	Private	Va. Cont. Line	3 yrs.	Jan. 5, 1785
3689	Wolfinbuger, Philip (William Reynolds, assee.)	200	Private	Va. Cont. Line	war	Jan. 11, '85
3704	Watson, James	100	Private	Va. Cont. Line	3 yrs.	Jan. 20, '85
3711	White, William	100	Private	Va. Cont. Line	3 yrs.	Jan. 20, '85
3733	Word, Hugh	200	Private	Va. Cont. Line	war	Feb. 7, 1785
3734	Wolf, Andrew	200	Private	Va. Cont. Line	war	Feb. 7, 1785
3736	Welch, John	200	Sergeant	Va. Cont. Line	3 yrs.	Feb. 7, 1785
3769	Whitaker, Thomas	100	Private	Va. Cont. Line	3 yrs.	Mch. 5, 1785
3786	Warren, Gabriel	100	Private	Va. St. Line	3 yrs.	Mch. 25, '85
3804	...er, Edward (William Reynolds, assee. of David Valentine, who was assee. of)	2500	Major	Va. St. Line	3 yrs.	Apr. 12, '85
3805	...ller, Edward (William Reynolds, assee. of David Valentine, who was assee. of)	2833⅓	Major	Va. St. Line	3 yrs.	Apr. 12, '85
3808	Wright, Thomas	200	Private	Va. Cont. Line	war	Apr. 16, '85
3820	Watts, William	100	Private	Va. St. Line	3 yrs.	Apr. 22, '85
3875	Whitsell, Jacob	100	Private	Va. Cont. Line	3 yrs.	May 10, '85
3889	Wood, James	1111	Colonel	Va. Cont. Line	3 yrs.	June 11, '85
3894	Wilkins, Thomas	200	Private	Va. Cont. Line	war	June 16, '85
3897	Waterfield, John (William Reynolds, assee.)	200	Private	Va. Cont. Line	war	June 21, '85
3907	Wilson, James (William Reynolds, assee. of Robt. Wilkins, legal rep.)	200	Private	Va. St. Line	war	June 21, '85
3917	Wheatley, William	200	Private	Va. Cont. Line	war	June 21, '85
3949	Watkins, Jesse	100	Private	Va. St. Line	3 yrs.	Aug. 10, '85
3955	Webb, Joseph (William Reynolds, assee.)	100	Sailor	Va. St. Navy	3 yrs.	Aug. 12, '85
4022	Watts, Samuel (William Reynolds, assee.)	200	Corporal	Va. Cont. Line	3 yrs.	Dec. 5, 1785
4033	White, Jesse	100	Private	Va. Cont. Line	3 yrs.	Dec. 10, '85
4035	Wilkinson, John (Alex. Wylly, assee.)	200	Private	Va. Cont. Line	war	Dec. 12, '85
4058	Waddy, Thomas	200	Private	Va. Cont. Line	war	Dec. 31, '85
4085	Ward, William	100	Private	Va. Cont. Line	3 yrs.	Jan. 19, '86
4088	Wilson, Whitfield (Alexander Wiley, assee.)	200	Private	Va. Cont. Line	3 yrs.	Jan. 21, '86
4091	Walker, Thomas	100	Private	Va. Cont. Line	3 yrs.	Jan. 23, '86
4100	Wren, Robert	100	Private	Va. St. Line	3 yrs.	Jan. 29, '86
4128	Wilson, James	100	Private	Va. Cont. Line	3 yrs.	Mch. 18, '86
4139	West, Beriah	200	Corporal	Va. Cont. Line	3 yrs.	Apr. 5, 1786
4146	White, Benjamin (John White, heir at law)	100	Private	Va. Cont. Line	3 yrs.	Apr. 19, '86
4157	Wood, John L.	100	Private	Va. St. Line	3 yrs.	May 12, '86
4182	Waring, Henry (Thos. Waring, heir at law)	2666⅔	Lieutenant	Va. Cont. Line	3 yrs.	June 29, '86
ⓐ4236	Winn, Harrison (Henry Hayes, assee.)	200	Private	Va. Cont. Line	war	Dec. 16, '86
4248	Wood, Edward	100	Private	Va. Cont. Line	3 yrs.	Jan. 5, 1787

LAND BOUNTY WARRANTS.   83

Warrant.	Name.	Acres	Rank	Department	Term	Date
4254	WHITE, Anthony W. (duplicate issued 2d of June, 1797, and delivered to John Hopkins)	6666⅔	Lieut.-Col	Va. Cont. Line	3 yrs.	Jan. 29, '87
4259	WILLIS, William	200	Sergeant	Va. Cont. Line	3 yrs.	Jan. 21, '87
4262	WALLACE, Edmund (William Reynolds, assee.)	100	Private	Va. St. Line	3 yrs.	Mch. 25, '87
4287	WOOD, William	100	Private	Va. Cont. Line	3 yrs.	Apr. 7, 1787
4306	WRIGHT, Jarrott	200	Corporal	Va. St. Line	3 yrs.	Aug. 20, '87
4309	WILSON, John (John Wilson, heir at law)	2666⅔	Lieutenant	Va. Cont. Line	3 yrs.	Oct. 1, 1787
4318	WEBSTER, Richard	100	Private	Va. Cont. Line	3 yrs.	Oct. 23, '87
4326	WOOD, John (Sarah Wood, heiress)	100	Private	Va. Cont. Line	3 yrs.	Nov. 3, 1787
4328	WALKER, John (Mary Walker, widow)	100	Private	Va. Cont. Line	3 yrs.	Nov. 3, 1787
4355	WHITE, James	400	Corporal	Va. Cont. Line	war	Dec. 22, '87
4356	WAIL, Wilmore	100	Private	Va. Cont. Line	3 yrs.	Dec. 28, '87
4361	WILLIAMS, Daniel	200	Private	Va. Cont. Line	war	Jan. 10, '88
4366	WILLIS, James (William Reynolds, assee. of Eli Peed, rep. of)	100	Sailor	Va. St. Navy	3 yrs.	Jan. 17, '88
4375	WALDEN, Spencer (Wm. Reynolds, assee. of Jeremiah Munday, assee. of the rep. of)	100	Private	Va. Cont. Line	3 yrs.	Jan. 23, '88
4395	WILLS, George	200	Private	Va. Cont. Line	war	Mch. 31, '88
4408	WALLER, John	200	Sergeant	Va. Cont. Line	3 yrs.	June 27, '88
4426	WIATT, Edward (William Wiatt, rep.)	100	Private	Va. St. Line	3 yrs.	July 17, '88
4430	WARREN, Drury (Turner Morris, assee. of Jno. Bailey, assee. of Ed. Davis, assee. of R. Burnett, assee. of the rep. of)	100	Private	Va. Cont. Line	3 yrs.	Aug. 4, 1788
4453	WATKINS, David (William Reynolds, assee. of Rich. Burnett, assee. of the rep.)	100	Private	Va. Cont. Line	3 yrs.	Apr. 8, 1789
4491	WALCH, David	200	Matross	Va. Cont. Line	3 yrs.	Mch. 24, '90
4495	WOODS, Alexander (Henry Christian, assee.)	200	Private	Va. Cont. Line	war	May 27, '90
4501	WALLACE, Thomas	2666⅔	Lieutenant	Va. Cont. Line	3 yrs.	Oct. 22, '90
4509	WAYNE, Benjamin (John Hume, assee. of Francis Graves, assee. of)	100	Private	Va. Cont. Line	3 yrs.	Dec. 7, 1790
4536	WHITE, Randolph (Patrick Doran, assee.)	100	Private	St. Line	3 yrs.	Nov. 10, '91
4537	WILLSON, Thomas	2666⅔	Lieutenant	St. Line	3 yrs.	Nov. 10, '91
4552	WOOLDRIDGE, Joseph	100	Private	St. Line	3 yrs.	Nov. 26, '91
4561	WILLIAMS, John	4000	Captain	St. Line	3 yrs.	Dec. 22, '91
4566	WARREN, John	100	Private	Cont. Line	3 yrs.	Jan. 31, '92
4573	WOOD, Benjamin (the rep. of)	200	Private	Cont. Line	war	May 5, 1792
4586	WINSTON, Robert	100	Private	St. Line	3 yrs.	Oct. 2, 1792
4593	WILLS, Nathaniel (Robert Macans, assee.)	200	Private	Cont. Line	war	Nov. 9, 1792
4595	WALKER, John (Jones Allen, assee.)	200	Private	Cont. Line	war	Nov. 26, '92
4599	WHITT, Shadrack (John Whitt, heir at law)	200	Private	Cont. Line	war	Dec. 13, '92
4605	WALLACE, Nathaniel (Wm. Bigger, assee. of the rep. of)	200	Private	Cont. Line	war	Jan. 25, '93
4619	WILSON, Henry	100	Private	Cont. Line	3 yrs.	Aug. 5, 1793

Y

164	YOURS, William	200	Corporal	Va. Cont. Line	3 yrs.	Mch. 8, 1783
201	YANCEY, Robert	1000	Captain	Lt. Drags. in Va. Cont. Line	3 yrs.	Mch. 26, '83
202	YANCEY, Robert	3000	Captain	Lt. Drags. in Va. Cont. Line	3 yrs.	Mch. 26, '83
275	YOUNG, Frederick (Dr. James McClung, assee.)	200	Sergeant	Va. Line	3 yrs.	Apr. 3, 1783
612	YOUNG, Henry	4000	Captain	Va. Cont. Line	3 yrs.	May 21, '83
763	YARRINGTON, Oliver	100	Private	Va. Cont. Art.	3 yrs.	June 6, 1783
1020	YOUNG, Nathan	200	Sergeant	Va. Cont. Art.	3 yrs.	June 23, '86
1052	YOUNG, John	200	Private	Cont. Line	war	June 24, '83

84 LAND BOUNTY WARRANTS.

Warrant.	Name.	Acres	Rank.	Department.	Term	Date.
1730	Yarbrough, Charles	2666⅔	Lieutenant	Va. Cont. Line	3 yrs.	Sept. 8, 1783
1977	Yowell, Samuel	100	Private	Va. Cont. Line	3 yrs.	Nov. 26, '83
2115	Young, Samuel	100	Private	Va. Cont. Line	3 yrs.	Dec. 13, '83
2554	Yager, Henry	100	Private	Va. Cont. Line	3 yrs.	Feb. 20, '84
2630	Young, William (Daniel Flowerree, assee.)	200	Sergeant	Va. Cont. Line	3 yrs.	Feb. 24, '84
2876	Young, Robert	100	Private	Va. Cont. Line	3 yrs.	Apr. 5, 1784
2921	Yancey, Layton	2666⅔	Subaltern	Va. Cont. Line	3 yrs.	Apr. 12, '84
3070	Yancey, Ludwell	100	Private	Va. Cont. Line	3 yrs.	May 11, '84
3127	Yancey, Lewis	100	Private	Va. Cont. Line	3 yrs.	June 5, 1784
3132	Yancey, Robert	666⅔	Captain	Va. Cont. Line	7 yrs.	June 5, 1784
3170	Young, Duncan	400	Private	Va. Cont. Line	war	June 17, '84
3957	Yearly, Samuel (William Reynolds, assee.)	200	Sergeant	Va. Cont. Line	3 yrs.	Aug. 12, '85
3967	Yager, John	200	Private	Va. Cont. Line	war	Aug. 12, '85
3978	Yancey, Absalom	100	Private	Va. Cont. Line	3 yrs.	Oct. 5, 1785
4023	Yancey, James (William Reynolds, assee.)	200	Corporal	Va. Cont. Line	3 yrs.	Dec. 5, 1785
4084	Yates, John	2666⅔	Lieutenant	Va. St. Line	3 yrs.	Jan. 18, '86
4321	Yates, George	2000	Surg.'s Mate	Va. St. Navy	3 yrs.	Oct. 26, '87
4322	Yates, George	666⅔	Surg.'s Mate	Va. St. Navy	3 yrs.	Oct. 26, '87
4385	Young, Thomas	4000	Captain	Crockett's Reg	3 yrs.	Feb. 4, 1788

Z

1539	Zimmerman, William	200	Sergeant	Cont. Line	3 yrs.	Aug. 9, '83
3945	Zimmerman, John (William Reynolds, assee.)	100	Private	Va. Cont. Line	3 yrs.	Aug. 10, '85

Note—In some instances, manifest inaccuracies, either in the number of Acres, in the Rank, or in the Term of Service, will be detected in the foregoing list, but such errors occur in the copies from which this list was made and it was thought better, as a rule, to adhere to the official records and present a faithful digest of their contents, than to attempt any correction of such errors, however palpable.

Most of the names in the above list are faithfully reproduced, but a number of them were difficult to decipher and the names actually given in such cases represent only the compiler's best guess, and it is not pretended that the true original name is in every case catalogued or spelled with infallible accuracy. In a few instances it will be found that the same name is variously spelled in a single warrant.

www.ingramcontent.com/pod-product-compliance
Lightning Source LLC
LaVergne TN
LVHW051705080426
835511LV00017B/2739